The Strategic and Operational Planning of Marketing

Gordon E. Greenley

University of Birmingham

McGRAW-HILL Book Company (UK) Limited

London · New York · St Louis · San Francisco · Auckland
Bogotá · Guatemala · Hamburg · Johannesburg · Lisbon · Madrid
Mexico · Montreal · New Delhi · Panama · Paris · San Juan
São Paulo · Singapore · Sydney · Tokyo · Toronto

Published by
McGRAW-HILL Book Company (UK) Limited
MAIDENHEAD · BERKSHIRE · ENGLAND

British Library Cataloguing in Publication Data

Greenley, Gordon E.
   The strategic and operational planning of
   marketing.—(McGraw-Hill marketing series)
   1. Marketing—Management
   I. Title

   658.8'02   HF5415.13

ISBN 0-07-084154-3

Library of Congress Cataloging-in-Publication Data

Greenley, Gordon E.
   The strategic and operational planning of marketing.

   (The McGraw-Hill marketing series)
   Bibliography: p.
   Includes index.
   1. Marketing—Management.   2. Marketing.   I. Title.
II. Series.
HF5415.13.G72   1986   658.8'02   85-23298
ISBN 0-07-084154-3

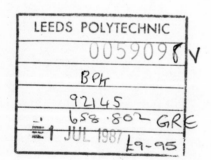
12345RJA89876

Typeset by Eta Services (Typesetters) Limited, Beccles, Suffolk, and
printed and bound in Great Britain by R. J. Acford.

To my wife, Pamela, and my daughter, Amanda Kate

CONTENTS

PREFACE

The discipline of marketing now appears to be entrenched as a *force majeure* in the competitive actions of companies, as well as being well established within the literature. Attention to the importance of formal planning has also been developing within the literature, although current evidence indicates that planning is not, at the present time, competently carried out by the majority of companies. The overall objective of this book is to provide a comprehensive treatment of the planning of marketing at both the strategic and operational levels of management, and it is aimed not only at students, but also at managers involved with the planning of marketing.

The book is aimed at postgraduate students studying marketing, strategic management, business policy, and organizational behaviour, as well as at students following marketing and business policy options on first degree programmes. This includes those pursuing a master's degree, post-graduate diploma, or research degree at either the master's or doctoral level. Of equal importance is that the book is also aimed at candidates for the Institute of Marketing's Diploma in Marketing. Here the content provides exhaustive material for the formal areas of teaching, but also includes treatment of additional areas of study that are invaluable for preparation for the case study examination. Managers involved with the planning of marketing are also seen to be important consumers, as the book is practically orientated through a series of illustrations of the application of planning concepts. These include company illustrations in the text, plus a number of company case study exhibits.

The approach taken in this book is seen to differ from other current texts concerned with the planning of marketing. Approaches taken in these other texts tend to fall into the following classifications:

- The management of the individual marketing mix elements, with only a cursory treatment of planning
- Separation of corporate planning into strategic and operational planning, with marketing appearing only as a component of operational planning
- A treatment of strategic planning, where the inputs of the marketing function are highlighted
- The amalgamation of marketing into strategic management as overall and grandiose company management

The basis of the approach taken in this book differs from these classifications, being derived from the principle that marketing is a management process. It recognizes that both strategic and operational management have different, but equally important, roles to play within organizations. This combination results in the book's overall approach that the management process of marketing needs to be planned at both strategic and operational levels, as reflected in the book's title. Also, within the literature a trend is developing in which strategy is evolving as the major consideration within the management process. This approach is not adopted in this book as other functions of management are seen to be of equal importance. From this basis, the range of text objectives dictated the resultant format of the book, which is in five parts as follows:

Part One An introduction to the concept of planning relative to marketing
Part Two A treatment of strategic planning involving the marketing process
Part Three A treatment of the operational planning of marketing
Part Four Processes involved in the planning of marketing
Part Five The implementation and control of plans

A feature of the book is that the major principles of each chapter are illustrated by their application into company situations, aimed at enhancing the understanding of managers and the learning of students. Here case studies of 'well-known companies' are used to actually explain and illustrate, rather than merely presenting a case study in total without directly relating the relevent concepts. These case studies are available through the Case Clearing House of Great Britain, and consequently are available through other worldwide case clearing organizations. Therefore, the added advantage is that readers can also pursue an understanding of the planning concepts within the context of the many complex issues apparent within these organizations.

The author owes his gratitude to the many colleagues who have helped and given encouragement in the preparation of this book. Of particular importance is that given by Professor Roger Mason, Professor Stephen Littlechild, David Shipley, Dr Gordon Foxall, Adrian Halstead, and Alan Matcham.

Gordon E. Greenley

OUTLINE

The overall aim of Part One is to introduce major concepts and issues that provide the basis for other parts of the book. In Chapter 1 various definitions of marketing are examined, particularly emphasizing marketing as a process. This chapter also examines the nature of planning as a function of management. In Chapter 2 the planning framework to be used throughout the book is established within the context of both its preparation and its implementation. The role of marketing within this framework is given as a prelude to the rest of the book.

ONE

BASIC CONCEPTS

Learning objectives are to:

1. Understand the concept of marketing.
2. Understand the nature of marketing as a management process.
3. Appreciate the nature of planning relative to management.
4. Become familiar with the major features of planning.
5. Gain an outline of the approach to be taken within this book.
6. Recognize major concepts that have been introduced.

Anyone involved with the business literature will be aware of the considerable attention to, and development of, that part devoted to marketing. Consequently, the vast body of knowledge covers all aspects of the individual marketing-mix elements and contains many explanations of the nature of marketing and its consequences for organizations. Within recent years there has also been an increase in interest in the area of planning, although here there has been a tendency to link planning to the concept of strategy. The result is that the literature now contains many labels incorporating these two words, and this has resulted in a lack of commonality of terminology. Indeed, writers such as Carroll[1] observe the abuse of the word strategic within the literature, in that it has become a 'grandiose synonym for the word important'. Consequently, the aim of the first two chapters is to address this situation, by establishing a framework of planning to be used throughout the book.

This situation is also reflected in the planning of marketing within organizations. The results of research carried out by the author (which will be discussed at appropriate places within the text) have revealed a wide variation in the understanding of marketing and planning concepts, which has also been reported by other researchers. This variation is not only from company to company; variations are also to be found between marketing personnel within the same organization and involved in the same product line. Again the word strategic emerges as being a synonym for important, although the majority of personnel fail to give an adequate explanation of their understanding of the concept.

THE MARKETING CONCEPT

All basic texts on marketing propose a definition of the concept, although it is not intended to enter an exhaustive discussion of the advantages or otherwise of these, but to establish the basis for the approach taken in this book.

A recent trend has been for authors to differentiate between micro-marketing and macro-marketing. For example, McCarthy[2] sees the former as being concerned with the firm internally, while macro-marketing is described as being concerned with a social process that directs the flow of goods and services within the society. Although the latter is obviously an important role of marketing, in the context of this book it is seen as being a consequence of the utilization of marketing by organizations and not a benefit that would be directly planned for by a company. However, the importance of a company setting objectives relative to social responsibility is discussed in Part Two, and indeed this illustrates the general principle that the planning of marketing cannot be in isolation from other influential factors.

Therefore the focus of this book is on the internal company requirement to utilize marketing. Stanton[3] defines marketing as being 'a total system of interacting business activities designed to plan, price, promote and distribute want-satisfying products and services to present and potential customers'. This definition exhibits many important features of marketing. The internal nature is referred to as the interacting business activities, themselves incorporated into a system the nature of which is significant for this book and will be developed in Chapter 2. The other aspects of this definition are concerned with the implementation of the elements of the marketing mix, directed towards customers. Many company examples of the utilization of marketing are available. IBM UK claim that they are a marketing-orientated organization.[4] The UK retailing group Habitat organize their business around a set of basic marketing criteria. These include offering well-designed and well-produced products to identified potential customers, while ensuring that price is comparable to product quality and customer acceptance.[5]

The definition of the Institute of Marketing[6] is that marketing is the management process responsible for identifying, anticipating and satisfying customer requirements profitably. This definition is seen as being pertinent to the basis of this book owing to its direct reference to marketing as a management process. However, although it goes on to explain what this process aims to achieve, relative to customer requirements, it does not develop an explanation of the nature of the management process. However, this gives the starting point for the basis of the approach taken in the book and indeed the nature of the process is developed later in this chapter. Similarly, the definition adopted by the American Marketing Association[7] refers to marketing as being a process of planning and execution.

Further guidance comes from the work by Kotler.[8] His simple definition of marketing as being human activity directed at satisfying needs and wants is indicative of this activity being a process. Here the interpretation can be of a management process, as required for the text, or as a macro-process, as previously discussed. However, Kotler also defines the concept of marketing as being 'management orientation that holds that the key task of the organization is to determine the needs and wants of target markets and to adopt the organization to delivering the desired satisfactions more effectively and efficiently than its competitors'. (Reproduced by permission of Prentice-Hall Inc.) Here the process of marketing is an orientation of management and a key feature is that it permeates throughout the company. Indeed, this is central to the planning of marketing at both strategic and operational levels, as will be emphasized in subsequent chapters. Another key feature is that of adapting the organization to meet the requirements of the marketing process. The planning systems to be developed in conjunction with marketing orientation have a combined effect on the organizational structure, which will be discussed in Part Four. A lack of such management orientation had a major effect on the Swiss watch industry. When cheap quartz watches became available, the Swiss companies failed to react to both their new competitors and the resultant changes in customer needs. The result was a reduction in their worldwide market share from 30 to 9 per cent. However, the industry did react, with the establishment of a consortium, Asuag-SSIH, to reorientate management thinking and to develop new products to meet the new market needs.[9]

[The final definition to be considered is also by Kotler,[8] being his definition of marketing management: 'the analysis, planning, implementation and control of programmes designed to create, build and maintain mutually beneficial exchanges. . . .' Here the nature of management is described in the form of analysis, planning, implementation and control, relative to marketing in its role of customer satisfaction.] *2nd part*

All these separate definitions can be combined to give an overall understanding of the nature of marketing as a management process. Hence the process involves human activity within the organization as the focus is on the micro-approach. This human activity involves an orientation of managers towards the needs and wants of customers, which permeates throughout the organizational structure. As the human activity also involves the utilization of the principles of management, marketing as a process operates within a framework of analysis, planning, implementation and control. This involvement throughout the organizational structure shows that interacting business activities are involved, but, as illustrated throughout the book, these are both lateral within the structure and horizontal across functional areas of responsibility. The aim of utilizing marketing as a management process is to achieve an end result, namely satisfying customer requirements while achieving a level of profitability acceptable to the company. However, end results relative to the planning of marketing are a major issue that is given continued consideration throughout the text. The major features of this understanding are given in Fig. 1.1.

Micro-approach of internalization

Human activity of orientation towards customers

Permeation throughout the organizational structure

Framework of analysis, planning, implementation and control

Laterally interacting business activities

Horizontally interacting business activities

Marketing utilized to achieve end results of customer satisfaction, plus profits or other end results

---

Figure 1.1 Marketing as a management process

THE NATURE OF PLANNING

We have already seen that Kotler[8] uses the concept of planning in the context of the management of marketing. Current knowledge relative to the functions of management appears to be based upon the work of Fayol,[10] published in 1949, which gives management as being based upon the following:

Planning Examining the future and drawing up a plan of action.
Organizing Establishing a human and physical frame to enable the undertaking to achieve results.
Commanding Activating the organization.
Co-ordination Drawing together all activity and effort.
Controlling Seeing that everything occurs in conformity with establishing rules and expressed command.

Consequently, the role of planning was established as a function of management, or one of the tasks to be carried out by managers. Development of involvement within these tasks has occurred subsequently and indeed has provided the basis for the expansion of the management literature. Many explanations consequently appear and, for example, writers such as Ansoff and Brandenburg[11] give three related classes of management activity, as follows:

Planning Formulation of guidelines and constraints for the organization and evaluation of these guidelines into budgets, activity schedules and assignments.

Implementation Communication of plans to the individuals responsible for carrying out the activities, and motivation plus leadership in the execution of desired courses of action.

Control Measurement of performance in the execution of desired courses of action and determination of appropriate corrective measures to ensure the achievement of desired results.

Such a three-stage approach is almost universally accepted, having the advantage of providing a simple basis which explains the nature of management, although the extensive concepts and issues pertinent to these stages are as complex and involved as any study derived from human behaviour.

This explanation of the stages, by Ansoff and Brandenburg, exhibits several features. Planning is given as being concerned with guidelines and constraints, although perhaps more simply these can be classified as being intended activity to be carried out in the future. The inclusion of evaluation is indicative that managers are able to develop alternative activities and make a choice as which to pursue. Examples given of types of activities are budgets, schedules and assignments. Parts Two and Three are concerned with the development of such planning activities and the importance of choice, or decision making. As planning requires decision making it is also apparent that, having made decisions, managers are then committed to their planning, as reflected in the following definition of planning by Warren:[12] 'Planning is essentially a process of preparing for the commitment of resources. . . .' Therefore, although commitment to planning is essential for its utilization, as will be discussed in Part Four, flexibility for some change also needs to be a feature, in order to counteract contingency situations that were not anticipated at the time the planning was prepared.

The implementation stage brings the planning into action, and involves the individuals within the organization who are to carry out the various parts of the plans. This area of study is discussed in both Parts Four and Five of the book. As the various parts of the planning are carried out the performance of such activities can be assessed, which is the concern of the management activity of control. As mentioned above, this also requires the instigation of corrective actions, should the activities initially planned and ultimately implemented not produce the planned levels of performance. Such control measures relate to the flexibility of planning as previously mentioned, and the whole area of control is concluded in Part Five.

A slightly different approach to the stages of management is taken by Hussey,[13] which serves to highlight other important features. He classifies the tasks of management into three areas as follows:

Deterministic Those tasks concerned with the creative, planning and arranging functions, including the determination of objectives, policies, procedures and organizational structures.

Motivational Tasks which motivate the organization, including communication, leadership and personal development.

Directing Implementation, co-ordination and controlling.

We should note here, first, that planning is creative in nature. Alternatives relate to different sets of activities to tackle aims of the company or problems that develop, that can be considered to be unique in the way they relate to the organization. Creativity in planning is also important in the actions of competing organizations. Here it can lead to novel approaches to customer requirements, making products or services more suitable and attractive than those offered by other companies.

The second feature to note is that certain planning concepts are defined as being activities of planning, which are, as previously discussed, necessarily related to the organizational structure. Another is that planning alone is not sufficient: motivation of personnel at the planning stage is necessary to ensure that realistic and useful plans are prepared. It is also necessary at the stage of implementation to ensure that the plans are followed, as well as at the control stage to ensure that corrective action is both identified and implemented. Again, all these features will be covered throughout subsequent chapters of the book.

Planning now having been established as a function of management, other aspects of its nature need to be described before we discuss the planning framework in the next chapter. One such aspect is described by Ackoff.[14] This is the view that planning is decision making about action to be carried out in the future, at a time before the action is to be implemented. This simple fact has many obvious implications in that, at the time of planning, it is impossible to know just exactly, for example, what level of expenditure will occur within a particular market or how economic factors will affect demand. A general rule, based on simple logic, is that the further into the future planning extends, the less certain predictions can be. However, firms often experience unpredicted changes within only months of initiating plans, which can cause immediate planning problems. This, however, does not mean that long-range planning is of little value, and indeed any planning can be based only upon current understanding (until such time as prophecy becomes an exact science), and must be continuously adjusted through control procedures and revised at appropriate time-intervals. This theme of planning being concerned with the future is discussed by Hausler,[15] who describes planning in two stages as follows:

- A preview of future fields of action, a search for order and goals in the future, and a search for fields of performance for the future mobilization of resources.
- Methodological preparation for action, including the development of strategies, or guidelines for future action.

This emphasizes that planning is concerned not only with specific areas of activity, given as being goals, searches and strategy, but also with the mobilization of resources. Therefore planning is a commitment not only to activity, but also to an allocation of resources, particularly as presented in the form of expenditure, which can be both current and capital. Again, such issues will be discussed within the text. At ICI Fibres the future of their business is now planned with a marketing orientation. Starting in 1980, they used planning to establish and satisfy the needs of their markets, and to determine goals and strategies to develop new products that customers need. Their previous approach to their business has been to develop products that had not been planned in relation to customer needs.[16] This reflects the first of Hausler's stages of planning, as given above. The US Company, Tandem Computers, consider that long-range planning gives stability to their business. However, the firm does record some failures in their overall business success during the early 1980s, with inadequate planning of product launches having been given as a failure. This reflects Hausler's second stage of planning, relating to preparation for action.[17]

A more comprehensive approach in explaining the nature of planning is given by Steiner.[18] This approach is based upon different roles that planning can fulfil within a company, including specific activities as already discussed. These differing roles of planning are given by Steiner as follows:

Generic planning Here planning systematically examines future alternatives and decisions are made based upon these alternatives.

Planning as a process This process starts with objectives, defines strategy and policies to achieve objectives, prescribes sub-plans in detail, establishes an organization to implement the plans, and provides for a review of performance.

Planning as a philosophy This is the view that planning creates patterns of logic and managerial attitudes for the continued development of the company.

Planning as an integrating framework The emphasis here is on a comprehensive and uniform programme of plans for the entire organization, over a long period of time. This gives integration of plans within the company, leading to an overall plan for the entire organization.

The value of this approach is that it integrates many of the planning issues already developed. In addition, planning as a philosophy and as a framework are important concepts. The former emphasizes that throughout the company planning contributes to development in a systematic and logical manner, affecting, as already mentioned, the very attitudes of managers that are essential to its utilization. As an integrating framework, planning allows for continuity of this business logic, establishes the parameters for the various business functions, and gives co-ordination to their diverse activities, leading to an overall or corporate force that can be sustained in the future.

Some of these issues are also discussed by Loasby,[19] who presents a range of advantages of planning. The first is that planning requires managers to understand the future implications of present decisions, placing the focus on issues such as future action to be taken, the effects these decisions will have on future options and the problems that may be created in the future by these decisions. The second advantage is that, by assessing future events, their effects on current decisions can be estimated. For example, the probability of future expansion in the activity of competitors has numerous implications for current decisions. The final advantage of systematic planning for the future is that the process itself allows for motivation and mechanism in the planning process. Discipline, systematic methods and assumptions are, by necessity, developed in planning. This latter advantage is also outlined by Heroux,[20] who considers that planning has a major effect in providing a degree of discipline and formality which may not otherwise exist, leading to a fuller awareness and understanding on the part of managers as to their job function within the company. Additional advantages of planning are given in Chapter 11, which discusses its effectiveness.

The major features of planning developed in this chapter are presented in Fig. 1.2, while Case Study 1 (page 11) illustrates some of these features. The main thrust in this examination of the nature of planning has been relative to its role as a function of management. Planning is established as being related to current activities and decisions about future action. These activities, in their preparation, allow for a systematic and disciplined approach to the manager's role within the company. They themselves relate to areas such as objectives, guidelines, strategies, actions, budgets and organizational considerations. Planning also plays four major roles within organizations and advantages are seen to accrue as a consequence. The full details of the activities of planning are presented in Parts Two and Three.

The final issue concerning the nature of planning relates to the organization of managers within a company. This is normally within a hierarchy, with delegation of authority moving down the hierarchy from the board of directors. However, at each level the managers still need to carry out the functions of management in order to exercise their authority, so that the function of planning is applicable to all levels of management. The organizational arrangements referred to by Ansoff and Brandenburg are concerned with the planning the company expects from each level of management and how these separate sets of planning are integrated into the overall planning of the company. This is the overall planning process of the firm and can be considered

Planning is:

- A function of management

- Intended activity for the future

- Developing alternatives, decision making and commitment

- Sufficiently flexible for contingency situations

- Creative in nature

- A range of specified activities

- Dependent upon the motivation of personnel

- Decision making about future action

- Concerned with resource mobilization and expenditure commitments

- Classified as being generic, a process, a philosophy and a framework

- Focused on the consequences of future action

- Concerned with discipline, formality and systems

- A contributor to the motivation of personnel

Figure 1.2   Major features of planning

to be within a hierarchy such as the organizational structure. This gives, in the terminology of Hausler, the order and preparation for action, while in the terminology of Steiner it gives a programme of plans plus an overall company plan. These concepts of different levels, programmes and types of plans are discussed as the framework of planning in the next chapter.

RATIFICATION OF TERMINOLOGY

The final part of this chapter is concerned with a ratification of the concepts of planning and management as used in this book. This is considered to be necessary, as some writers tend to use the terms planning and management synonymously, as do some managers. Here planning has tended to be conceived as the overall function, encompassing the functions of implementation and control; within this context management becomes the personal qualities of managers in co-ordinating this encompassing function.

An example here is the approach of Hussey[13] to corporate planning (the nature of which will be examined in the next chapter), namely that such planning incorporates all the functions previously discussed as management, and the establishment of the principle that such planning is the complete management task; consequently, corporate planning is management.

However, the approach taken within this book is that management is the encompassing discipline and that planning is a function of management, albeit an important one. This view is taken because the role of planning, as previousy illustrated, is distinct from the implementation of action and the control of performance. All three areas are seen to be of equal importance, as each plays a specific role, although, of course, all are interdependent. Sophisticated plans are unlikely to be effective without adequate implementation and control. Similarly, unplanned action which is not controlled is also likely to have little effect.

Finally, one major aspect of the relationship of planning to the other functions of management needs to be highlighted, as this often causes confusion with students of planning.

This is that the areas of implementation and control generally appear within plan formats. The explanation here is that both these areas constitute activities that are to be carried out in the future and it follows that they too need to be subjected to planning. Indeed, this is the approach taken in this book, with Part Five being devoted to these areas of study.

SUMMARY

This chapter has examined certain basic concepts concerned with both marketing and planning. In the former, the micro and macro approaches were outlined and the micro approach was given as being pertinent to this book. Various aspects of marketing were examined relative to market requirements and the concept of marketing as a company and management orientation was discussed. Finally, marketing as a process was discussed and established as a major basis for the development of the book.

The nature of planning was presented as being a major function of management. The major features of planning were also discussed. Here planning was seen to be a range of intended activity to be implemented in the future, developed through being creative in preparing alternative courses of action and through decision making and commitment to finalized plans. Planning can also be classified as being generic, a process, a philosophy and a framework. Planning involves systems, discipline and formality, and although it contributes to the motivation of personnel, it also requires their motivation in both its preparation and its implementation. However, management is applicable to the different levels of a company's managerial hierarchy, so that planning is also applicable at different organizational levels.

The approach taken in the book is that management is the encompassing discipline, of which planning is a function, although some sources describe planning as being the encompassing discipline. However, the activities of both implementation and control need to be planned as future activities, although the approach is not to include them as being part of planning.

CASE STUDY 1: IRISH CREAM LIQUEURS*

Case outline

The study is concerned with the phenomenal success of a range of Irish cream liqueurs developed by R. & A. Bailey & Co. Ltd, a subsidiary of the Grand Metropolitan Group.

Illustration

The chairman and managing director of Bailey stated that planning as part of their managerial process has been of vital importance to their success. The focus of planning relative to current decision making that will affect future performance is indicated twice in this case study. The initial marketing opportunity relative to cream liqueurs was identified through the process of the board disciplining their approach to the long-term future of the business, the result being the identification of this opportunity within the liqueur market. Second, having gained marketing success, their planning was again directed to the long-term future to pursue worldwide market potential by widening distribution, pursuing market development, and aiming for worldwide product acceptance.

The alternatives developed were based on market-segment need differentiation, in that the alternative products to be developed were for those people who do not like either the taste of alcohol, or the high alcoholic strength of most spirits. Consequently, the planning then exhibited decision making to participate in these segments with related commitment to these potential customer needs. Creativity in their planning was reflected in the development of their product concept, using a blend of Irish whiskey and Irish cream, with an image of quality and sophistication to reflect the quality of Irish life, which was a unique product concept at the time. This creativity also reflects the motivation of the personnel, although the MD stresses the enthusiasm and excitement generated by the people developing the product.

Discipline and formality in their approach are shown in the utilization of a rigorous market research programme. This was based upon customer acceptance testing, through product tastings directed at both the trade and consumers. The aspects of resource mobilization and expenditure commitments are featured throughout the case study, as the company progressively expanded its production capacity for market development in other countries. Finally, flexibility in their planning is reflected in that, due to excessive demand, they were required to adjust their operations in order to satisfy incoming orders.

* Derived from Barra O'Cinneide, Irish Cream Liqueurs. Copyright © 1981 Barra O'Cinneide.

REVIEW QUESTIONS

1. Do you consider that marketing is the most important business function and how would you justify your opinion?
2. How would you explain the difference between marketing orientation and marketing as a management process?
3. Discuss the range of outcomes as a consequence of companies utilizing marketing as a business function.
4. Why is planning a function of management?
5. Do you consider that any of the features of planning are more important than the others? Explain.

REFERENCES

1. P. J. Carroll, 'The link between performance and strategy', *Journal of Business Strategy*', **2**, 4, 3–20, 1982.
2. McCarthy, E. J., *Basic Marketing*, Irwin, Homewood, 1981.
3. Stanton, W. J., *Fundamentals of Marketing*, McGraw-Hill, New York, 1967.
4. 'Nixon's IBM', *Management Today*, January 1985.
5. 'Conran's New Habitat', *Management Today*, November 1983.
6. 'Editorial definition', *Quarterly Review of Marketing*, **8**, 1, October 1982.
7. The American Marketing Association, *Definition of Marketing*, Chicago, 1985.
8. Kotler, P., *Marketing Management: Analysis, Planning, and Control*, 5th edn, Prentice-Hall, Englewood Cliffs, 1984.
9. 'The Swiss put glitz in cheap quartz watches', *Fortune*, 20 August 1984.
10. Fayol, H., *General and Industrial Management*, Pitman, London, 1949.
11. H. I. Ansoff and R. G. Brandenburg, 'The design of optimal business planning systems', *Kommunikation*, **III**, 4, 163–88, 1967.
12. Warren, E. K., *Long Range Planning: The Executive Viewpoint*, Prentice-Hall, Englewood Cliffs, 1966.
13. Hussey, D. E., *Corporate Planning: Theory and Practice*, Pergamon, Oxford, 1976.
14. Ackoff, R. L., *A Concept of Corporate Planning*, Wiley, New York, 1970.
15. J. Hausler, 'Planning: a way of shaping the future', *Management International Review*, **2**, 3, 12–21, 1968.
16. 'ICI's new yarn', *Management Today*, February 1984.
17. 'Tandem's twofold task', *Management Today*, November 1984.
18. G. A. Steiner, 'Current trends in planning in business and government', *European Business*, **25**, 33–6, July 1967.
19. B. J. Loasby, 'Long range formal planning in perspective', *Journal of Management Studies*, **4**, 3, 300–8, October 1967.
20. R. L. Heroux, 'How effective is your planning?' *Managerial Planning*, **30**, 2, 3–16, September/October 1981.

THE PLANNING FRAMEWORK

Learning objectives are to:

1. Appreciate key issues in developing a planning framework.
2. Understand the differences between the various types of planning introduced.
3. Understand the structure and reasoning behind the adopted planning framework.
4. Appreciate the features of strategic and operational planning, including the role of marketing.
5. Appraise the role of business policy.
6. Recognize major new concepts that have been introduced.

In Chapter 1 the concept of planning as an integrating framework was introduced from the work by Steiner.[1] The value of such a framework was given as its integrating nature, which encompasses all areas of a company, yielding a uniform programme of plans for the entire organization over a long period. The aim of this chapter is to develop and define such a framework of planning as may be applicable throughout an organization. There are three major reasons for the establishment of such a framework. First, it provides a basis for the explanation of the planning of marketing at various levels in a company and as such reflects the structure of the book. Second, it reviews important issues that have been developed within the literature, providing a consolidation of important works. Finally, it provides a framework for the structuring of planning, which can be applied universally into specific company situations.

Chapter 1 also introduced the concept of a hierarchy of planning within companies, related to the managerial hierarchy, and the planning framework developed in this chapter includes this. Again, one aim of this is to allow firms to be able to apply such a planning hierarchy to their own managerial hierarchies.

A major consideration in this chapter, and indeed in subsequent chapters, is variation in terminology within the literature. Consequently, meanings have been extracted and used which represent current usage both in the literature and in organizations. However, each concept is given a definition and references to the literature have been selected in accordance with the development of a planning framework as outlined above.

FRAMEWORK CONCEPTS

This section is concerned with the examination of some key planning concepts as a prelude to defining the planning framework. The development of planning within the literature over the past two decades tends to be reflected here, although the adopted framework is developed from recent developments within the literature.

The total planning within a company is seen by Ansoff and Brandenburg[2] to involve the following:

– The complete set of documents designed to guide the behaviour of the members of the firm.
– The process by which these documents are conceived, prepared and revised.

The first indicates that the plan documents specify future action to be carried out by the various managers concerned. As the documents contain the detailed activities they are the end results of the planning process and give the guidance for continuous activities. The existence of an integrated set of plans for all areas of the company ensures the co-ordination of action. The second statement concerns the way in which the company organizes its planning, as opposed to the content of plans. This is the process of planning, in which planning exercises are carried out at a time before the period in which the resultant plans are to be applicable. However, the planning process also includes the revision of plans, not only those for future planning periods but also current plans, although within contingency parameters.

The concept of developing different plans for different levels of the managerial hierarchy is discussed by Janzen.[3] He gives five arbitrary levels of management, ranging from the board of directors (level A), through a hierarchy, to the level of department manager (level E). At this stage the meanings of the various levels of management and plans are not developed, as the aim is to give an overall understanding of the planning process. The various stages given by Janzen are as follows:

Planning level A: formulation of objectives
(board of directors)
                B: strategic planning
                C: tactical planning
                D: performance planning
                E: operational planning

Here the process starts with an overall definition of the aims or objectives of the company by the board of directors. At the strategic planning level the directors, and probably senior managers, are concerned with planning the overall direction and approach that the organization will take in total, as its all-embracing plan to achieve the company objectives. Planning levels C, D and E represent the plans of different divisions and departments of the organization, representing their planned action, as a contribution to the total company plans, established in the strategic planning. At each progressive stage within this planning hierarchy, managers at lower levels within the managerial hierarchy become progressively involved with planning. In addition, the planning activities become more specific when moving down the hierarchy, as specific objectives and actions are planned for individual product lines, plus individual products and brands. Definitions of these types of planning will be finalized in the next section of this chapter.

Another approach to the complete planning process is given by Fierheller.[4] He classifies planning at three different levels within the managerial hierarchy, as follows:

Corporate planning prepared by the board of directors.
Business planning prepared by senior executives, but with inputs from other levels.
Profit planning prepared and built up from all levels of management, finalized at board level.

This approach has the advantage of being more universal than that of Janzen and therefore is more readily applied into company situations. Here there are two levels of planning, corporate and strategic, but although other levels of management are seen to participate, there is no designation of specific planning below senior executive level, which is seen to be a weakness in this designation. However, a further strength is the integration of planning through profit planning, although, as will be illustrated later, such integration can also be achieved through an established planning framework.

A different approach is taken by Ansoff and Brandenburg[2] in presenting an overall planning process. Here they classify three types of plans: strategic, operational and administrative. Their suggested approach is that they prescribe a company's total planning process as being made up, in total, of these three plans, but that in addition these three types of plan should be developed for each level of management. The implication here is that, at each level of the company, managers need to face both strategic and operational issues, as well as organizing administration. However, the company overall still has a need to integrate each level of management and therefore they prescribe an overall encompassing strategy, an integration of all levels of operations and an integration of all levels of administration. This approach features the advantage of allowing for a development of the full potential of planning from all levels, as well as giving full potential for integration. This allows for ease of application to individual company situations, regardless of the degree of complexity of the managerial hierarchy. However, the disadvantage is that such a process is likely to lead to a complex system, confusing issues of demarcation, and creating problems where each level of planning provides inputs to the next level.

Alternatively, the total planning process within an organization can be related to periods of time as opposed to levels of management. An example here comes from the work of Godiwalla, Meinhart and Warde.[5] They consider that planning should be effected as a process by all executives, at all levels of the managerial hierarchy. The approach requires the establishment of three ranges of objectives and a set of time-related plans, as follows:

- Organizational objectives and their associated long-term plans.
- Specific goals and their associated medium-term plans.
- Performance objectives and their associated short-range and tactical plans.

This approach obviously has the advantage of allowing for participation by all managers. However, the disadvantage is a lack of structuring relative to an integrating framework and the managerial hierarchy. This can lead to a lack of plan integration, as, for example, illustrated in early planning at Nestlé, described by Brey and Gabsa.[6] Here the company planning featured long-range plans from individual business functions, which were then merely consolidated into an overall plan, without any overall direction.

DEVELOPING THE FRAMEWORK

Having examined these initial key planning concepts, we now turn our attention to developing the planning framework to be utilized within the book. The starting point is that the overall organizational planning process is referred to as corporate planning, which comprises both strategic and operational planning. Each of these types of planning can be simply explained as follows, while their relationship is given in Fig. 2.1.

Corporate planning The overall integrated planning system within an organization, incorporating strategic and operational planning.

Strategic planning An examination of the organization as a whole, followed by the planning of its future posture, shape and size.
Operational planning The planning of the manufacture, marketing and deployment of resources for the organization's current operations or business functions.

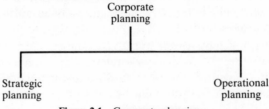

Figure 2.1   Corporate planning

A definition of corporate planning that is typical of this approach has been given by Hussey,[7] as follows:

> A comprehensive, continuous process of management looking towards the future, which is implemented within a formal framework and which is responsive to change in the external environment. It is concerned with both strategic and operational plans and, through participation, develops plans at the appropriate levels within the organization. It includes methods of monitoring and control and is concerned with both the short and long term.

This definition encompasses many of the concepts developed so far. The nature of planning as a function of management is emphasized, with an orientation to future action, which is continuous within the organization. The 'formal framework' equates to an integrating planning system, while responses to changes in the external environment are emphasized. The multiplexity of the total environment in which planning is utilized is a major feature of planning systems. Indeed, the effects of the environment on planning are continuously referred to throughout the text. The Hussey definition also emphasizes the importance of participation in planning, which will be discussed in Part Five. The orientation of the definition to the development of plans at appropriate levels does not give an indication as to location within the hierarchy, but this will be discussed later in this chapter. However, there is perhaps confusion as to the inclusion of control in a definition of planning, as opposed to it being a separate function of management. This is interpreted to mean the planning of control, as opposed to its exercise, as already established as a principle within the book. Finally, the Hussey definition refers to the consideration of time periods relative to planning. However, it is not clear as to which periods are pertinent to the different forms of planning, although this will also be discussed later in the chapter. Attention will now be given to a deeper understanding of both strategic and operational planning.

Strategic planning

From the above explanation a major stage of strategic planning involves an investigation, analysis and examination of the total environment of the organization. Both internal and external environments are included and considerable attention has been given in the literature to the effects of external variables on planning efforts, while the effects of economic recessions have forced organizations into assessing such effects. When such an examination is completed, the heart of strategic planning can be tackled. This is seen by Hussey[8] as being the overall objectives for the organization and the means by which these objectives are to be attained. These objectives and means are seen by Denning[9] as being the future posture of the organization, interpreted to mean the company's future state or condition, relating certain criteria to this posture such as size, profitability, rate of innovation and product-market posture. These objectives, within strategic planning, can also be considered to be the intended future direction of the firm, in the context of the types of business that are desired, size of operation and company image. However, they can also be considered to be desired levels of achievement, so that they also affect confidence in the future of the organization, both internally and externally. The overall means by which these objectives are to be obtained is normally referred to as strategy, so that the inclusion of strategy within strategic planning is the next stage. However, here there is immediate confusion within terminology, although this will be tackled in Part Two.

The emphasis given by Ackoff[10] is that strategic planning is differentiated from other planning in that its consequences have an enduring affect on the organization, being broad issues that relate to the long term. Therefore the concern is with a relatively long period, with decisions made now having consequences on the organization a long way into the future. Although strategic plans are likely to be modified as part of the control process at intervals over this period of time, decisions on commitment to the deployment of resources and courses of action may not be modifiable within the short to medium term. Because of this influence of the affects of strategic planning, Denning[9] and Higgins[11] identify the responsibility for strategic planning as lying with top management, as opposed to the functional managers, or at the top levels of the managerial hierarchy. Higgins also emphasizes the long-term nature of strategic planning as a major feature.

Finally, Taylor[12] stresses that strategic planning not only allows the firm to tackle adverse conditions arising in its business environment, but also allows it to exploit opportunities arising in the environment. Therefore, the concern is not solely directed at overcoming variables that affect the desired direction of the organization. Indeed, the major thrust of strategic planning is in allowing for the identification and selection of opportunities that not only allow the firm to pursue its desired direction, but which also dictate the determination of the desired direction. This is seen to be the major advantage and justification for the utilization of strategic planning, which, as a logical process, acts as a catalyst in the identification of opportunities, but also includes a process for selecting those to be pursued.

The major features of strategic planning are presented in Fig. 2.2, and illustrated in Case Study 2 (page 23).

Strategic planning is concerned with:

– Exploiting opportunities

– The future shape, size and posture of the firm

– An examination of the firm as a whole

– Assessing the affects of environmental variables

– The responsibility of top management

– Developing overall objectives and strategy

– Enduring consequences for the firm's future

Figure 2.2   Major features of strategic planning

Operational planning

This concerns not changing the strategic criteria, such as product-market posture, but planning the existing areas of business upon the foundation of the current base of resources. Therefore major changes of direction are not included, although modifications to production processes are, while new-product launches within the same product line and market entry within existing product lines are also within the scope of operational planning. Although the current base of resources is applicable, this does not exclude a reallocation of expenditure and/or manpower within the scope of current operations. Likewise, the attainment of additional finance for, say, a new product launch will be included as such an action would be within the province of operational planning. Here the plans are the responsibility of functional managers, as the concern is the operation of these functions into the future. These areas of business are given by Higgins[11] as marketing, production and manpower. However, Hussey[8] sees them as being marketing, production and an administration plan, the latter being aimed at approaches of continuously improving profitability.

In his definition of corporate planning, Hussey[7] emphasizes the relevance to both the short and long term. Operational planning, owing to its very nature, necessarily relates to the short term, in that it is founded upon the current base of operational resources. However, looking into the long-term future necessitates not only the establishment of strategic plans, but must also include, as reflected by the Society for Long Range Planning,[13] a translation of strategic plans into programmes of implementation within the business functions, which is very much the function of operational planning. Therefore operational planning involves not only short-range, one-year plans but also operations into longer periods of time. Consequently, writers such as Scott[14] identify both long-range and short-range operational planning, while many writers refer to the latter as tactical planning. Figure 2.3 shows the relationships developed so far.

The major features of operational planning are presented in Fig. 2.4 and are illustrated in Case Study 3 (page 24).

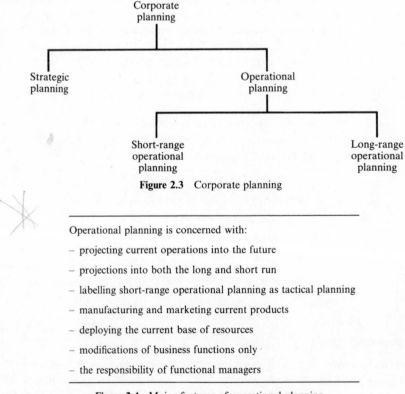

Figure 2.3 Corporate planning

Operational planning is concerned with:

– projecting current operations into the future

– projections into both the long and short run

– labelling short-range operational planning as tactical planning

– manufacturing and marketing current products

– deploying the current base of resources

– modifications of business functions only

– the responsibility of functional managers

Figure 2.4 Major features of operational planning

THE ADOPTED FRAMEWORK

This section is concerned with the establishment of the planning framework to be adopted in the book, building on Figs 2.1 and 2.3. The approach taken is first to examine the stages involved in both strategic and operational planning and then to establish the resultant planning framework.

The stages of strategic planning

An examination of the major texts that address strategic planning reveals variation in the terminology used by different authors. Similarly, there is apparent variation in the different stages of strategic planning proposed by these writers. However, an examination of these recent major texts by writers such as Byars,[15] Harvey,[17] Higgins,[18] Hofer and Schendel,[19] and Johnson and Scholes[20] shows similarity of major stages. Consequently, the major stages of strategic planning adopted within this book are given in Fig. 2.5. Traditionally, the strategy and objectives of the company in total have been known as corporate objectives and corporate strategy. However, this means that the word corporate is included within the strategic planning process, causing confusion within the terminology. There has been a trend within the literature to be more specific in terminology, and this approach has been adopted here, so that the labels organizational objectives and organizational strategy refer to the company in total.

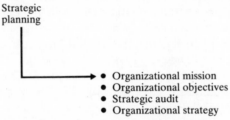

Strategic
planning

- Organizational mission
- Organizational objectives
- Strategic audit
- Organizational strategy

Figure 2.5   The stages of strategic planning

The role of marketing within strategic planning is seen as being a contribution to all stages. Although writers such as Ansoff[21] and Abell and Hammond[22] tend to see marketing and some stages of strategic planning as being synonymous, this is not the view taken in this book. Although, obviously, the role of marketing is taken to be critical, the roles of the other business functions are also seen to be of equal importance. Consequently, the planning of finance, manufacturing, purchasing and manpower are seen to have their own important and unique roles within strategic planning, alongside the role of marketing.

In stages one and two, establishing organizational mission and objectives, marketing is central to the organization's future direction, being based on the basic tenet of orienting the organization towards the market-place. In determining the organization's overall objectives the marketing process plays a major role. As will be seen in Chapter 4, the range of objectives a firm can select are either directly or indirectly affected by the marketing process. Again, the orientation of such objectives to the market-place is of central importance.

The strategic audit stage is concerned with an examination of the firm as a whole, relative to the external environment. In the former the expertise of marketing personnel is a major contribution, as is the strength of established marketing practices, such as brand image, product range, sales force and distribution effectiveness. The external environment aspect of the strategic audit can be considered as being simply a continuous appraisal of both opportunities and threats.

Opportunities in particular need to be market opportunities, and therefore marketing skills are needed for their identification, while marketing criteria need to be used to establish their viability for exploitation. Threats can be considered to be any variable that has the potential of adversely affecting company performances. Sales volume and market share are obviously two major measures of such performance, so that marketing skills are, again, required both to identify such threats and to contribute to corrective action to tackle such threats.

Finally, organizational strategy is concerned with the overall approach the firm will take to achieve its organizational mission and objectives. As these aims are oriented to markets, it follows that the means of achievement also needs to be oriented to markets and hence to marketing issues. Indeed, as will be seen in Chapter 5, the contributions of marketing become specific within the individual stages of developing an organizational strategy.

The stages of operational planning

An examination of the major texts that address marketing operational planning also reveals a variation in the utilization of terminology and the proposed range of stages involved. The major stages adopted within the book are given in Fig. 2.6, which has been synthesized from current major texts by writers such as Cravens,[23] Jain,[24] Kotler,[25] Luck and Ferrell,[26] and McDonald.[27]

Traditionally, within companies, this range of planning stages has represented the work of the marketing department for the forthcoming year, hence the use of the marketing label within the stages, which also, of course, serves to differentiate from other operational planning carried out in other functional departments, such as finance. The split between the long- and short-range components is stressed in Fig. 2.6 to illustrate the relationships, although company practice tends to include both marketing strategy and tactics within the same marketing plan document. Indeed the sequence within the plan document would normally be to present the objectives before both the strategy and tactics. The different roles performed by marketing strategy and marketing tactics will be explained later in the book.

This area of operational planning has come to be known as marketing planning within many organizations and in some parts of the literature, generally being related to the annual marketing plan, so that the phrase 'marketing planning' does not include strategic planning concepts.

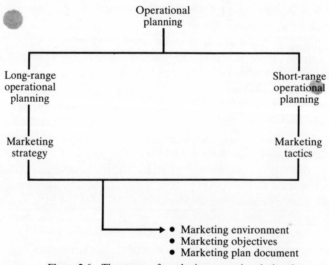

Figure 2.6 The stages of marketing operational planning

Consequently, within the planning framework of this book the term marketing planning has been abandoned in favour of referring to the planning of marketing at either the strategic or operational levels. At this stage of the book the reason for this approach should be obvious to the reader, it being based upon the different roles played by both strategic and operational planning within organizations, plus the role of marketing within each form of planning. However, the full ramifications due to this approach will, of course, be fully expounded in subsequent chapters.

The planning framework and book presentation

Although the nature of the planning of marketing at both the strategic and operational levels has been defined, such planning is obviously carried out within the context of the other functions of management and within the totality of the organization. Consequently, Fig. 2.7 presents the total planning framework adopted in the book, in which these contextual variables, or considerations, are related to the planning stages. These are given as relating firstly to the process that the organization uses internally to achieve its planning, and secondly to the implementation of the plans.

The total planning framework from Fig. 2.7 is presented within the book as follows:

Part Two   Strategic planning
Part Three Operational planning
Part Four The planning process
Part Five Implementing and controlling plans

Within the individual chapters of each part the areas given in Fig. 2.7 are examined in turn.

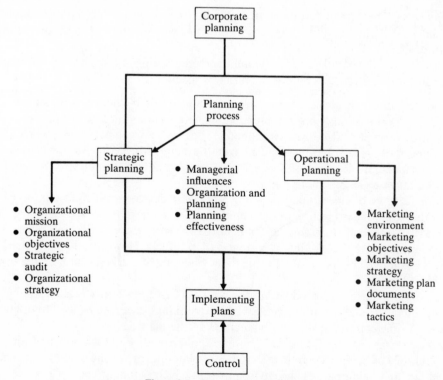

Figure 2.7   The planning framework

THE ROLE OF BUSINESS POLICY

The concept of policy, and more specifically that of business policy, has not been mentioned so far. The concept of business policy has also been given considerable treatment within the literature and is also used within organizations. However, there is confusion about the use of the concept. Indeed, Ansoff[28] recorded in 1971 that there was confusion regarding the meanings of policy and strategy, while more than a decade later Leontiades[29] was discussing the same confusion. Indeed, many writers and organizations use the concepts of strategic planning and business policy synonymously. This, however, is not the approach taken in this book. The approach taken here is that policy can be simply explained as being 'the way the company does things', whereas objectives and strategy can be simply explained as being 'what they are to do' and 'how they are to do it'. Byars[15] explains policy as being general guidelines to managers for decision making, whereas Harvey[17] defines it as being advanced decision making to cover a prescribed set of conditions. Business policy is discussed again in Chapter 3, although a further treatment is to be found in a recent article by Greenley.[30]

Consequently, the book approaches policy as being a set of guidelines in which the organization's planning must be carried out. A fuller treatment of the role of business policy and its affect on planning will therefore be given in Part Two.

SUMMARY

The first section of this chapter examined certain key planning concepts as a prelude to developing a planning framework. The adopted planning framework can be summarized in the following classifications:

Corporate planning The overall and integrated planning system within an organization.
Strategic planning An examination of the organization as a whole, followed by the planning of its future posture, shape and size.
Operational planning The planning of the manufacture, marketing and deployment of resources for the organization's current operations, or business functions.

The major features of strategic planning were developed in the chapter. A major thrust was given as being the exploitation of opportunities, along with an assessment of the potential affects of environmental variables. Also involved is an appraisal of the organization as a whole, as well as the development of overall objectives and an overall strategy. Marketing was taken as having a contribution to make at all stages of strategic planning, although the roles of other business functions were taken to be of similar importance.

The major features of operational planning were also developed. This is concerned with current operations and the projection of the manufacture and marketing of these into the future. This projection is into both the long run and short run. Here the contribution of marketing obviously appertains to the marketing of current-base products. However, the term 'marketing planning' was abandoned in favour of referring to the planning of marketing at both the strategic and operational levels.

The planning framework adopted within the book was given in Fig. 2.7. Here strategic and operational planning are set within the context of the planning process to be used to prepare the plans, and within the context of the implementation of the plans.

Finally the chapter examined the role of business policy relative to the planning framework. This was established as being a separate role to that of planning, providing a set of guidelines for decision making, and being part of the environment in which planning takes place.

CASE STUDY 2: CARNATION FOODS COMPANY LTD*

Case outline

The case study highlights the development of Carnation UK away from its traditional product of evaporated milk.

Illustration

The necessity for strategic planning to assess the effects of environmental variables is illustrated in this case study. The UK company had traditionally been dependent on one product, evaporated milk, but the UK market and the company's margins were rapidly declining. The chief cause was a change in consumer tastes since the war, but there was also an over-capacity situation in the industry, government control of milk prices, and the questionable effectiveness of Carnation's approach to advertising. Consequently their examination of the firm as a whole had changed from being defined as 'the manufacture and sale of evaporated milk' to a broader base of businesses, although these were not explicitly defined in the case study. However, another aspect here is an orientation from the US parent company of defining their business in terms of levels of profitability as opposed to products and markets.

Consideration of the firm's future shape, size and posture is also highlighted. The US parent company had achieved rapid growth and it is implicit that further growth was being pursued. The implications for the UK firm were to achieve growth themselves, while experiencing greater intervention from the USA company in the management of all its subsidiary companies. A major directive here was for product-line expansion, and to diversify away from the traditional product into other markets. Consequently, the feature of opportunity exploitation took three directions in the UK company. The first was to enter the expanding pet-food market, while the second was to enter the similarly expanding slimming-aids market with a US-based product ('Slender'), that featured a potentially high gross margin in excess of 40 per cent. The final opportunity was pursued in the coffee-whitening market with another US product, 'Coffee-Mate'.

Overall objectives are described within the case study as being focused on profit margins and profitability, particularly as a directive from the parent company. However, evidence of other overall objectives is not apparent. The overall strategy appears to have been oriented to diversification away from the traditional product of evaporated milk, through the development of products already being marketed by other Carnation companies in other countries. Finally, the feature of top management involvement in these issues is emphasized throughout the case. This included the president of the Carnation International Division, US corporate staff, the managing director of Carnation UK, and its marketing director.

---

* Derived from Kate Gillespie and Ulrich E. Wiechmann, Carnation Foods Co. Ltd, Case 9-578-075. Boston: Harvard Business School. Copyright © 1978 by the President and Fellows of Harvard College

CASE STUDY 3: CARNATION FOODS COMPANY LTD*

Case outline

The case study illustrates some of the marketing issues in the operational planning of two of Carnation's product lines.

Illustration

The role of operational planning in projecting current operations into both the long and short future is illustrated in several places in the case study. The product aimed at the coffee-whitening market, Coffee-Mate, was test-marketed in the Midlands over a five-year period, to provide a basis for projecting this particular marketing operation over subsequent years. This was successful in testing product acceptance, price and size of jar, allowing for a decision to be committed to marketing the product into the future on a national basis. The test market also gave a short-term sales forecast for the first year of the national launch, although the actual sales for this period were almost double the forecast, allowing for a reappraisal of a subsequent projection into the long-run future of this particular marketing operation. In subsequent years of the national launch, consumer attitude surveys were used in order to investigate product attitudes and how these would be likely to affect future sales, particularly in relation to the test marketing of a competitive product from Cadbury's, Britain's largest food company. However, five years after the national launch Carnation were also attempting to project into the future the likely affect of a tripling of raw-materials costs relative to necessary price increases of Coffee-Mate, and how such increases would affect sales and gross margins. Test marketing was also used for two new products to be aimed at the pet food market, again as a basis for projecting such marketing operations into the future.

Examples of current marketing operations are also evident. A range of product benefits of Coffee-Mate were identified and two jar sizes were initially introduced, although this was increased to three, the latter also reflecting the feature of operational planning relative to modifications to individual business functions. Considerable attention was given to price, relative to jar size, competition and raw materials costs. Television advertising was an important part of the marketing operations, with a projected image of being superior to milk, giving a taste of cream to coffee, and being highly convenient. Promotion to the trade was also important, and Carnation were able to offer higher margins and a smaller space investment than Cadbury's.

Little information is given in the case of the feature of deployment of current base resources. However, over the three-year period preceeding Coffee-Mate's national launch a constant level of expenditure was allocated to advertising, despite increasing prices for advertising time and space.

Finally, the feature of functional managerial responsibility is highlighted. Here the managing director was seeking to develop the initiative for the development of the operations of Carnation UK from within his managerial hierarchy, and not from corporate staff within the US parent company.

* Derived from Kate Gillespie and Ulrich E. Wiechmann, Carnation Foods Co. Ltd, Case 9-578-075. Boston: Harvard Business School. Copyright © 1978 by the President and Fellows of Harvard College.

REVIEW QUESTIONS

1. What do you consider to be the key issues for consideration in developing a planning framework?
2. How would you defend the Ansoff and Brandenburg approach to a planning framework?
3. Discuss the differences between planning at the strategic level and planning at the operational level.
4. Discuss the major features of strategic planning, emphasizing which you consider to be central issues.
5. Explain the role of operational planning and outline how you think it relates to other levels of planning.
6. 'The term "marketing planning" has been abandoned.' Discuss.

REFERENCES

1. G. A. Steiner, 'Current trends in planning in business and government', *European Business*, **25**, 33–6, July 1967.
2. H. I. Ansoff and R. G. Brandenburg, 'The design of optimal business planning systems', *Kommunikation*, **III**, 4, 163–88, 1967.
3. L. T. Janzen, 'Systematic planning and re-organisation', *Long Range Planning*, **4**, 2, 58–62, December 1971.
4. G. A. Fierheller, 'Planning in the medium-sized company', *Managerial Planning*, **29**, 16–19, January/February 1980.
5. Y. M. Godiwalla, W. A. Meinhart and W. A. Warde, 'General management and corporate strategy', *Managerial Planning*, **30**, 2, 17–29, September/October 1981.
6. A. Brey, and G. Gabsa, 'Integrated long range planning at Nestlé', *Long Range Planning*, **5**, 2, 44–6, June 1972.
7. D. E. Hussey, 'How to plan success', *Management Today*, 107–9, November 1978.
8. Hussey, D. E., *Corporate Planning: Theory and Practice*, Pergamon, Oxford, 1979.
9. Denning, B. W., *Introduction to Corporate Planning: Selected Concepts*, McGraw-Hill, London, 1971.
10. Ackoff, R. L., *A Concept of Corporate Planning*, Wiley, New York, 1970.
11. Higgins, J. C., *Strategic and Operational Planning Systems: Principles and Practice*, Prentice-Hall, London, 1980.
12. B. Taylor, 'The concept and use of corporate planning', in Taylor, B., and J. R. Sparkes (eds), *Corporate Strategy and Planning*', Heinemann, London, 1977.
13. Society for Long Range Planning, 'Editorial definition', *Long Range Planning*, **14**, 2, April 1981.
14. Scott, B. W., *Long Range Planning in American Industry*, American Marketing Association, Chicago, 1965.
15. Byars, L. L., *Strategic Management*, Harper and Row, New York, 1984.
16. Glueck, W. F., and L. R. Jauch, *Business Policy and Strategic Management*, McGraw-Hill, New York, 1984.
17. Harvey, D. F., *Strategic Management*, Merrill, Columbus, 1982.
18. Higgins, J. M., *Organizational Policy and Strategic Management*, Dryden, New York, 1983.
19. Hofer, C. W., and D. Schendel, *Strategy Formulation*, West Publishing, St Paul, 1978.
20. Johnson, G., and K. Scholes, *Exploring Corporate Strategy*, Prentice-Hall, London, 1984.
21. Ansoff, H. I., *Corporate Strategy*, McGraw-Hill, New York, 1968.
22. Abell, D. F., and J. S. Hammond, *Strategic Market Planning: Problems and Analytical Approaches*, Prentice-Hall, Englewood Cliffs, 1979.
23. Cravens, D. W., *Strategic Marketing*, Irwin, Homewood, 1982.
24. Jain, S. C., *Marketing Planning and Strategy*, South-Western, Cincinnati, 1981.
25. Kotler, P., *Marketing Management*, 5th edn, Prentice-Hall, Englewood Cliffs, 1984.
26. Luck, D. J., and D. C. Ferrell, *Marketing Strategy and Plans*, Prentice-Hall, Englewood Cliffs, 1979.
27. McDonald, M. H. B., *Marketing Plans*, Heinemann, London, 1984.
28. H. I. Ansoff, 'Strategy as a tool of coping with change', *Journal of Business Policy*, **1**, 4, 3–7, 1971.
29. M. Leontiades, 'The confusing words of business policy', *Academy of Management Review*, **17**, 1, 45–8, 1982.
30. G. E. Greenley, 'A teaching framework for business policy', *Business Education*, **6**, 1, 53–62, 1985.

TWO

STRATEGIC PLANNING

3. Organizational mission
4. Organizational objectives and the strategic audit
5. Organizational strategy

OUTLINE

Part Two is devoted to an examination of the stages of strategic planning. Chapter 3 is concerned with the organizational mission as the initial stage of all corporate planning. Chapter 4 examines the overall aims of the total company in the form of organizational objectives. This chapter also addresses the examination of the company's total environment, particularly within the context of its affect on the achievement of organizational objectives. This part of the book concludes with an examination of organizational strategy in Chapter 5, as the overall means of achieving the organizational mission and objectives. Throughout Part Two the role of the marketing process is emphasized in relation to each of the stages of strategic planning. Additionally, the marketing orientation required in formulating these stages is discussed, along with the marketing orientation that their adoption is likely to instil.

THREE

ORGANIZATIONAL MISSION

Learning objectives are to:

1. Appreciate the influence of various groups of people on mission.
2. Understand the role of internal stakeholders.
3. Appreciate the role of business policy relative to corporate planning.
4. Understand the nature and function of organizational mission within strategic planning.
5. Recognize major concepts that have been introduced.

In Fig. 2.5 from Chapter 2, the location of organizational mission was indicative of the starting point of strategic planning. Although a theme developed within the book is that the stages of planning do not necessarily follow in sequential order, the premise is established that this is the logical starting point of all planning within an organization.

The organizational mission plays two major roles, the overall purpose and overall direction of the firm. (The specific roles will be established later in the chapter.) The establishment of and subsequent changes to such purpose and direction are likely to be affected by the various different groups of people associated with the firm, often labelled stakeholders, particularly the major decision makers within the organization. Here the aspirations, expectations and values of individuals become an initial input to the planning process. Indeed, the affect of such human influence, regardless of how it is motivated, cannot be detached from the establishment of each of the planning stages, a theme which is also developed throughout the book.

Consequently, this chapter firstly addresses stakeholder influence on organizational mission as an initial input to the planning process. Such influence is also seen to be important relative to the other stages of both strategic and operational planning, being a further reason for its location at this point in the book. However, such influence is examined further and in more detail in Part Four, after the examination of all stages of planning.

In Chapter 2 the role of business policy of providing a set of guidelines was established. Such guidelines are seen as being part of the influence of the stakeholder group of internal major decision makers. Consequently, the nature of business policy is also discussed in the chapter, before the formal examination of organizational mission.

STAKEHOLDER INFLUENCE

As stated, the various groups of people likely to affect organizational mission are often referred to as stakeholders. Indeed, the concept extends to relate to the organization as a whole. A definition of a stakeholder is given by Freeman[1] as follows: 'any group or individual who can affect or is affected by the achievement of an organization's purpose'. Such a definition is extremely wide and allows for the inclusion of many groups of people, some of which are likely to be outside the scope relative to planning. However, the major principle relative to planning is to identify those people who have the potential of affecting planning, or who are likely to be affected by it. The extensiveness and variation of such stakeholder groups is illustrated in Case Study 4 (page 43).

Despite such wide variations writers such as Freeman[1] have attempted to generalize the major groups of stakeholders. The different groups he suggests are presented in Fig. 3.1, although here they are presented in a different format and are grouped into three major sections. The interests, or stakes, that the individuals within these different groups will have will obviously vary from group to group. Market-place stakeholders are obviously concerned with trading and contractual relationships and as such will have a direct effect on planning. The internal stakeholders are principally concerned with the benefits they will receive from the firm and will also have a direct affect on planning. The interests of the external groups are varied and are likely to have varying degrees of effect on planning.

Market-place stakeholders
Customers
Competitors
Suppliers

External stakeholders
Government
Political groups
Financial community
Trade associations
Activist groups

Internal stakeholders
Owners
Decision makers
Unions and employees

Figure 3.1 Major stakeholder groups

The remainder of this section of the chapter examines the effects these groups are likely to have on planning whereas Chapter 4 examines in detail the approaches to be taken towards the total environment. Also, the principle is established that it is the internal stakeholder group that has the greatest effect on planning and therefore is the subject of the greatest attention. Consequently, internal stakeholder groups are allotted a complete section within this chapter.

Market-place stakeholders

The expectations of customers towards the company's products obviously have a central affect on planning and indeed are central to the total marketing effort. Consequently, the understanding of these expectations through the utilization of marketing is entirely pertinent at this initial stage of strategic planning. The potential affects of customer expectations are illustrated by the US drug company Smith Kline and their product Tagamet, which is a cure for ulcers. Following a seven-year monopoly in the USA through patent protection, the product is facing competition from the UK firm Glaxo Holdings. A major objective within the planning of Smith Kline is market share, but the company realizes that the erosion of this by Glaxo will be affected by the expectations of the 120 000 physicians in the USA who prescribe the bulk of ulcer medication.[2] Approaches to be taken, to understand the expectations of customers, are classified as being part of marketing operations and as such are examined in Part Three.

Similarly, the expectations of competitors also have an effect on company planning. Their expectations relative to the share of the market they wish to obtain will affect their planning of marketing, while their effectiveness in achieving this desired market share is likely to affect the subsequent planning of the other companies in the market. Using the example of Smith Kline, the expectations of Glaxo relative to market share will no doubt have affected their marketing activities, the success of which will need to be considered in the future planning by Smith Kline in order to maintain their market dominance. Again, marketing is normally required to assess the affects of such competitive actions, and again such approaches are examined in Part Three.

The expectations of suppliers probably have less of an effect on the planning of the majority of companies. Unless, for example, a supplier is unable to provide adequate quantities of components to expand output to meet the growth of sales volume required within the planning, it is more than likely that both quality and quantity of suppliers will be negotiated relative to planning requirements. Indeed, the function of procurement has an equal responsibility relative to planning, at both the operational and strategic levels. However, despite this general principle, it must be recognized that situations can arise where suppliers are able to affect a firm's planning. For example, the Central Electricity Generating Board in the United Kingdom relies upon supplies of coal from the National Coal Board in order to be able to continuously provide its product to its customers, and consequently the importance of this stakeholder is well recognized by the CEGB.[3]

External stakeholders

Owing to the diversity of the different groups within this classification, a diversity of effects can be applicable relative to planning. The expectations of government relative to the nationalized industries are obviously very different to that of, say, the privately owned companies in the retail trade. Similarly, the expectations of government relative to the overall performance of British industry differs from the expectations of the financial community. The only feasible common principle that can probably be established relative to the possible effects that expectations from this group can have on planning, is that each organization needs to be continually aware of changes that are likely to occur in these groups so that they can be in a position to be able to forecast likely effects on their planning. Such an approach to assess this type of change is discussed in Chapter 4.

An example of the effects of external stakeholder groups on planning comes from the European textile industry. During the period 1975 to 1980 an excess of production capacity had developed, companies had suffered deficits, and planning into the future was obviously difficult. In 1978 the major producers, together with the European Commission in Brussels, agreed to reduce production capacity within the industry by 15 per cent. Further cuts in capacity were required of companies in 1982, which were achieved under the auspices of CIRFS (the European man-made fibres association). Further restrictions were also initiated within the industry for the period 1983 to 1986 by the MFA (Multi-Fibre Arrangement), under the auspices of the European Commission, restricting increases in production capacity within EEC countries. These restrictions were supported in the UK by the British Textiles Confederation.[4] Therefore the planning of companies within this industry is affected not only by market conditions, but also by the expectations of these stakeholder groups operating to control the future development of the industry.

Again, marketing can be seen to play a role in the assessment of the effect of some of these expectations. In the above example, marketing personnel within companies in the textile industry would be responsible for forecasting changes in customer requirements, and, in this case, changes in the level of market demand. Having identified the trend that would have been developing in the seventies, the firms would have been in a position of not only predicting the planning they would need to do as a consequence, but also predicting the action that would be likely from these external groups, namely that the resulting trend would necessitate institutions such as the European Commission acting to reduce production capacity within the industry.

INTERNAL STAKEHOLDERS

After the initial examination of stakeholder groups earlier in this chapter, the principle was established that it is the internal groups that are likely to have the greatest effect on planning. Indeed, this principle is restricted still further to that of the major decision makers. The justification for establishing this principle will become apparent later in the section, but is also supported within the literature by writers such as McCarthy, Minichiello and Curran.[5] As a result, most of this section is devoted to these particular groups, although attention is firstly given to the other internal stakeholder groups listed in Fig. 3.1.

Owners and unions

The power that the owners have relative to affecting planning arises from their voting rights. In large organizations where the owners are a different group of people from the decision makers, such power is likely to be less than that where the owners are also the directors. In the former, where there are many owners, each with a relatively low level of shareholding, such power will be restricted merely to appraisal of past performance, which will have only an indirect affect on future planning, plus voting relative to future board members. In such a situation the diverse ownership is probably unorganized as far as concentrating their power to affect planning goes. However, the situation is different where a large proportion, say 30 to 40 per cent, of the shares represent a common owner. Here the power is more concentrated and organized around the owner, so that voting rights can be exercized to influence the planning, or even specific aspects such as mission, objectives and strategies. Examples of stakes that companies often obtain in the ownership of others are common within the financial press, while the influence of the British government as a stakeholder in the ownership of nationalized industries is also well reported. Where ownership and directorship are common, the power to influence the firm's planning is also common. While the two different roles may provide different criteria for those decision makers in their planning, the approach adopted in this book is that it is part of the same process and can therefore be equated to the processes to be discussed in the next section.

The effects that unionization of employees can have on an organization have been well documented, although studies of its effects specifically on planning are not apparent. Obviously, activities such as strikes can drastically affect the achievement of short-term objectives, and may also affect current investment for planned future growth. However, other potential effects relate to participation in planning by the unions in order to represent directly their stake within individual companies through taking part in the formulation of objectives and strategies. Such partnership in planning appears to be a neglected area within the current body of knowledge and one likely to benefit from a deeper understanding. An example of a development in this direction has been reported in the case of the Chrysler Corporation in the United States. Here a union president was offered a seat on the board of directors, reportedly the first in a major US corporation. A prominent issue was the resistance to and disagreement with the offer among senior executives, a leading concern being that there would be a conflict of interests, between those of the company and those of the union.[6]

Decision makers

The effects that decision makers within a firm can have on planning have been discussed in the literature. Christensen, Andrews and Bower[7] have stressed that executives are often more influenced by what they personally want to do than by what the company is capable of doing. Here the implication is that the personal values and opinions have a stronger influence on planning than does a planning process where alternative objectives and strategies are logically and systematically developed and where justifiable decisions are made. If we extend this concept we can conceive a potential conflict situation where the values and expectations of executives who are the planning decision makers conflict with the planning process. The nature and influence of these managerial values and expectations will be considered in the next section, since the remainder of this one examines the nature of the planning decision makers as a prelude to a survey of their influence.

From company to company, considerable differences are evident regarding the managers who participate in both strategic and operational planning. A major reason why such differences occur is that there tend to be major differences between the organizational structures of firms. Such differences in structure and their direct affect on planning are examined in Part Four, although the identification of such managerial groups will be tackled at this point. Simplistically, such groups can be classified as follows:

– The board of directors.
– Specialist planning personnel.
– Senior managers.
– Operational managers.

Several permutations of participation of these four groups within the stages of strategic planning are possible. The board may merely set a mission and objectives, leaving the rest of the planning to the planning personnel, where these are employed, or to senior managers. Alternatively, the planning personnel may have total responsibility, or when specialist planners are not employed the board may assume total responsibility. In such cases, of what is commonly labelled the 'top-down' approach, the participation of senior and operational managers will be limited, possibly to merely providing information such as forecasts and market performance. Another approach is that operational plans are prepared first and 'passed upwards', to be used in compounding an overall strategic plan; the ultimate alternative for this 'bottom-up' approach is that the strategic plan is prepared by senior and operational managers in draft form for final approval by the board. While such involvement clearly gives these managers participation which is likely to be beneficial to them (again to be pursued further in Part Four), Hall[8] has high-lighted the weakness of such a total 'bottom-up' approach. This is that, owing to pressure from their normal duties, such managers do not have the time or inclination to systematically consider alternatives, so that resultant plans are likely to be limited.

Additional permutations of participation occur where companies are divided into different divisions, or organized into different product groups or market groups. Such divisions have been labelled strategic business units (SBUs) within the literature. Here there can be an overall strategic plan for the organization and separate operational plans, or indeed each SBU may be sufficiently large enough to merit its own strategic and operational plans. Again, despite the approach taken, there can be several variations in which decision makers participate in these plans. Consequently, the overall implication to emerge from this discussion is that within this stakeholder group of decision makers there is considerable variation from organization to organization both in the types of executives to be involved and in the individual roles they play in the planning process.

Another approach taken in the literature has been to attempt to classify managers into a range of different management styles. One such approach is by Hall, O'Leary and Williams[9] who have developed a classification based on the dimensions of decision adequacy on the part of the decision maker, plus his concern for the commitment of others to his decisions. This provides a decision-making grid of five major management styles into which managers can be placed. A similar two-dimensional grid approach is taken by McClelland and Burnham,[10] using the dimensions of the decision maker's need for achievement and his need for power, which also results in five major management styles into which managers may be placed. However, despite such attempts to quantify human behaviour, three major problems have not been overcome. These are individual personality differences such as individual values, expectations, and attitudes towards planning itself. The last named will be examined in Part Four, whereas attention is now given to values and expectations.

Values and expectations of decision makers

This examination of the values and expectations of executives has been developed from the extensive literature concerned with organizational behaviour. The aim is to outline how values and expectations affect the planning of marketing, which also links with the examination of managerial attitudes towards planning given in Part Four.

The overall principle to be established in this section has been epitomized by Chang and Campo-Flores.[11] This is that executives are unable to separate their feelings, emotions and personal preferences from logical analysis when making decisions, with the major consideration being the executives' personal values. Therefore it must be remembered that, although planning can be logically set out in stages, as given in Part One, the process is carried out by people, and the ramifications of human behaviour are apparent in planning just as they are in other human activities.

Human values have been defined by writers such as Williams[12] as being a component part of attitudes, with the previous experience of individuals having a major affect on the formulation of their attitudes. Consequently, executives' experiences of either the success or failure of planning, or the success or failure of marketing, are likely to affect how they currently value the need for either planning or marketing. An example here is the recently reported change in values of the top executives of the Ford Motor Company in the United States. Here there has been a 'forced' change of attitudes to make executives more marketing orientated by making their cars more 'driver orientated' and the executives more aware of the performance and handling of cars.[13]

A fuller explanation of the factors likely to affect the values of executives within the company situation has been offered by Johnson and Scholes.[14] These factors are classified into three groups as follows:

- External influences of the values of society and peer groups to which individuals belong.
- The nature of the business, with the market situation and product range being particularly important.

– The company culture, including company age and history, managerial style, plus planning and control systems.

Here the implication is that the very nature of the markets and products affect the values of executives towards marketing, which is perhaps in opposition to marketing orientation, which itself can be taken as being a form of value establishment in order to serve markets by developing products. However, the example of the Ford Motor Company given above reflects the principle given by Johnson and Scholes. Similarly, the planning the company has used, and its history of success, themselves have an effect on planning. In both cases there is a reverse cause-and-effect relationship: the planning affects managerial values, which in turn affect subsequent planning. An example of another company-culture effect on managerial values comes from a recent report relative to the UK subsidiary of Toshiba, the Japanese television company. Here the chief executive aims to make all managers feel important and to instil a sense of purpose and direction into all personnel.[15] This aspect of company culture is likely to affect managerial values in a way favourable to planning; it emanates directly from the first stage of organizational mission (as will be seen later in the chapter).

The expectations of executives relative to their employment is discussed in the literature as expectancy theory by writers such as Gray and Starke.[16] Expectancy theory is one of a range of theories within the literature to explain the motivation of people towards work. Briefly, the theory is concerned with the outcome that individuals desire to achieve from the working environment, plus their belief as to the probability that they will achieve these outcomes. Here the general implication is that if executives expect the utilization of planning and marketing to have a positive affect on the performance of the company, then these expectations are likely to motivate the executives to strive to achieve effective planning. The British engineering firm Wadkin illustrates the use of expectations in order to motivate managers towards planning. The firm has established five major criteria which it expects to improve currently, such as higher product quality and distribution effectiveness, and managers are motivated towards achieving these desirable outcomes.[17]

Throughout the organization it is likely that executives will have different values and expectations. However, some are likely to be similar and such a group of executives represents a coalition of common values and expectations. Regardless of differences, if planning is to be completed then agreement must be reached by various levels of groups of managers who are responsible for completing the various stages throughout the corporate planning. Fuller attention to the affects of such coalitions and group dynamics will be addressed in Part Four. However, there is one area of coalition agreement relative to values and expectations that needs to be examined. This is concerned with the guidelines that the board of directors establish within which all planning must be carried out. In Part One this was explained as being the business policy of the organization, to which fuller attention is now given.

BUSINESS POLICY

In earlier works within the literature the concept of business policy was referred to as the overall management of the company, as, for example, given by Learned et al.[18] and Christenson, Andrews and Bower.[19] Here stages of overall company objectives and strategy were included within business policy, with no clarification of different levels of planning. This approach to business policy is also reflected in other works, such as Glueck[20] and Thomas.[21] This broad approach to the concept of business policy clearly enters the sphere of strategic and operational planning. Indeed, as the body of knowledge relative to these forms of planning has developed, so the confusion referred to above regarding the role of policy within organizations has developed also.

One approach to the narrowing of the scope of business policy is given by Chang and Campo-Flores.[11] Their approach is to classify business policy as being part of strategic planning. Within this context, business policy is given as being made up of four areas. The first two refer to the overall company objectives, while the other two areas are given as being the company purpose, plus a range of guidelines. However, the last is interpreted as being no more than specific issues from strategic planning.

The establishment of the role of business policy relative to the adopted planning framework is based upon several definitions of policy advocated within the literature. For example, Tilles[22] used the phrase 'decision rule' as a guide to the making of strategy when explaining policy. Similarly, Byars[23] uses the concept of general guidelines, while Higgins[24] refers to policy as guidance created to ensure the successful formulation, implementation and control of planning. Similarly, Higgins[25] refers to guidelines or codes to take action, while Quinn[26] defines policy as a set of rules or guidelines that express limits within which action should occur. The common theme which unites these writers is that business policy is seen as the set of guidelines to be used within the company, the guidelines being applicable throughout the range of corporate planning, as well as in the implementation and control of plans.

The nature of the type of guidelines to be included within business policy is well developed by Brech.[27] Here the approach is that the organization develops its own set of guidelines, but within a framework of four interrelated facets. The first two facets relate to areas that are labelled the ethical foundation. The first of these is concerned with standards of fair trading. This covers the principles upon which the firm conducts outside relations with other firms or individuals, plus society as a whole. This is obviously a wide area for the development of guidelines. In the former the range of firms can include suppliers, competitors, agencies and official bodies. Policies aimed at individuals are likely to be dominated by those relating to customers, where a range of marketing policies relating to the product, selling and advertising, and distribution efficiency can be developed. The general rule for policies concerning the society as a whole is that they are applicable where the firm is likely to incur a social cost. An obvious example here is pollution, but others may include excessive profit margins and the utilitarian value of products. The second part of the ethical foundation comprises standards of employment, involving conditions of employment and dealings with employees. This is obviously the concern of the personnel function, although developed guidelines are likely to be applicable to all employees.

The third facet in the development of the guidelines of business policy is channels and methods of trading. Again, these policies are mostly marketing related, with examples being policies towards direct sales, selling agents, exporting, retailing and wholesaling. These would include direction as to the type of situation in which each particular method would be chosen,

---

Business policy is concerned with:

– A separate area of attention to the planning framework

– Rules to be used by managers in decision making

– Deferred decisions triggered by specific situations

– Rules for limiting the actions of employees

– Policy guidelines related to an ethical foundation, channels and methods of trading, plus internal arrangements

---

Figure 3.2 Major features of business policy

plus guidelines relating to the conditions in which they would be used. The final facet covers internal arrangements, providing guidelines for the internal administration of the organization. Here policy guidelines cover the company's approach to management practice and internal effectiveness and efficiency.

Having examined the role of business policy within the adopted planning framework, further formal treatment within the book is not offered. However, throughout the text reference will be made, where applicable, to the effects of business policy on the planning of marketing. The major features of business policy are summarized in Fig. 3.2.

ORGANIZATIONAL MISSION

In its broadest sense, an organization's mission can be taken to be the reason why it is in business. Traditional micro-economic theory gives this reason as being profit maximization, and indeed many businessmen will give such a reason as being to make money or to earn a profit. However, the complexities of modern companies mean that such a simplistic explanation is far from adequate. The well-quoted, but nevertheless appropriate, approach given by Drucker[28] for firms to pursue is to pose two questions, the answers to which will give a basis for defining a company's mission. These questions are: What is our business? and What should our business be?

Although the answers to such questions provide the prime purpose for existence, they are not adequate for practical purposes. The Directors of ICI recently addressed both these questions and in both cases the answer was that they are in the chemical business.[29] Similarly, Patek Philippe, Swiss manufacturers of expensive and exclusive watches, very much define their purpose not as being in the jewellery business, but as being watchmakers.[30] While the prime purpose of the company is obviously identified, the range of involvement could be extensive. Chemicals can range from plastics to pharmaceutics to petroleum, and while such a scope falls within the business of ICI it is not suitable for many smaller chemical firms. The prime purpose of Patek Philippe has, perhaps, a limiting effect, albeit purposely selected. A mission of being in the jewellery business would have allowed for expansion into other markets, but instead their decision has been limited to the product of watches only.

Basis of organizational mission

While the prime purpose needs to be defined, other considerations affect the definition of mission. Such an approach has been given by Kollat, Blackwell and Robeson,[31] being based upon stakeholder expectations, the environment, and the distinctive competences of the firm. Stakeholder expectations have already been discussed at the beginning of this chapter. However, in determining the mission the most dominant group is likely to be the directors, although they clearly need to accommodate other expectations in its definition. The other considerations affecting mission determination are as follows:

The environment The full range of environmental issues affecting strategic planning are to be examined in the next chapter, after which the effects of such issues on mission will be more clearly understood. For now, the main issue is that it is in the environment that there will develop both the opportunities and threats that the company is likely to experience in the future. Slow growth, or indeed decline, in traditional industries may not be acceptable to a company, prompting a shift into other industries. Stagnation in petrochemicals, say, could lead ICI to consider engineering industries, while the decline in the world market share of the Swiss watch industry may force Patek Philippe to change its mission towards other jewellery products. Conversely, growth opportunities in a firm's traditional markets would not cause a shift in emphasis. For example, the British Oxygen Company has maintained its mission relative to the business of being primarily in the business of supplying oxygen, acetylene and other major gases to industry.[32]

Distinctive competences These can be the prime consideration for many firms and can evolve from many aspects of the business. Indeed, for many firms these may be due to the very nature of their business and their experience and knowledge of that business, plus an acquired dominance within the market-place. The example of BOC, quoted above, serves as an example in that they have a major competence in the supply of industrial gases, resulting in a high degree of domination within the market-place. Distinctive competences can also be developed through the marketing function. Well-established brand names such as Rolls-Royce, Guinness, Royal Doulton and Cadbury provide a competence that will allow for the development of the respective firms in the future. Similarly, the nature of the product range can be the major strength, with the previously quoted example of Patek Philippe's products providing the basis for the future business. Other marketing competences can also be developed and utilized for defining mission, such as a low pricing policy, well-established market share, an extensive understanding of the market place, efficient selling and distribution systems, and expertise in communicating to customers.

Competences can also arise within other areas of the firm that can be used for the mission. Availability of finance from a parent company may allow for expansion into other industries, or may allow for the pursuance of leadership in the market place. Leadership can also be included within the mission relative to technological developments within the technical specification of products, or the technical nature of production processes.

In addition to these considerations for the basis of an organizational mission, Kotler[33] suggests that the history of the organization plus its available resources should also be major considerations. Such considerations are likely to affect an organization's mission as follows:

Organizational history Where a company has a history of participation in a particular industry then it obviously follows that the total culture is embedded in this historical development. Many of its employees will see themselves as working within the chemical industry, the watch industry, or whatever. The managers of the firm will have developed expertise within the industry which has developed over the prevailing period and has been built into its culture. For manufacturing companies their factories and capital equipment will have been developed to serve that industry, while financial structuring will also be geared for participation within that industry.

Consequently, apart from any practical considerations of reorientating the physical assets of a firm to other industries, the values and expectations of the decision makers, as already discussed earlier in the chapter, are likely to be dominated by this historical participation. The change of attitudes required to move away from such a base can be difficult to achieve, but will be examined in Part Four of the book. However, such a change is likely to be achieved through consideration of alternative organizational strategies that the firm could pursue, which are to be discussed in Chapter 5. Where such an effect does develop then it would require a modification to the mission, which again highlights that in practice the stages of planning do not necessarily follow in sequential order.

Resource availability For many organizations it is likely to be a practical reality that a lack of resources will not allow for any movement away from the prime purpose. While conglomerates like Unilever and ICI are able to consider changes of direction, Morgan Cars would probably not be able to obtain resources to change its mission to transportation and hence pursue market opportunities relative to, say, aircraft or ships. A general rule for any organization is that, if a mission is to be considered that will take it away from its traditional industry, then the whole financial structure of the organization needs to be examined, regardless of whether finance for such a venture is to be pursued either internally or externally. Here there is often a great temptation for students of strategic planning to advise on grandiose missions without due attention to this vital contribution to be made by the financial function.

The final consideration to be proposed as a basis for defining the organizational mission is the responsibility of the organization to the world in general and the society in which it operates in particular. The importance of a social policy has already been mentioned in the first section of this chapter. As was emphasized by Taylor,[34] organizations as part of society need to address moral issues relative to contributing to solving the problems of society. Such an obligation can be taken to be almost at the heart of the reason why a firm is in business. The pursual of profit is at the cost of consumption of the world's finite resources, so that a moralistic approach to such consumption needs to be reflected in the definition of the firm's mission. Additionally, the many groups of people with which the firm must deal with as stakeholders also expect the firm to act with responsibility, and again such an approach needs to be initiated at the mission stage of planning. An example of an organizational mission that takes into account responsibility is that of the Japanese television manufacturer Toshiba. This company considers that it contributes to a richer and healthier life and to the advancement of society through the creation of new values based on human respect. This it aims to achieve by being customer-orientated, by utilizing resources effectively and by providing staff with the opportunity to realize thier potential.[15]

In this example, responsibility within the mission has a direct bearing on the utilization of marketing in that it has contributed to customer orientation. Indeed, this is compatible with many definitions of marketing where social responsibility is recognized, such as the definition of macro-marketing by McCarthy[35] as already discussed in Chapter 1, and as discussed by writers such as Bell[36] in explaining the nature of marketing. However, despite the moral issue of responsibility leading to customer orientation, a failure of the organization to act responsibly can also affect its reputation. Consequently, irresponsible acts that are publicized in the press can cause the formulation of adverse attitudes on the part of customers, which can lead to adverse affects on sales volume and market share. From this point of view, the stressing of responsibility within the basis of the organization's mission would be clearly advantageous.

Aims of organizational mission

Having examined considerations that can affect the definition of organizational mission, attention is now given to aims that can be pursued in its establishment. A range of six aims that can be sought from an organizational mission are given below. While all six could be pursued, this would be less than likely for most firms. The six aims are:

Purpose As already discussed, this is the prime purpose for existence; an example is ICI being in the chemical industry. However, the purpose should also give direction for the future and in the case of ICI this is related to developments in high technology within the industry.[29] For some companies the direction could be a change into other industries, or indeed it may be to continue as previously. This aim of the organizational mission is obviously dependent upon marketing. The purpose and direction can only be viable and ultimately successful given both market potential within the industries in which the firm wishes to participate and the marketing expertise needed to pursue such opportunities. Although ultimate marketing orientation may dictate that the opportunities should be identified before the industry is selected, firms that are not able to change their industry of participation will then obviously need to focus on segmentation of that industry to identify areas of greatest potential relative to their particular situation.

Philosophy This is explained by Byars[23] as establishing the values, beliefs and guidelines that the organization will aim to use to conduct its business. Such ramifications were discussed in the first section of the chapter, but this aim of the mission is to ensure that those that are finally adopted are utilized within subsequent stages of the planning.

Another view of philosophy is that it represents the overall approach to the business. For example, although the business IBM is in has changed over the years, its philosophy has continued to be based upon three principles, namely respect for individuals, customer service, and the pursuance of all tasks in a superior fashion.[37] Here the importance of marketing is again emphasized in that customer service is held to be a major value within IBM's philosophy. A different emphasis on values and beliefs is taken by the J. R. Crompton company, producers of paper for teabags. Here a major value within their philosophy is to remain as a family business while improving efficiency and profits.[38] Again, such a philosophy is reliant on marketing, in that marketing effectiveness can be seen as being part of internal efficiency, while the utilization of marketing, as discussed in Chapter 1, obviously contributes to profits.

Vision This aim of the organizational mission is complementary to purpose and philosophy. However, writers such as Johnson and Scholes[14] have highlighted the importance of this particular aim. This is the aspect of looking into the long-run future and being able to envisage where the company is likely to be at a particular point in the future. This is likely to go beyond that which can be formally forecast from a current data base, and so is a feature of mission that needs to be imaginative in estimating both purpose and philosophy over a long period. Here a lack of formal forecasting means that certain marketing approaches are not applicable to this particular aim of mission. However, as market forces are obviously also going to be important over this period of time, it then follows that such vision needs to be developed by decision makers who are themselves marketing-orientated.

Business domain This particular aim of mission has been well discussed by Abell.[39] Although the mission establishes the overall purpose, Abell suggests that it can also aim to be more specific by highlighting the customer groups to be served, the customer needs to be met and the technology needed to service these needs. Using the previous example of Patek Philippe, the company serves wealthy consumers, the need extends beyond simply time keeping, while the technology uses traditional escapement movements. Alternative business domains could include other income-bracket markets with their associated needs, and the utilization of microchip technology.

Although such alternatives are necessary for consideration for decision making in planning, being so specific at this particular stage is likely to be premature. As will be explained in later chapters, organizational and marketing strategies are concerned with this type of decision making, and indeed being too specific at the mission stage may lead to a restriction of opportunities in later stages of the planning. However, this discussion will be addressed again in the appropriate chapters.

Market-base Here the aim is that the mission should epitomize marketing orientation in that it should be focused on markets, encompassing the marketing issues already discussed, and should not be focused on products. Such an aim arose out of the well-quoted and established concept of marketing myopia as developed by Levitt.[40] A tenet from this work is that market-based definitions of a business are superior to product definitions of a business. In the example of Patek Philippe such an approach has not been taken. It will be recalled that their business is defined in product terms, in that it is defined as being that of watchmakers with the emphasis being on the quality and performance of the movements incorporated into the watches.

Motivation The final aim that can be pursued in the establishment of an organizational mission is that it can contribute to the motivation of personnel within the organization. A sense of purpose and direction allows employees to relate their personal contribution to the overall direction of the organization. Within the philosophy certain aspects can be related directly to the welfare of personnel, as seen in the examples of IBM and Toshiba, which have a direct bearing on motivation. Similarly, when the company is able to demonstrate that it is concerned about the long-run future and that it is able to define its business relative to the markets it serves, then again such an approach is likely to affect the motivation of personnel.

Finally, considerations that can be made in defining an organizational mission, plus the aims that can be pursued, are summarized in Fig. 3.3. Some of these aims are also illustrated in Case Study 5 (page 44).

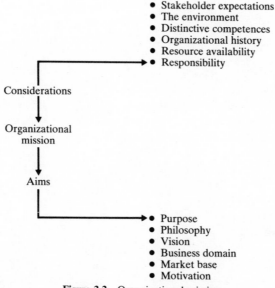

Figure 3.3 Organizational mission

SUMMARY

This chapter has been concerned with organizational mission as the first stage in strategic planning.

The first area of examination was the various groups of people who are likely to influence not only the formulation of the mission, but also planning in general. These groups were classified into market-place stakeholders, external stakeholders and internal stakeholders. The latter were considered to be the most important relative to planning, with decision makers being the key group. An initial examination of the various groups of decision makers was made, as was their values and expectations in influencing planning.

The role of business policy was also discussed. This was seen as being part of the values and expectations of the board of directors. Here the role of business policy is seen as providing guidelines for planning which can apply throughout preparation, implementation and control.

The final area of examination was the organizational mission itself. The formulation of an organizational mission was taken to be based upon stakeholder expectations, the environment, distinctive competences of the company, organizational history, resource availability and social responsibility. Finally, the aims of the mission were identified. These were classified as being purpose, philosophy, vision, business domain, market base, and motivation.

CASE STUDY 4: THE CRUCIBLE THEATRE, SHEFFIELD*

Case outline

In 1971, Sheffield Corporation opened its new civic theatre, named The Crucible. The product can be considered to be the service of entertainment in the arts, which requires marketing as does any other customer offering.

Illustration

The case study illustrates the extensiveness and variation of stakeholder groups that are able to affect the planning of the marketing of the theatre. These groups have been arranged in three classifications as follows:

Market-place stakeholders
– Theatregoers segmented by geographical area and social class.
– Art education for schools.
– Children's entertainment.
– Other customer needs such as a restaurant, bars, and *ad hoc* entertainment (e.g. World Snooker Championships).
– Sponsoring organizations of these *ad hoc* entertainments.
– Concessionary consumers, namely children, students and senior citizens.
– Competition, which is wide, varied and extensive in that the theatre represents only 1 per cent of entertainment.
– Booking agencies such as libraries, the 'Artspur Agent' system, and the 'Crucible Link Organization'.

Internal stakeholders
– Board of Trustees of the Theatre, including members from Sheffield Council, the University, and the Trades and Labour Council.
– Management Committee, responsible for operational decisions.
– Financial Sub-committee, responsible for monthly financial control.
– The theatre director.
– The heads of department.
– The Planning Committee responsible for the entertainment.
– The actors' union Equity.

External stakeholders
– Arts Council.
– National Council for Civil Theatres.
– Yorkshire Arts Association.
– University of Sheffield.
– Trades and Labour Council.
– Sheffield Metropolitan District Council.
– Sheffield Yorkshire County Council.
– The newspaper the '*Sheffield Star*'.

* Derived from H. K. Scholes, The Crucible Theatre, Sheffield. Copyright © 1976 by H. K. Scholes.

CASE STUDY 5: HEUBLEIN INC*

Case outline

The case is based on a US company whose major product is the Smirnoff brand of vodka. The case includes many complex strategic planning issues, but aspects of organizational mission are highlighted.

Illustration

At an early stage within the case, Heublein's president comments on the company's business as follows:

> Although liquor products account for most of our sales, we consider ourselves to be in the consumer goods business, not the liquor business. Liquor is a consumer good just like toothpaste and is sold in the same way. To be successful in this business you need three things: a good product, good distribution for customer convenience, and good advertising to tell customers why they should buy.

The purpose of the business is clearly stated as being that of consumer goods, which obviously gives greater breadth of direction than merely being involved with liquor. However, a criticism is that such a definition is perhaps too broad, although this was restricted to only a particular range of food products beyond its liquor products. Company philosophy is reflected in the explanation in that they are obviously orientated towards servicing customers. This is highlighted elsewhere in the case in that they also value the ability to be able to effectively market consumer products, which they also consider to be a major strength of the company. At another place in the case they also emphasize that part of their philosophy is to value high-quality standards both in the purchase of their raw materials and in the production of their final products.

The historical development of Heublein illustrates some interesting changes in mission. By the time of prohibition in 1920 the company had some food products, but closure of their liquor plant forced a change of direction towards food products. During the early 1960s Smirnoff accounted for almost 70 per cent of sales, so that again the company took a change of direction within its mission.

The visionary nature of their mission is also illustrated. They were able to foresee the continued market domination of the Smirnoff brand, while they were also able to predict a decline of their share of the cocktail market, even though this market was expanding, but resulting in an overall increase in cocktail sales.

Although the applicability of the business domain aim of mission was challenged in the chapter, the case does illustrate that Heublein's domain is defined as being primarily affluent young adults. Finally, the aim of making the mission market based is reflected in their orientation to marketing issues. As already stated, the serving of customers and continued communications to them is emphasized, likewise throughout the case study their prime purpose of being in the business of consumer goods as opposed to being producers of liquor.

---

* Derived from Charles W. Hofer and Norman Berg, Heublein, Inc. (A), case 9-313-125. Boston: Harvard Business School. Copyright © 1972 by the President and Fellows of Harvard College.

REVIEW QUESTIONS

1. Why is it that several groups of people are able to influence planning?
2. 'When executives do their planning they cannot separate their own values from the firm's values.' Discuss.
3. Differentiate between strategic planning and business policy.
4. How would you recommend that an organization should prepare for the formulation of its mission?
5. Do you consider that any of the aims of mission are more important than the others?
6. Examine the proposition that only the organizational mission can be the starting point of corporate planning.

REFERENCES

1. Freeman, R. E., *Strategic Management*, Pitman, Boston, 1984.
2. 'Smith Kline's ulcer medicine holy war', *Fortune*, 19 September 1983.
3. 'Power complex at the CEGB', *Management Today*, May 1984.
4. 'ICI's new yarn', *Management Today*, February 1984.
5. D. J. McCarthy, R. J. Minichiello and J. R. Curran, *Business Policy and Strategy*, Irwin, Homewood, 1983.
6. 'The risk in putting a union chief on the board', *Business Week*, 19 May 1980.
7. Christensen, C. R., K. R. Andrews and J. L. Bower, *Business Policy*, Irwin, Homewood, 1978.
8. W. K. Hall, 'Strategic planning models: are managers really finding them useful?', *Journal of Business Policy*, **3**, 2, 33–42, 1973.
9. J. Hall, V. O'Leary and M. Williams, 'The decision grid', *California Management Review*, **III**, 2, 43–54, 1964.
10. D. McClelland and D. Burnham, 'Power is the great motivator', *Harvard Business Review*, **54**, 2, 100–10, 1976.
11. Chang, Y. N., and F. Campo-Flores, *Business Policy and Strategy*, Goodyear, Santa Monica, 1980.
12. Williams, T. G., *Consumer Behaviour*, West Publishing, St Paul, 1982.
13. 'Ford's fragile recovery', *Fortune*, 2 April 1984.
14. Johnson, G., and K. Scholes, *Exploring Corporate Strategy*, Prentice-Hall, London, 1984.
15. 'Toshiba's British switch', *Management Today*, March 1984.
16. Gray, J. L., and F. A. Starke, *Organizational Behaviour*, Merrill Publishing, Columbus, 1984.
17. 'How Wadkin Worked clear', *Management Today*, May 1984.
18. Learned, E. P., C. R. Christenson, K. R. Andrews and W. D. Guth, *Business Policy*, Irwin, Homewood, 1969.
19. Christenson, C. R., K. R. Andrews and J. L. Bower, *Business Policy*, Irwin, Homewood, 1973.
20. Glueck, W. F., *Business Policy: Strategy Formulation and Management Action*, McGraw-Hill, New York, 1976.
21. Thomas, R. E., *Business Policy*, Philip Allan, Oxford, 1977.
22. Tilles, S. 'How to evaluate corporate strategy', *Harvard Business Review*, **41**, 4, July-August 1963.
23. Byars, L. L., *Strategic Management*, Harper and Row, New York, 1984.
24. Higgins, J. M., *Organizational Policy and Strategic Management*, Dryden Press, New York, 1983.
25. Higgins, J. C., *Strategic and Operational Planning Systems*, Prentice-Hall, London, 1980.
26. Quinn, J. B., 'Formulating strategy one step at a time', *Journal of Business Policy*, **11**, 3, 42–63, 1981.
27. Brech, E. F. L., *The Principles and Practice of Management*, Longman, London, 1975.
28. Drucker, P., *Management: Tasks, Responsibilities, Practices*, Harper and Row, New York, 1973.
29. 'ICI thrives on self-inflicted culture shock', *Fortune*, 1984, April 16.
30. 'Patek Philippe's Better Time', *Management Today*, February 1984.
31. Kollat, D. T., R. D. Blackwell and J. F. Robeson, *Strategic Marketing*, Holt, Rinehart and Winston, New York, 1972.
32. 'BOC goes west', *Management Today*, January 1984.
33. Kotler, P., *Marketing Management: Analysis, Planning and Control*, Prentice-Hall, Englewood Cliffs, 1984.
34. Taylor, B., *Strategic Planning for Social and Political Change*, in Taylor, B., and J. R. Sparkes (eds), *Corporate Strategy and Planning*, Heinemann, London, 1979.
35. McCarthy, E. J., *Basic Marketing*, 7th edn, Irwin, Homewood, 1981.
36. Bell, M. L., *Marketing Concepts and Strategy*, 3rd edn, Houghton Mifflin, Boston, 1979.
37. F. T. Cory, 'The remaking of American business leadership', *Think Magazine*, November-December 1981.
38. 'How Crompton took the strain', *Management Today*, March 1984.
39. Abell, D., *Defining the Business: The Starting Point of Strategic Planning*, Prentice-Hall, Englewood Cliffs, 1980.
40. Levitt, T., 'Marketing myopia', *Harvard Business Review*, 45–56, July-August 1960.

FOUR

ORGANIZATIONAL OBJECTIVES AND THE STRATEGIC AUDIT

Learning objectives are to:

1. Understand the nature and roles of organizational objectives.
2. Become familiar with the different types and groupings of organizational objectives that can be established.
3. Understand the role of the strategic audit.
4. Be able to recognize the areas of analysis required for both external and internal appraisals.
5. Recognize major concepts that have been introduced.

In Part One the overall aims that a company strives to achieve were labelled organizational objectives, whereas the strategic audit was given as being concerned with an examination of the firm as a whole in relation to the external environment.

As will be developed later in the chapter, the organizational objectives provide an extension of the organizational mission by providing specific levels of achievement. They also provide a link into the operational planning in that they provide a basis for the formulation of objectives at the operational level. Therefore organizational objectives can be considered to have two major roles. The strategic audit is the strategic planning stage of information collection. Again, there is a dual role in that information collected will be used both in order to prepare the various stages of strategic planning and also to provide an information input into operational planning.

In the approach taken in this book the establishment of organizational mission and objectives have been prescribed as stages to precede that of the strategic audit. However, it could be argued that the audit should be the first stage as it provides essential information necessary for the formulation of mission and objectives. Indeed, there is a difference of opinion in the literature, with one school of thought prescribing that an audit–objectives sequence should be the approach, while the other prescribes an objectives–audit sequence, as followed in this book. Here the rationale is that by establishing overall aims first the required direction is being established, which is not being restricted by constraints from existing environments. However, the opposing argument is that the organizational objectives must be realistic relative to constraints. Here again is an example of one of the themes of the book, that the stages do not necessarily follow in sequential order. Consequently, both stages are likely to be done together, with each providing an input to the other.

THE NATURE OF ORGANIZATIONAL OBJECTIVES

The utilization of objectives by companies has been given considerable attention within the literature, having been developed from early publications at the turn of the century. The result has been the development of a process of management with objectives as the core, called management by objectives or MbO. Major works relative to MbO have included classical writings within the management literature, such as those by Drucker,[1] Odiorne[2] and Miller.[3] However, subsequent weight of treatment of MbO has led many executives to become sceptical of the use of objectives, as some claims to success have not always been fully justified. The approach taken in the book is that objectives have an essential role to play in planning, but that this role is no more important than the roles played by other stages of planning.

The central theme of MbO is quite simple: aims or levels of achievement are stated for a particular period of time and, as that period of time passes, actual levels of achievement are measured against the planned levels given in the objectives. The utilization of this principle is illustrated in a report concerning ITT in the United States. This company is stated to have paid particular attention to short-term results relative to their objectives and particularly that of growth of earnings per share. The approach was to measure this growth on a quarterly basis in order to achieve the growth objective at the end of the time period.[4] Indeed, this is the principle of the utilization of objectives that is at the heart of planning, which will be developed within the book.

Other aspects of MbO are worthy of consideration at this stage, although a full treatment is outside the scope of the book. The first is that managers at all levels should participate in the formulation of objectives, which is likely to affect their motivation towards the achievement of these objectives. The second is that areas of responsibility are then designated relative to these objectives, followed by the designation of sub-objectives which identify the levels of expectation relative to these responsibilities. Again, participation by all concerned is deemed to be part of the process. Third, MbO is a system of managing that needs to be an integral part of the job of the manager and is not an additional task. Finally, a major feature of MbO is that it is results-orientated, which again can have a positive affect on managerial motivation.

The system of MbO dictates that different, but integrated, objectives need to be set for different levels of management within an organization. This results in a hierarchy of objectives, to which attention is now given relative to be role of organizational objectives.

The hierarchy of objectives

A major contribution to explaining the hierarchy of objectives within companies is that by Granger.[5] The aim of Granger was to develop a conceptual framework of the full range of objectives within organizations which is totally embracing for all levels of personnel. Consequently, the hierarchy ranges from the aims of individual personnel to the overall major aim for the company being in business, as given in the organizational mission. Within this hierarchy the various operating departments will also have aims, but the consequences of such a hierarchy are twofold as far as the company is concerned. The first is that each level of objectives must relate to higher levels so that all objectives ultimately contribute to the major aim of the organization, as given in the mission. The second is that the organization itself is a vehicle for the achievement of objectives within the hierarchy, relative both to the operating departments and also to individual personnel.

This principle of a hierarchy of objectives is reflected within the planning framework adopted in the book. The overall major aim is represented within the organizational mission, followed by organizational objectives as the next level in the hierarchy, followed in turn by marketing objectives, as illustrated in Fig. 4.1. Within this hierarchy the three levels of formal objectives are related to the personal objectives of the hierarchy of people within the organizational structure. The direction of the planning objectives is down the hierarchy, but as will be discussed in the examination of the strategic audit, operational planning can also affect organizational objectives, so that an upwards influence is also possible. An example here is from the Firestone Tyre and Rubber Company where record losses had resulted up to 1980. Owing to the situation, short-term objectives to correct the situation were paramount, while the long-term organizational objectives were neglected.[6]

Level of objective   *Type of aim*
Personal objectives of owners → Organizational success

Organizational mission → Purpose

Personal objectives of directors → Performance and personal achievement

Organizational objectives → Performance of company

Personal objectives of senior managers → Performance and personal achievement

Marketing operational objectives → Performance of marketing function

Personal objectives of marketing personnel → Performance and personal achievement

---

Figure 4.1 A hierarchy of objectives

Although personal objectives originate at source, both top-down and bottom-up influences can also prevail. Personal influences will be discussed in the next section, but another issue that will affect the hierarchy is when the company is organized into different divisions or strategic business units (SBUs). Here there may be overall organizational objectives, each SBU may be designated an operational unit and hence each SBU would have different operational objectives. However, if each SBU is large enough it may be that each has separate organizational and operational objectives. A further examination of the effect of organizational structure on planning is given in Part Four.

Personal influence on organizational objectives

In the last chapter the principle was established that it is difficult for executives to separate their feelings, emotions and personal preferences from logical analysis in decision making. The same situation is prevalent in setting organizational objectives, in that personal objectives influence the formal objectives to be established for the organization. Writers such as McCarthy, Minichiello and Curran[7] observe that such influence relative to objectives is greater from senior executives, who claim a tendency for such executives to force their own expectations into organizational objectives. However, such personal influence does not necessarily need to be detrimental. The report of the negotiations for the merger of Kraft and Dart Industries (including Tupperware containers and Duracell batteries) was reported to have been engineered by Kraft's chief executive, who was seeking faster growth. However, for both companies there were advantages; for Kraft a wider product range and for Dart a potential smoothing of volatile sales.[8]

Vancil[9] emphasizes that executives need to recognize such influence and attempt to identify any conflict between their personal aspirations and feasible levels of achievement for the organization. Here the implication is simply that personal and organizational aims should be compatible. Growth of the organization should be pursued only if it can be justified in terms of both market opportunity and company capability, although the achievement of such growth can also affect personal aims of achievement. An example of matching personal objectives with the aims of the organization comes from a report concerning Interbank, the umbrella organization for Master Card. A major objective was to regain market share lost to Visa and to improve the image of Master Card. Part of the strategy adopted was to replace some key personnel, although the chief executive aimed to match the personal career objectives of new executives with the aims of Interbank.[10]

The roles of organizational objectives

Many of the reasons why organizational objectives are needed will perhaps be apparent already. In the early MbO literature many of the writers devoted efforts towards justifying why objectives are needed. Indeed, reasons given by writers such as Granger,[5] Levinson[11] and Reif and Bassford[12] are still applicable. Therefore the roles of organizational objectives can be considered to be basically the following:

- A guide to action by stating what needs to be achieved as an extension of the organizational mission.
- A means of measuring and judging performance.
- A device for organizational control and integration.
- Linking other objectives in the organization into a hierarchy.
- The enhancement of communications between levels of management.
- A vehicle for adapting to both internal and external constraints.
- The provision of a challenge to personnel.
- To foster motivation within personnel through participation.
- To relate the performance of individuals to the overall performance of the company.

These roles of organizational objectives can be classified into those concerned with the process of planning and those concerned with the people of the organization. On the above list all but the last three roles are concerned with the process of planning, while the last three are concerned with people.

The roles of organizational objectives can be seen to be wide and varied. Those involving the process of planning vary, from being concerned with direction and action as an extension of the organizational mission to being concerned with control mechanisms, or to being a vehicle of communication and for adapting to constraints. Roles concerned with people vary from providing a challenge and motivation to linking performance within the managerial hierarchy. Although these roles can be taken to be the major reasons the inclusion of organizational objectives in strategic planning, it is in addition inherent that they appertain also to the role of organizational objectives in providing part of the strategic plan framework for operational planning. As will be seen in Part Three, the marketing operational objectives link into the organizational objectives as part of the contribution of the marketing function to overall company performance. The ultimate utilization of the organizational objectives is to exercise control over the performance of the company relative to these desired levels of achievement. In simple terms, this is concerned with a comparison of actual performance against the planned levels of performance given in the organizational objectives, analysis of the reasons for any variations, and the instigation of any corrective action. The process of control will be examined in Part Five.

TYPES OF ORGANIZATIONAL OBJECTIVES

Within the literature there has also been a relatively high level of attention given to the types of objectives to be set for the company in total. A major contribution was from Ansoff,[13] who considered that these objectives can be classified as being both economic objectives and non-economic or social objectives. The former he relates to profitability, so that such objectives can be set in terms of, for example, sales growth, return on investment, return on assets, and profit margin. Non-economic objectives are those not concerned with profitability. They relate to both the internal operation of the company, in particular employee relations, and to the external environment, which tends to be dominated by objectives relative to social responsibility. Another approach taken in the literature, such as advocated by Hussey,[14] is to establish primary objectives relative to profitability and secondary objectives relative to any other aims the organization desires to pursue.

Other writers have each listed a range of organizational objectives that they recommend companies should establish. Although many writers have suggested that all objectives should be quantified in order to allow for specific measurement and control, the trend has been to recommend both quantitative and qualitative objectives. However, there is agreement that they should all be related to specific periods of time to allow for measurement and control. Such listings of objectives have been used as a basis to develop the range to be recommended in this book, as given by writers such as Hofer,[15] Thompson and Strickland,[16] Pearce and Robinson[17] and Ansoff.[18]

This range of organizational objectives is given in Fig. 4.2, which is divided into four groups of objectives. Within each group a set of objectives is given along with the ways in which these can be measured. While the full range of organizational objectives is probably not exhaustive, it is likely that most organizations will not establish all measures as given. Each of these objectives is discussed as follows:

Market leadership Like the other two objectives in this group, market leadership is developed out of the overall direction formulated in the organizational mission, giving the company a marketing orientation at the very core of the business. Hence the company's ability to be the market leader is based upon its marketing expertise, although other variables also need to be taken into account. If leadership cannot be the aim, then a decision needs to be made on which aim to pursue, as, for example, from a range given by Kotler:[19] market challenger, follower or nicher. Innovation and technological advances also need to be market-based if they are to be successful, as outlined by any basic marketing text. Consequently, the aims of achieving technological advances and subsequent product innovations need to be relative to market requirements, to similar competitive aims and to the company's marketing expertise. An example of a firm pursuing such objectives is the US company Gould, manufacturers of electronic and electrical products. Here the company has previously aimed to develop technological advances and innovation, so that it now enjoys market leadership in the markets in which it participates.[20]

Market spread Here knowledge of markets through the marketing function is essential in order to set objectives in this area. If the aim is to increase the spread in order to reduce risk then research is likely to be needed to give information to enable a decision to be made on which markets etc. to enter. An example of the need to aim for increased market spread comes from the world's largest tyre manufacturer, Goodyear. Despite market dominance in terms of market share, the company realizes that its reliance on supplying car manufacturers, representing low market spread, means that its performance is vulnerable to changes in demand for new cars.[21]

Group 1 Directional objectives

Market leadership, measured by:	competitive position
	degree of innovation
	technological advances
Market spread, measured by:	number of markets
	number of customer groups
	number of industries
	number of countries
Customer service, measured by:	product utility
	product quality
	product reliability

Group 2 Performance objectives

Growth, measured by:	sales revenue
	volume output
	profit margin
	contribution
Profitability, measured by:	return on capital employed
	return on assets
	profit margin on sales revenue
	return on shareholders funds

Group 3 Internal objectives

Efficiency, measured by:	sales on total assets
	stock turnover
	credit period
	liquidity
	department costs on sales
Personnel, measured by:	employee relations and morale
	personal development
	average employee remuneration
	sales revenue per employee

Group 4 External objectives

Social responsibility, measured by:	corporate image
	price/profit relationship
	resource utilization
	public activity
	community welfare

Figure 4.2   Range of organizational objectives

Customer service   Again, this objective is an aim towards making the firm marketing-oriented, in that this aim is to ensure that its customers are offered products which represent their requirements. Such an objective has been recently adopted by Ford. Here it was reported that the most important organizational objective is product quality and not return on investment as in previous years. The justification is that product quality is so central and important to customer needs that only by aiming for and achieving the required quality will the company be able to achieve its performance objectives.[22]

Growth   In order to be able to set growth objectives it is necessary to be able to forecast market trends, so that again the marketing process needs to be adopted. Sales revenue forecasting can be achieved only from a full understanding of the nature of the markets, while other growth objectives are dependent upon this forecast. In the previous example of Gould, the obtained market dominance has allowed them to pursue and obtain high annual sales growth objectives.[20]

Profitability Objectives within this area are obviously of prime importance as a basic necessity for survival. Again, marketing orientation is important, as once more the forecasting and achievement of sales revenue are the responsibility of the marketing function, and as the volume of sales obviously has an important effect on the volume of profit. Levels to be aimed for are based upon the trend of previous levels of achievement, but can also be related to the performance of other comparable organizations (an issue to be pursued further in Part Five). However, improvements in profitability are also affected by how market factors affect sales revenue. Many examples of profitability objectives are evident, although the Ball Corporation in the USA is an example of such importance in that a certain level of profitability is required from all areas of its business, regardless of market share of growth potential.[23]

Internal Again, many of the objectives within this group are affected by marketing, particularly the attainment of sales revenue with time, its associated stock levels of finished products, and obtaining payments from customers. The importance of personnel within planning has already been an issue within earlier chapters, and as a major feature of the book will be discussed in later ones.

External As marketing is concerned with communications externally, it follows that marketing orientation is important in fostering social responsibility. The ethics of communication are a direct concern, although there is a particular contribution to the corporate image that the firm aims to attain. The previously quoted company Interbank also serves as an example here. The company had identified an adverse image of Master Card relative to Visa, so that a major aim was to change its corporate image.[10]

The utilization of organizational objectives from this range, by a major company, is illustrated in Case Study 6 (page 61).

EVIDENCE OF ORGANIZATIONAL OBJECTIVES

Within the literature there have been several reports of research carried out to investigate the organizational objectives established by companies. Evidence from the research of Grinyer and Norburn,[24] Kudla,[25] Ringbakk,[26] Bhatty,[27] and Shetty[28] is discussed below, being presented within the range of objectives format as given in Fig. 4.2 above.

Group 1 Directional objectives

With the exception of the Grinyer and Norburn investigation, the research has indicated less than half the respondents setting objectives in this area. However, market leadership showed a high level of incidence within these firms. Here there is perhaps a problem of classification of objectives in that many of these objectives could be classified as being marketing objectives by some firms. Consequently, the incidence of such objectives will also be examined in Part Three.

Group 2 Performance objectives

In all the surveys these were considered to be the most important and such objectives were set by almost all firms, with profitability being set by nearly all of these. Growth objectives also showed a high level of incidence, although there were wide variations in level. Shetty found that 82 per cent of firms have a growth objective, whereas the Ringbakk and Bhatty surveys found within the region of only 30 per cent.

Group 3 Internal objectives

Here the Shetty survey found that 60 per cent have objectives concerned with personnel and 50 per cent with efficiency. The other surveys found that the companies appear to consider these objectives to be less important and a low level of incidence was reported.

Group 4 External objectives

Social responsibility objectives were set by 65 per cent of the companies in the Shetty survey and by 43 per cent in the Grinyer and Norburn survey. The other researchers reported little attention to such objectives, with firms claiming to find difficulty in setting these objectives.

Differences in the results of the surveys are obviously partly explained by the differences in research methodology used. However, overall the indications are of a domination of organizational objectives concerned with performance, although directional objectives are important to many firms. There are perhaps two consequental implications of these results. The first is that the results of such sample surveys are only an indication of utilization and do not give a comprehensive explanation of levels of incidence. The second is that a lack of utilization is indicative of companies not taking advantage of planning methodology. The reasons for such non-utilization will be examined in Part Four.

ROLE OF THE STRATEGIC AUDIT

In the introduction to this chapter the dual role of the strategic audit was highlighted, being that of information collection, both for the preparation of the individual stages of strategic planning and as an input to operational planning. Accordingly, this treatment of information collection needs to be considered in conjunction with that given in operational planning in Part Three. Within the literature there has been a tendency to split the collection of information into (1) an external appraisal of the total environment in which the company operates and (2) an internal assessment of the company. Both assessments need to be related to the current situation, and to the forecasts of trends that are likely to affect future situations.

The importance of the collection of information has been emphasized by many writers, such as Houlden,[29] which is that it provides the basis for making decisions relative to each stage of planning. However, the development of such collection has itself developed into a discipline of management information systems. Such systems of information collection are for all levels of management, to be used not only for decision making in planning but also for feedback for monitoring and control. Indeed, this aspect is treated as vital in this book; it is discussed in Part Five.

Within the external appraisal, the role of the strategic audit is concerned with both the identification and the forecasting of both opportunities for company development and threats from variables that may be detrimental to the achievement of objectives. Internally, the role of the strategic audit is to assess the strengths of the company in exploiting opportunities and overcoming threats, as well as any inherent weaknesses that may affect the approach to such opportunities and threats. This process has been labelled SWOT analysis by many writers: strengths, weaknesses, opportunities and threats.

THE EXTERNAL APPRAISAL

Several approaches have been recommended for an external appraisal. That taken by Bates and Eldredge[30] is an analysis of the general environment followed by a further analysis of the specific environment of the company's markets. The general environment is seen as providing likely or potential opportunities or threats, whereas the specific is seen as providing direct and immediate opportunities or threats. In both cases, the emphasis taken in this book is that we are concerned with the marketing implications of both environments, relative to both strategic and operational planning.

The general environment

Here the general principle is that the external environment can be split into areas of similar effect upon the organization, such as are shown in Fig. 4.3. All four areas have the potential of affecting

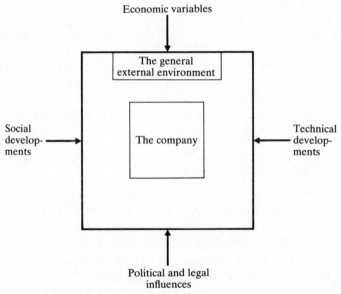

Figure 4.3 The general external environment

any organization, both in that they represent the workings of the outside world and because the majority of firms cannot affect the workings but must take a reactive position. Each area has the potential of affecting different industries in a different way and each will provide different potential opportunities and threats. One general rule is that each company needs to be able to develop an ability to monitor trends that are likely to affect its business. Another general rule is that a marketing orientation to the interpretation of such trends is needed. The central principle is that anticipation of threats to markets or opportunities to develop other markets will require consequential marketing activity to be developed within the planning. Aspects of both opportunities and threats arising from these areas are as follows:

Economic variables There are many examples of how the economic recession of the early 1980s has affected many companies. Toshiba found that the size of the market for television sets in the UK was drastically reduced due to the recession, but particularly due to the strength of the pound and high levels of inflation.[31] Similar effects can also be due to high levels of unemployment, and low levels of consumption and investment. The economic policies of government also need to be studied, as investments in particular industries and can create new opportunities, whereas inflation control policies can have a severe affect on demand within some industries.

Technical developments Where developments in technology affect the nature of products then such changes are pertinent to customers and therefore require a marketing orientation. Technical developments that give product advantages relative to competitors represent an opportunity, while similar product advantages developed by competitors represent a threat. Technical developments within an industry can also have effects: during the early seventies the UK textile industry was threatened by an over-capacity situation, caused partly by technical developments in production.[32] Opportunities for new or expanding markets can arise when industries develop, such as with the movement to advanced production systems in many sectors, which have resulted in new markets for numerous ranges of equipment.

Political and legal influences Here there can be wide-ranging influences, from general legal rulings to specific and direct rulings related to specific industries. An example of the former is the law relating to consumer protection. To some firms this may pose a threat, but to others it will be an opportunity to improve their products relative to customer requirements and social movements. The direct intervention of government in the consumption of tobacco is an obvious threat to that industry, whereas political pressure from interest groups relative to food additives has posed threats to the food industry. However, government support for certain industries can result in opportunities for suppliers as those industries expand.

Social developments As standards of living increased after the Second World War, many opportunities developed for new markets particularly concerned with consumer durables. However, by 1984 companies such as Black & Decker were identifying a market threat in that nearly every household now has a power drill, which represents saturation of this market.[33] Therefore one social development has created both opportunities and threats. Social attitudes can have similar affects. A movement to the consumption of health foods by an increasing proportion of the population would provide threats to some firms but opportunities to others.

Overall companies need to be able to monitor trends in the general external environment so that they can assess the likely affects on their business and take consequential action in their planning. For many firms, knowledge of such effects is likely to have been acquired through experimental learning. However, developments have been made within the literature relative to forecasting trends in these areas such as in the book by Higgins[34] and it is likely that firms would benefit from the use of these methods.

The specific environment

Here the appraisal is specific to the industries and markets with which the firm is associated. The areas to be considered in this appraisal are given in Fig. 4.4. Knowledge of customers, market trends, and competitors is obviously the responsibility of the marketing function. Such information would normally be generated through the marketing function of marketing research and would be included in the operational marketing plan. Therefore appraisals from these areas would normally be in the form of an input from the operational planning. An examination of these areas will be given in Part Three. However, in appraising the specific external environment all four areas need to be included.

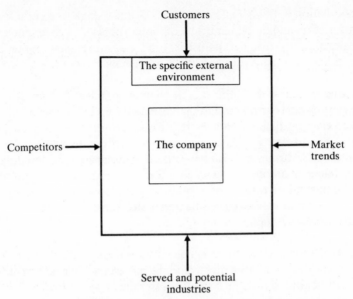

Figure 4.4   The specific external environment

In appraising industries the considerations should be the same for both the industries being currently served and those that may be potentially served. For the latter the starting point of a search should be the framework established within the organizational mission and objectives. However, an appraisal of an unconsidered industry may prompt redirection, which is again an example of the interrelation of the stages of planning. In making the appraisal two areas need to be considered:

Industry life-cycle   The concept of the product life-cycle (PLC) is well established in the literature. However, markets within industries also show a pattern of initial establishment to growth, maturity and decline. The previously quoted example of the power drill market is also applicable, in that having gone through a period of expansion the market has now reached maturity. The approach of Black & Decker was given as an expansion into the world market with a standardized global product.[33] Some industries may also be in decline, such as shipbuilding and coal mining, although this could be a temporary depression in the cycle as in the PLC. However, this illustrates the major problem with all life-cycle analysis, that at a particular point in time a forecast needs to be made of the direction the curve will take. Nevertheless, it must be realized that there is a tendency for markets to follow such a pattern, so that some assessment needs to be made of the current situation.

Industry structure   This is concerned with the companies that participate in the industry. Writers such as Christensen *et al.*[35] have identified five major groups of companies. The first is the range of competitors, where an understanding of each would, as previously mentioned, be provided from marketing research. The second group is that of companies with the potential to enter as additional competitors. Here an assessment needs to be made of barriers to entry. The third group is concerned with companies that can provide substitute products, where an assessment of the ability of such products to satisfy customer needs is required. The final two groups are suppliers and buyers in the industry, whose ability to affect marketing plans needs to be assessed.

THE INTERNAL APPRAISAL

The role of the internal appraisal has already been established as identifying an organization's strengths and weaknesses. Many writers have suggested areas to consider, with Hussey,[36] for example, giving a checklist as follows:

– Trends of previous results.
– Profits identified by products and markets.
– Identification of potential risks.
– Manufacturing strengths and weaknesses.
– Rationalization of resources such as factories, plant, machinery, and buildings.
– Identification of financial resources.
– Analysis of the allocation of resources.
– Assessment of the suitability of the organizational structure.
– Efficiency of managerial systems.
– Key corporate strengths and weaknesses.

The approach taken in this book is to recommend an internal appraisal based upon three major areas of consideration that will require a full internal appraisal of the organization, namely:

– Position analysis.
– Operations analysis.
– Capability analysis.

Position analysis

This part of the appraisal is concerned with both the financial structure of the company and its performance relative to its associated planning. For both areas, the analysis needs to include the trends of both previous structure and performance, and forecasts of those anticipated for the future. In both the financial structure and performance the final analysis is concerned with the identification of strengths and weaknesses. Making such identifications is perhaps suggestive of a simple process. A trend of falling profits for a particular product group may be indicative of a weakness, while an increasing market share for another product group may suggest a strength. However, in the former case this might be within a difficult external environment with a declining market size, while the latter may not be sufficient to meet levels of growth specified in the organizational objectives. Therefore, in determining strengths and weaknesses it is perhaps important to compare trends with past levels of achievement, the prevailing external conditions, and the future aspirations as emphasized in the organizational objectives. In the case of the prevailing external conditions, the total environment is obviously important, but a vital comparison is that with other firms operating in the same environment. These can be direct competitors, other firms operating in the same industry, or firms of similar size. Such comparisons can be made by referring to the specialist firms that publish performance analysis within a range of industries, which allows for company comparisons with industry norms.

The financial structure This analysis is concerned with the inflow of funds necessary for the implementation of the company's planning. Within some organizations the financial structure is seen as a constraint to planning. However, the approach taken in this book is that finance needs to be planned at both the strategic and operational levels, just as marketing does, and therefore the financial structure is part of the strategic planning. Consequently, any financial constraints are incorporated into the planning. Although this area is really outside the scope of the book, Bates and Eldredge[30] suggest an analysis in the following areas:

- Integration of finance into corporate planning
- Growth of profitability and trends of risk
- Financial strength to tackle the external environment
- Allocation of resources through capital budgeting
- Effective budgeting to control operations and evaluate planning

Organizational performance Here there should be an initial assessment of key performance criteria, analysed by divisions, SBUs, markets and products, although the breakdown for each company will depend upon its organizational structure. Typical key performance criteria are given in Fig. 4.5, which can be used for either products or markets. Again, trends can be

---

Market criteria
Total market size
Market share

Product critieria
Price per unit
Variable cost per unit
Contribution per unit
Fixed cost per unit
Profit per unit

Financial criteria
Sales value
Variable costs
Contribution
Fixed costs
Total profit

Figure 4.5 Key performance criteria

established of previous performance relative to these criteria, plus forecasts of anticipated future performance. The aim of the analysis is again to identify strengths and weaknesses, so that, for example, each product can be analysed in relation to previous performance which can then be compared with industry norms and organizational objectives. The other part of the organizational performance assessment should be an appraisal of the success of previous planning. The success in the level of achievement of objectives needs to be examined and the reasons for any variances must be determined. Similarly, the suitability of the organizational strategy also needs to be examined with the aim of making improvements for the future.

The total position analysis is particularly related to the control function of planning and will be pursued further in Part Five.

Operations analysis

This appraisal is concerned with an assessment of the contribution of each of the functional operations to the total corporate performance, and the marketing operations are obviously central to the focus of the book. Strengths and weaknesses of marketing can be identified by the marketing personnel, or it may be more effective to employ persons other than these. The marketing audit is a tool for completing such an appraisal, but as this is linked to a control procedure it will be examined in Part Five. However, the major criteria that need to be examined to analyse the contributions of marketing are given in Fig. 4.6. Again, any of these areas can be indicative of either strengths or weaknesses. As with the analysis from all functions, decisions then need to be made as to how the strengths can be utilized in both organizational and marketing strategies and how the weaknesses can be overcome. An illustration can again be drawn from Black & Decker. Their marketing strengths of a strong brand image and worldwide franchises became the basis for future marketing strategy.[33] Such affects will be discussed further during the examination of each of these strategies.

Marketing research
Ability to be able to identify customer requirements and to develop knowledge on the required marketing

Products
Suitability of current products relative to customer requirements, plus ability to be able to develop and implement changes

Price
Current prices relative to profitability and market price levels

Selling and distribution
Appropriateness and effectiveness of both plus an appraisal of the total service offered to customers

Advertising and sales promotion
The role of communications within the marketing mix relative to expenditure and competitive communications

---

Figure 4.6 Criteria for analysing marketing operations

Capability analysis

The general ability of an organization to effectively serve its markets at its desired levels of performance and relative to its competitors represents the overall capability of the firm. Such capability is seen by Ansoff[18] to be central in the internal appraisal and indeed central to the success of organizations. Capabilities are classified into those within the operating business functions and those relating directly to managers' capability. The former equates to operations analysis as previously discussed, so that further treatment is not required.

Management capability is concerned with strengths and weaknesses within the management structure. The first examination made is of the organizational chart, and how this division of labour influences the effectiveness of planning and its implementation. Such issues will be fully examined in Part Four. The second examination is of what has been labelled by Ansoff the responsiveness of management. Here the analysis requires an assessment of the general disposition within the company towards responding to change (such as increased competition), the competence of the managers to tackle the response, plus the capacity of managers to be able to handle the volume of work required to respond to change. The reported diversification of Goodyear into the energy industry was accompanied by support for the decision, but was also accompanied by a caution as to top managements' capacity to manage the diversification.[21]

The final examination of management capability is given by Ansoff as a management capability profile, providing a framework for the analysis of strengths and weaknesses in this area. This is a checklist to identify the strengths and weaknesses in and around management capability, the effect of organizational climate on capabilities, and competences in the firm that will affect capability. A full discussion of capabilities is given in Part Four.

An approach to both external and internal appraisals for a strategic audit is illustrated in Case Study 7 (page 63).

SUMMARY

Chapter 4 has addressed the roles of organizational objectives and the strategic audit. Although the relative sequence of these two stages was examined, the approach has been to locate objectives first, despite the established theme that the stages do not necessarily follow in sequential order in practice.

The nature of organizational objectives within a hierarchy of objectives was identified, while the process of management by objectives was highlighted. The personal influence of managers on organizational objectives were discussed, while the reasons why objectives are needed were classified into nine major roles. Finally, four major groupings of organizational objectives were presented, being directional, performance, internal and external, with a range of objective measures within each.

The role of the strategic audit was given as providing information for the stages within corporate planning. The external appraisal in the audit was split between general environment and specific environment, both featuring areas requiring assessments. The internal appraisal was given as requiring analysis concerned with the organization's position, operations and capability. Again there were further areas of assessment within each analysis.

CAST STUDY 6: HEWLETT PACKARD (B)*

Case outline

Hewlett Packard are a US electronics company whose products include computers, calculators, instruments and medical equipment. They are probably best known to the general public for their educational computers and calculators. The case highlights the successful growth of the company and how they have utilized both objectives and strategies.

Illustration

The case describes Hewlett Packard as being one of the current giants of the high-technology electronics industry, a position they have achieved through sustaining high levels of annual growth. This has been achieved while retaining a people-orientated organization, where individual creativity and initiative are encouraged within an open and informal environment, which also allows for flexible work methods. However, such a situation is utilized for the achievement of both company and personal objectives.

The overall company objectives were first formalized in 1957 and it is emphasized that they have been important in guiding growth, developing technology and in the 'betterment of society'. The case reports an updating of these objectives in 1977, although it is claimed that there was little change from the originals. The range of organizational objectives has been extracted from the case and classified into the range of objectives format as presented in Fig. 4.2 above.

Group 1 Directional objectives Considerable emphasis has been placed on objectives from this group. Market leadership in the form of innovation has been continuously aimed for and achieved. Market spread has also been an important objective. A basic organizational objective has been to enter new fields, and by 1975 they were established in six different product-market scopes. Within instruments and computers further market spread was aimed for. In the former the need for precise measurement in many different industries and professions had been identified, giving further market spread. In computers, markets were spread across education, science and engineering, with the former having wide applications.

An original objective had been to provide products of the greatest possible value to gain and maintain customer respect and loyalty. Similarly, the aim had always been to give emphasis to all customer services. Both these customer objectives are well entrenched throughout the case.

Group 2 Performance objectives An original objective had been to earn sufficient profit to finance growth, while another had been to enter new fields that would be profitable.

Growth of sales during 1972 was at a level of 30 per cent, while that for 1973 was 40 per cent. The result was an increase in market share at the cost of reduced profitability. Consequently, the emphasis in the growth objectives was shifted to improving profit margins. This aim was achieved with net profit growing by 22 per cent per annum from 1975 to 1978, with a growth of sales of 21 per cent per annum.

Group 3 Internal objectives As outlined at the beginning of this report, Hewlett Packard have always aimed to be concerned about the people they employ. Here there were two original objectives. The first was concerned with personal success, job security, recognition, and job

* Derived from D. M. Crites and R. Atherton, Hewlett Packard (B). Copyright © 1979 Dennis M. Crites and Roger Atherton.

satisfaction. The second was concerned with aiming for managerial freedom, but directed to achieving well-defined and agreed objectives.

An indication of efficiency objectives is given relative to the 1973–4 period of 'redirection'. Specific aims were set relative to cost control, short-term debt reduction, and long-term debt avoidance. Overall they aimed for an across-the-company asset-management discipline.

Group 4 External objectives A social responsibility objective was included as one of the original range and was continuously maintained. This objective is relative to each nation in which Hewlett Packard operate. Here the aim is to honour their objligations to society by being an economic, intellectual and social asset.

CASE STUDY 7: THORPAC LTD*

Case outline

Thorpac was established as a family business to market packaging for home freezer owners who wish to prepare and freeze their own food. Consequently their business is related to the frozen-food industry, and the market for home freezers.

Illustration

This case study illustrates some of the many issues that need to be considered in the strategic audit. The sections given in Chapter 4 are illustrated as follows:

External appraisal

General environment Within their business Thorpac were experiencing an increased trend towards the use of convenience foods, along with an increasing ownership of home freezers. Other social trends were also affecting their market, including a trend towards urbanization, a higher proportion of working housewives and an increased willingness to experiment with foreign and exotic foods. The developing economic climate and levels of unemployment were also seen to have a likely effect on home cooking and freezing.

Specific environment At the time the company was launched the frozen food industry was at the start of its life-cycle and its structure featured many changes. During the seventies there was a dramatic increase in retail home freezer centres, selling both food and freezers, providing a market opportunity for Thorpac, plus an effective channel of distribution. Many manufacturers of foods developed frozen-food products for home freezers, ranging from small companies to large organizations such as Findus, Ross and Birdseye. Thorpac obtained their supplies from many companies, as a feature of the packaging industry was the supply of limited products from each manufacturer. The industry also developed a range of specialist magazines, giving a range of media for freezer owners.

   The growth in the ownership of home freezers was extensive during the seventies, representing an increase in market size for Thorpac products. Indeed the market for home freezer packaging was seen to be growing at about 5 per cent per annum at the time, with aluminium containers accounting for about a third of this market. Consumers perceived the major benefits of home freezers as being convenience and a more interesting variety of food consumption. Indications were that between 50 and 65 per cent of owners did some home preparation and freezing of foods, and would need the type of packaging supplied by Thorpac. However, it was also known that there was some confusion in that some people did not realize the difference between a refrigerator and a freezer. Thorpac faced competition from two smaller, but similar companies, as well as from Alcan Polyfoil and Tupperware. Although the latter were large organizations, they marketed different product ranges.

Internal appraisal

Position analysis At the time of the case a detailed split by individual product items was not available, so that a specific product position analysis could not be performed. However, Thorpac

* Derived from J. R. Nicholls, Thorpac Ltd. Copyright © 1976 by J. R. Nicholls.

were to introduce a new information system to give such an appraisal. The plastic bags/film product group was the most profitable, followed by aluminium containers.

A daily financial analysis was made by orders, invoices and a daily cashflow sheet was prepared. Monthly financial analysis was based on a monthly profit and loss account and a detailed report on stocks, costs and overheads. However, control of the cashflow was seen to be particularly important.

Operations analysis Several aspects of their marketing operations at that time are given in the case. The product range consisted of 100 individual items split into three groups based upon containers, plastic bags and accessories, such as knives and thermometers. Prices were considered to be comparable with those of competitors, while the policy of Thorpac is to not attempt control of the retail selling price of their products. Media advertising has been limited, although sales promotions such as exhibitions, trade deals and consumer 'freezer evenings' have been used successfully. The major channel of distribution to the consumer has been through freezer centres, accounting for up to 90 per cent of volume, although other retail outlets were being developed as significant channels.

Capability analysis Insufficient information is given in the case study to be able to illustrate this area of analysis.

REVIEW QUESTIONS

1. Why is it that the personal objectives of managers are interrelated with organizational objectives?
2. Justify the claim that objectives can provide many advantages to organizations.
3. Discuss the relative importance of the different measures for organizational objectives.
4. 'A strategic audit is of limited value as it is only based upon historical information.' Discuss.
5. 'The general external environment is nice to know but is of limited value for planning.' Discuss.
6. Where in the organization are strengths and weaknesses likely to be found?

REFERENCES

1. Drucker, P., *The Practice of Management*, Harper and Row, New York, 1954.
2. Odiorne, G., *Management by Objectives: A System of Management Leadership*, Pitman, New York, 1965.
3. Miller, E. C., *Objectives and Standards: An Approach to Planning and Control*, American Management Association, New York, 1966.
4. 'The de-geneening of ITT', *Fortune*, 11 January 1982.
5. C. H. Granger, 'The hierarchy of objectives', *Harvard Business Review*, **43**, 3, 63–74, 1964.
6. 'The pains of turning Firestone around', *Business Week*, 8 September 1980.
7. McCarthy, D. J., R. J. Minichiello and J. R. Curran, *Business Policy and Strategy*, Irwin, Homewood, 1983.
8. 'The man behind Kraft's merger', *Business Week*, 25 August 1980.
9. R. F. Vancil, 'Strategy formulation in complex organisations', *Sloan Management Review*, **17**, 2, 1–18, Winter 1976.
10. 'How a new chief is turning Interbank inside out', *Business Week*, 14 July 1980.
11. H. Levinson, 'Management by whose objectives?', *Harvard Business Review*, **48**, 4, 125–34, July/August 1970.
12. W. E. Reif and G. Bassford, 'What MBO really is', *Business Horizons*, **16**, 23–30, June 1973.
13. Ansoff, H. I., *Corporate Strategy*, McGraw-Hill, New York, 1965.
14. Hussey, D. E., *Corporate Planning*, Pergamon, Oxford, 1976.
15. Hofer, C. W., *Typical Business Objectives*, 9-378-726 Harvard Case Series, 1976.
16. Thompson, A. A., and A. J. Strickland, *Strategy Formulation and Implementation*, Business Publications, Plano, 1983.
17. Pearce, J. A., and R. B. Robinson, *Formulation and Implementation of Competitive Strategy*, Irwin, Homewood, 1982.
18. Ansoff, H. I., *Implanting Strategic Management*, Prentice-Hall, Englewood Cliffs, 1984.
19. Kotler, P., *Marketing Management: Analysis, Planning and Control*, Prentice-Hall, Englewood Cliffs, 1984.
20. 'Gould's golden gamble', *Management Today*, February, 1984.
21. 'The king of tyres is discontented', *Fortune*, 28 May 1984.
22. 'Ford's fragile recovery', *Fortune*, 2 April 1984.
23. 'The five-star management of Ball', *Management Today*, March 1984.
24. P. H. Grinyer and D. Norburn, 'Strategic planning in 21 UK companies', *Long Range Planning*, **7**, 4, 80–8, 1974.
25. R. J. Kudla, 'Elements of effective corporate planning', *Long Range Planning*, **9**, 4, 82–93, 1976.
26. K. A. Ringbakk, 'Organized planning in major US companies', *Long Range Planning*, **2**, 4, 46–57, 1969.
27. E. F. Bhatty, 'Corporate planning in medium-sized UK companies', *Long Range Planning*, **14**, 1, 1981.
28. Y. K. Shetty, 'New look at corporate goals', *California Management Review*, **XXII**, 2, 1979.
29. B. T. Houlden, 'Data and effective corporate planning', *Long Range Planning*, **13**, 106–11, 1980.
30. Bates, D. C., and D. L. Eldredge, *Strategy and Policy*, 2nd edn, W. C. Brown, Dubuque, 1984.
31. 'Toshiba's British switch', *Management Today*, March 1984.
32. 'ICI's new yarn', *Management Today*, February, 1984.
33. 'Black and Decker's gamble on globalization', *Fortune*, 14 May 1984.
34. Higgins, J. C., *Strategic and Operational Planning Systems*, Prentice-Hall, London, 1980.
35. Christensen, C. R., *et al.*, *Business Policy*, Irwin, Homewood, 1982.
36. Hussey, D. E., *Corporate Planning*, Pergamon, Oxford, 1976.

FIVE

ORGANIZATIONAL STRATEGY

Learning objectives are to:

1. Understand the nature of strategy relative to strategic planning.
2. Appreciate the different approaches available to formulate organizational strategy.
3. Obtain a detailed knowledge of the stages of strategy formulation.
4. Understand and appreciate the importance of the necessary considerations for organizational strategy selection.
5. Recognize major concepts that have been introduced.

In Part One it was outlined that organizational strategy is concerned with the overall approach to be taken to achieve both the organizational mission and objectives. The marketing orientation of this strategy was also outlined. Indeed, the previous chapters concerned with both organizational mission and objectives have emphasized their orientation to markets, so that it follows that the strategy to achieve these needs to adopt such an orientation, which will be emphasized throughout the chapter.

This chapter will also show how organizational strategy links with mission. It will be seen that it provides an extension of the mission roles of purpose and business domain, giving more specific detail to the company's direction. The chapter will also show how organizational mission links forward into operational planning and in particular how it relates to operational marketing strategy. Here there is a particular cyclical relationship between the two forms of strategy. The organizational strategy provides a framework for marketing strategy, although formulations in the latter can be indicative of direction to be established in the former. This again highlights one of the themes of the book, that the stages of planning are not necessarily discrete and sequential. However, both strategies are affected by changes within the environment. This provides a link into both the strategic audit and information that needs to be collected for operational planning.

As with the other stages of strategic planning, consideration is also needed of the effects caused by organization structure. Where there are different divisions or SBUs, different strategies may be required and their compatibility will also need to be considered. However, regardless of the different strategies needed, the chapter will show that different alternatives for the same SBU are possible to develop, and therefore decision making to select relevant strategies needs to be tackled.

EXPLAINING STRATEGY

The word strategy comes from a Greek word, *strategos*. The development of the meaning of the word has been well explained by Evered.[1] The strict meaning is that of a general in command of an army, *stratos* meaning army, and *agein* meaning to lead. Therefore in the company context organizational strategy is concerned with leading the overall organization. For example, the leading of Crompton, manufacturers of paper primarily for teabags, has been reported as requiring an overall strategy of leading the company to new uses for its specialist papers to reduce the business risk of relying on only one major market.[2] This explanation of strategy can be seen as being the broad means of achieving objectives, an approach taken by several writers in the literature.

The emphasis given by Andrews[3] is that the overall strategy is concerned with principal plans to achieve objectives in addition to defining the range of businesses to pursue. An example here is from the US firm Consolidated Foods. By the early seventies the firm had diversified into a wide range of businesses, resulting in an unwieldly organization. The major aim was then to make the company coherent, with a strategy of rationalization and selection of a range of businesses in which to participate for future company direction.[4]

A different emphasis is given by Hovell,[5] who sees strategy relative to the total organization as being the means by which a company shapes and directs its resource conversion process in order to achieve its objectives. The result is a reconciliation of objectives, resources, organizational structures, market opportunities and other environmental influences.

A range of features pertinent to organizational strategy has been proposed by Ansoff,[6] which is concerned with the following features:

- It gives direction to the company as opposed to immediate action.
- It stimulates the search for business opportunities.
- It provides a link between objectives and resources.
- It generates information, as well as requiring information for its formulation.
- Changes in objectives tend to affect changes in strategy.

The final issue in explaining strategy is the difference in terminology, to be found within both the literature and companies, relating to the concpet of the overall strategy, which has contributed to confusion in understanding and application. Some writers merely refer to strategy without any differentiation by levels of planning. The planning framework developed in Part One should allow the reader to realize the inadequacy of this approach. Other labels used for the overall strategy include the words master, enterprise and business. However, as will be seen in the next section, such labels have developed specific meanings within some parts of the literature and therefore cannot be used. Two common approaches are to use the labels corporate strategy and organizational strategy. However, as shown in Part One, corporate planning identifies the summation of strategic and operational planning, so that organization strategy is the chosen label for the overall strategy for the company in total.

APPROACHES TO ORGANIZATIONAL STRATEGY

Within the literature there are many prescribed approaches that are recommended to be adopted by companies in the formulation of their organizational strategy. Although there is some commonality across some of these approaches there are also major differences, so that confusion in understanding and utilization are perhaps to be expected. Consequently, five major approaches have been identified which are illustrated in this section (summarized in Fig. 5.1), while the next section will examine in detail the approach to be adopted in the book.

Directional approach
Selling out or divestment
Consolidation
Market penetration
Product development
Market development
Diversification

Component approach
Product-market scope
Growth vector
Competitive advantage
Synergy

Competitive approach
Aggressive-growth strategy
Defensive strategy
Neutral strategy
Mixed strategy

Hierarchy approach
Corporate level strategy
Line of business strategy
Functional area strategy

Typological approach
Stable growth
Growth
Mergers
Joint ventures
Harvesting
Retrenchment
Combination

Figure 5.1   The five major approaches to organizational strategy

Directional approach

This approach has been epitomized by Johnson and Scholes.[7] Their approach is to give six different directions that can be selected as the basis for the broad means of achieving objectives. These directions are:

Selling out or divestment This means selling to another organization a particular SBU or division, or perhaps a subsidiary company or even the total organization. Hence the direction is termination of a part of the business.

Consolidation Here the range of products and markets remain unchanged. Efforts are consolidated in the direction of, for example, maintaining market share, enhancing product quality and increasing promotions.

Market penetration Here the direction is to increase market share in current markets, probably with an objective of obtaining a dominant share.

Product development Again the direction remains within current markets, although products are extensively changed or new products are introduced.

Market development With this direction the approach is to retain current products but to channel resources into serving new markets with these products.

Diversification Here the direction requires two major changes. The first is that the company moves into markets that it does not currently serve, which will require products that may be either related to the current range or unrelated, this representing the second major change.

Component approach

Approaches within this classification recommend that strategy is developed by the consideration of several components, followed by a strategy formulation based on these. Probably the most respected and established approach is from the well-documented work by Ansoff.[8] He suggests four major components as follows:

Product-market scope This component specifies the industry in which the firm will participate and highlights the markets of participation plus the products needed. Consequently, the broad means of achievement is by the selection of business involvement.

Growth vector This component requires decisions on how the firm is to achieve growth. The alternatives are market penetration and development, product development, and diversification. The meanings of these alternatives are the same as those given above.

Competitive advantage Here the consideration is how the company is able to develop areas of expertise that can be used to the detriment of its competitors. Although advantages can be developed with most of the business functions, many of the more important are marketing-related.

Synergy This component is concerned with the firm utilizing strengths throughout the company, by each strength reinforcing the other, such as brand-image strengthening product-line extension, to give a total overall impact within the market-place. Here the consideration is of the development of such co-ordinating strengths, plus their utilization.

Competitive approach

Another group of writers suggest that the overall strategy should be approached from the point of view of how to tackle competitors. Examples here are from the works of Harvey[9] and Glueck and Jauch.[10] The approach recommended by Harvey depends upon whether the company seeks to be aggressive towards its competittors, decides to be defensive, or indeed is to remain neutral. This gives four groups of alternative strategies as follows:

Aggressive-growth strategy This alternative is concerned with attempts at market domination to both attack competitors and achieve increased growth. Several approaches are available in pursuing this alternative.

- Intensive growth is concerned with increasing volume sales and market share.
- Concentric diversification is concerned with growing into new markets but with related products.
- Conglomerate diversification is concerned with growing into new markets with new and unrelated products.
- Vertical integration is growth either backwards or forwards in the same distribution channel.

Defensive strategy This is sometimes called a retrenchment strategy, being used during periods of poor performance or excessive competition. Three alternative approaches are available:

– Turnaround strategy to improve performance.
– Divestment strategy to sell off part of the business.
– Liquidation strategy to liquidate or sell off its assets.

Neutral strategy Where companies dominate markets or where they are satisfied with their position relative to competitors, then this alternative is recommended. Two alternatives are available:

– Holding strategy to maintain current market share and growth.
– Harvesting strategy to generate cash by reducing costs, probably raising price and losing market share, aimed at improving cash flow by short-term cash gains.

Mixed strategy Here the firm would use combinations of the above strategies for different market segments, markets, countries, SBUs, divisions or subsidiary companies. This approach would be particularly applicable for larger firms that participate in a wide range of product-market scopes.

Hierarchy approach

Here the recommendation is to classify strategy at different levels within the company, extending the basic split of strategy within both strategic and operational planning as used in the book. The result is a range of strategies to be considered at different managerial levels. Such an approach is recommended by Thompson and Strickland[11] and Higgins.[12] The former give three levels, being corporate-level strategy, line-of-business strategy and functional-area strategy. The last is concerned with strategy within operational planning, so that it is not considered here. The other strategies are concerned with the following:

Corporate level strategy This relates to the organization as a whole and determines the businesses the company desires to be in. For this strategy nine alternatives are given:

– Single business concentration with ten alternative strategies.
– Vertical integration either backwards or forwards.
– Concentric diversification with six alternative strategies.
– Conglomerate diversification with six alternative strategies.
– Joint ventures with other organizations.
– Retrenchment.
– Divestment.
– Liquidation.
– Combination.

Line-of-business strategy This is the strategy to be developed for each of the particular businesses within the total corporate organization. Each business can be either a particular market, SBU or division. In determining this strategy, eight alternatives are given for different situations:

– Low market share companies with six applicable alternative strategies.
– Dominant firms with three different strategies.
– Growth markets with seven approaches.

- Weak or failing businesses with four strategies.
- Mature or declining markets with three approaches.
- Turnaround strategies with six alternative strategies.
- Risk strategies with six alternative strategies.
- Avoidance strategies with four alternatives.

Typological approach

In this approach the writers have merely listed the alternatives that can be selected without classifying them into groups, or without relating them to a particular orientation of strategy formulation. An example of such an approach is that given by Byars.[13] The range of alternatives that he gives is presented in Fig. 5.1, all of which have been identified within the other approaches. An emphasis within this approach is that firms need to consider several alternatives before decision making to select those to be pursued, in order to avail themselves of the possible opportunities.

From this comparison of approaches the approach to be adopted within the book was developed, with the aim of utilizing the strengths of the above approaches while developing a logical process. The adopted approach is illustrated in Fig. 5.2. There is obviously a strong influence from the

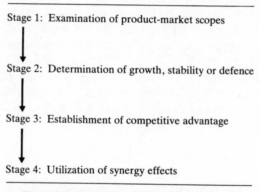

Stage 1: Examination of product-market scopes

Stage 2: Determination of growth, stability or defence

Stage 3: Establishment of competitive advantage

Stage 4: Utilization of synergy effects

Figure 5.2 Formulating organizational strategy

component approach as epitomized by Ansoff.[8] However, the growth vector is replaced by a stage of determining either a growth, stability or defence strategy. Here it is possible to pursue all three within different product-market scopes so that combinations of mixed strategies are possible. Figure 5.2 is also indicative of a sequential four-stage decision-making process and indeed this sequence is recommended. However, the sequence can also work in reverse order. For example, competitive strengths in brand image could be indicative of changing a stability strategy into a growth strategy. Finally, as will be emphasized fully in the next section, all stages of decision making in formulating organizational strategy require a marketing orientation, which is probably self-evident to most readers at this juncture in the book.

FORMULATING ORGANIZATION STRATEGY

This section is concerned with considerations of each of the stages of formulation of organizational strategy, as outlined in Fig. 5.2, whereas the next section addresses the selection of such strategy. Of particular importance in each of the stages are the ramifications of marketing orientation.

Stage 1 Product-market scope

Within the organizational mission the broad purpose and direction plus business domain were established. The product-market scope stage of organizational strategy is concerned first with being specific by identifying alternative businesses or industries in which the firm could feasibly participate. The second consideration is the identification of the range of product-market scopes available, each of which is identified by a different group of customer needs and their associated products. Companies operating in the manufacture of vehicles are likely to have product-market scopes of passenger cars, buses and coaches, lorries and trucks, plus agricultural vehicles. For each scope market customer requirements are different, so that products are consequently different, although all are concerned with transportation. Therefore, in formulating this stage of organizational strategy, consideration needs to be made of the range of scopes available.

Also to be considered is the relationship between these scopes. Here Spillard[14] has identified eight ways in which these scopes can be linked to give a 'common-thread' or business logic. One way is through a technological logic, such as the UK Central Electricity Generating Board. Here the scopes involve the technology of generating electricity, although nine scopes are identified relative to industrial groups such as iron and steel, heating, power, and steam-raising.[15] However, for some other firms the business link is more tenuous, although the advantage is that a wider spread of market opportunities are available. By the late sixties BOC participated in a wide range of product-market scopes such as industrial gases, engineering, road transport, fish farming, and pizza manufacturing.[16]

The need for marketing orientation within this stage is perhaps obvious in that businesses need to be seen as a grouping of different markets. The different scopes are based upon an understanding of different groups of customer needs and the products required to serve those needs, both of which are based upon marketing disciplines.

Stage 2 Growth

The next consideration is for growth within each scope, which is equally applicable in their initial selection and in subsequent decisions on continued participation. In practice growth, stability and defence logically need to be considered together.

In considering growth alternatives the famous Ansoff growth matrix (Fig. 5.3) is applicable.

Products / Markets	Present	New
Present	Market penetration	Product development
New	Market development	Diversification

Figure 5.3 Ansoff's growth component matrix. Reproduced by permission of McGraw-Hill Book Co.

Each of these alternatives provides the bases for growth in sales volume and/or market share as follows:

Market penetration Growth is achieved by increasing the market share of current products in current markets. Buzzell *et al.*[17] have found evidence to indicate improved profitability as a result of high market-share, which will be considered further in the next section.

Market development Growth is achieved by increasing sales volume through the identification of potential sales in additional markets. The example of Crompton, manufacturers of specialized paper for teabags, is applicable in that their proclaimed strategy for growth is to identify new markets for their well-established product.[2]

Product development This alternative is to achieve growth by introducing new products while remaining in the same markets. IBM had traditionally marketed mainframe computers to organizations, but pursued further growth by developing personal computers for individual managers within organizations.[18]

Diversification Here the approach to growth is to identify new markets that will accommodate such growth but to develop either new but related products or totally unrelated ones. To achieve growth that could not be achieved in the slow-growth tyre business, Goodyear recently diversified into oil and gas, and aerospace, while still searching for additional growth opportunities from diversification.[19]

Again the need for marketing is evident. All these growth opportunities require both an identification and an understanding of market needs and potential, again through marketing disciplines. Similarly, the recognition of products that would need to be developed in the last three approaches is basically a marketing exercise, while the pursuit of market penetration would be totally through marketing activities.

Stage 2 (continued) Stability

If growth is not to be pursued in a particular scope it may be because the firm is currently satisfied with performance, which usually occurs when it has achieved domination within the particular product market scope. In pursuing such a strategy there are two alternatives:

Holding strategy Here the firm is satisfied with current volume sales and market share which it strives to maintain. Procter and Gamble had previously attained domination in many markets and pursued a holding strategy. However, a recent report has outlined a decline in such domination in some markets, making such an approach less feasible.[20]

Harvesting strategy The alternative here is to use such domination to generate cash flow by cost reduction and possibly price increases. Although market share may decline, the approach is to make short-term cash gains.

In considering stability, marketing issues are also of central importance. First, the domination has to be recognized in terms of market standing, of comparative competitive marketing activities, and of the marketing activities needed if either strategy is to be adopted. In the case of holding this would require an assessment of the marketing needed to continue the domination of competitors. In the case of harvesting the effects of cost reductions, such as possible product degradation, on customers would need to be determined, as well as longer-term competitive standing relative to lost market share.

Stage 2 (continued) Defence

As mentioned in the last section, this approach is often labelled retrenchment. Where the firm is unable to grow within a particular product-market scope, or indeed where it is unable to maintain stability, it may be forced into a retrenchment strategy. In tackling its defence three major alternatives are available:

Turnaround strategy Here the company attempts to improve on its current competitive standing by improving its performance through improvements to its current operations, and marketing operations can be particularly important. Such an approach is reported to have been successfully pursued by International Harvester, manufacturers of agricultural equipment, by intensifying marketing during the late seventies in three major markets.[21]

Divestment strategy This is the opposite of investment for growth, where the firm sells off an SBU, division, or even a subsidiary, in order to defend itself by concentrating on other SBUs in which it is stronger.

Liquidation strategy This is similar to divestment, although the selling-off is normally to raise cash in order to defend against a weak position, often in relation to intense competition. However, liquidation of a particular SBU may be for less defensive reasons. The US company Gould, manufactures of electronic and electrical products, sold off its industrial products SBU and obtained 'well over the book value', although it exhibited market domination in other SBUs.[22]

The involvement of marketing disciplines in the turnaround strategy has been well emphasized above. For the other two strategies marketing skills are needed to ratify the firm's relative position within the markets of the SBU to be sold. Similarly, marketing skills will be needed to provide indications of markets to which the released resources should be allocated.

Stage 3 Competitive advantage

Decisions having been made at Stages 1 and 2, the third stage is concerned with how advantages can be gained over competitors. A basic split here is between those advantages that are marketing-related and those that originate from the other business functions. The importance of the former within this stage of the formulation of organizational strategy again shows the role of marketing orientation within strategic planning.

In developing marketing-related advantages there are several alternatives. The first is concerned with dominance of competitors. The example of Procter and Gamble dominating competitors through market share has already been noted.[20] Dominance can also be achieved by creating prohibitive costs for market entry, reducing unit cost for price advantage, or expanding capacity to swamp market demand. Patent protection of products can also achieve dominance over competitors.

A second approach to achieving competitive advantage is through expertise in marketing, especially in anticipating business opportunities and identifying product-market scopes. Marketing expertise has allowed the Ford Escort to become the best selling small car in the USA.

However, because of the element of price competition needed within the marketing mix each unit is sold at a loss, so that the cost of achieving such a competitive advantage obviously needs to be carefully determined.[23]

A third approach to competitive advantage has been emphasized by Ansoff[8] and is based upon the strength of products. These can be product benefits that provide superiority over the competition, or the development of breakthrough products that exhibit a radical and dramatic product performance relative to the competition.

Competitive advantages to be gained from the other business functions are considered to be outside the scope of the book, except where they have ramifications on marketing. For example Amstrad, manufacturers of low-cost audio equipment and televisions, utilize Far East manufacturers and assemblers, which they claim gives them lower manufacturing costs and higher quality than could be achieved in the UK. This obviously gives marketing the competitive advantages of both lower price and a reputation for performance and reliability.[24]

Stage 4 Synergy

The final stage in the formulation of organizational strategy is a consideration of company strengths and their amalgamation into combined capabilities. This is the '2 + 2 = 5' concept, where the combination results in a *force majeure* greater than where each strength is allowed to operate independently. Kollat, Blackwell and Robeson[25] see synergy as being the mutual effects of the various business areas within the firm, each reinforcing the other to provide a total corporate impact. As with the other stages of organizational strategy, marketing disciplines provide a key contribution to the formulation of this stage.

Ansoff[8] has identified several areas in which synergy can be identified and developed, two of which are selling and operational synergy, where marketing synergy is obviously important from the latter. An example here is from the power-tool manufacturers Black & Decker. In a recent report the firm claimed that their strengths of a worldwide franchise system and well-developed brand/corporate image would allow them to develop an extensive range of tools, appliances and consumer gadgets. Here the reinforcement from each product line would give operational synergy.[26]

Also applicable to marketing orientation in this stage of organizational strategy is management synergy, which is concerned with the combined experiences and expertise of managers. Such synergy has been achieved by the US container company Ball Corporation. Part of their strategy has been to utilize a smaller number of marketing executives than their competitors, but to ensure that these executives are knowledgeable about and committed to their markets, to give a combined, synergistic effect for capable management.[27]

Each of these four stages for formulating organizational strategy is illustrated in Case Study 8 (page 82).

Final considerations

Although these stages of strategy formulation have a range of alternatives, companies obviously need to be realistic in relation to constraints applicable to their individual situation. Therefore there are several final considerations that need to be made, although in practice these are likely to be tackled along with the consideration of each of the stages of formulation.

The first of these is the backwards integration of the organizational strategy into the other stages of strategic planning. The relationship to organizational mission has already been discussed, in that product-market scope represents an extension of the mission. However, the strategy also needs to be compatible with the achievement of organizational objectives. Indeed, the next section will examine the role of objectives in strategy selection, in that the latter is the broad means of obtaining organizational objectives.

The second consideration is the forward integration of organizational strategy into operational planning. As shown in Part One, organizational strategy will provide a framework for the operational marketing strategy. However, at this stage, the implications of this framework on marketing strategy need to be considered. Establishing parameters that are not feasible at the marketing operations level should obviously be avoided. Again there needs to be an input from operational planning, once more highlighting one of the book's themes, namely the interrelationship of the stages within corporate planning, as opposed to a one-way forward relationship.

Probably the final consideration is that the formulation of organizational strategy also needs to be realistic relative to constraints from the other business operations. Of particular importance is the constraint placed upon strategy by available finance. In particular, growth strategies can be formulated only if finance is available, although stability strategies could necessitate high expenditure on marketing operations. Similarly, developing competitive advantages may also be restricted by available finance as well as marketing feasibility. Similar arguments could also be followed relative to the other operations, with production capacity and capability constraints being of particular importance. These considerations emphasize the role that the other business operations have to play in strategic planning, although such planning is obviously outside the scope of the book.

SELECTING ORGANIZATIONAL STRATEGY

Having examined the alternatives available in formulating an organizational strategy, we can now address the process of strategy selection. Within the literature, over the past decade, there has been considerable attention to methodology based upon portfolio and matrix analysis. Such methods claim to provide a classification for each product situation, with the resultant label indicating the type of strategy to be pursued in each case. While such methods can be useful in strategy selection, other considerations are of equal importance. The process to be followed for organizational strategy selection is based upon four major areas of consideration, which are outlined in Fig. 5.4 and discussed in detail in the remainder of this section.

Previous and current strategies

For a given point in time, when organizational strategy is being selected, a current strategy will exist and previous ones will have been pursued. Regardless of the size of the organization or the number of products it markets, certain product-market scopes will have been applicable, growth, stability, or defence will have been pursued, competitors will have been tackled and certain synergies will have been developed. The level of sophistication of the development of strategies will vary from firm to firm. Indeed, writers such as Quinn[28] have stated that for many firms there has been a process of logical incrementalism where strategies have become more sophisticated and comprehensive over proceeding years.

For some companies it may be that the current strategy is appropriate for continuation into the future. Where there is satisfaction as to performance, or where growth is not valued, or where difficult competitive situations appertain, are all examples of where current strategies are likely to continue into the future. Another influence on continuation is the attitude of resistance to change on the part of managers. Such an attitude will be discussed further in Part Four, but the general human trait of resistance to change is also applicable to strategy selection. Particularly where

Previous and current strategies
Incrementalism of strategy development
Continuation of current strategy
Managerial resistance to change
Organisational constraints
Starting point for strategy selection

Organizational objectives and strategic audit
Previous achievement of objectives
Performance gap analysis
ROI and net profit margin approach
Environmental opportunities
Compatibility with other planning stages

Selection techniques
Boston Consulting Group matrix
General Electric's planning grid
Royal Dutch/Shell's directional policy matrix
Hofer's portfolio matrix
Pearce's selection matrix
Market share models

Timing considerations
Market evolution changes
Strategic window assessment
Time constraints on change

Figure 5.4 Considerations for organizational strategy selection

previous strategy is seen to have been successful, a changed strategy may be interpreted as a high-risk option so that attitude to risk can have an effect on strategy selection.

Also to be considered as part of the current organizational strategy are the constraints applicable to its operation and subsequent modification. The constraints from the other business functions, mentioned in the last section with regard to examining alternatives, become a reality in the selection process. Where financial resources are not available for growth it may be that the strategy cannot be changed, so that the firm continues with a stability strategy in current product-market scopes. The level of expenditure required to pursue diversification or entry into additional scopes would certainly need to be costed out by the financial function, while company policy relative to acceptable payback periods would need to be included in the decision to pursue such directions. Approaches to such resource determination and allocation relative to strategies are reported in the literature by writers such as Fogg.[29] Similarly, where the organizational structure cannot support major changes to strategy, then, if again the resource of management cannot be augmented, a constraint is placed on selection. The effects of organizational structure on strategy have been discussed by writers such as Chandler[30] and a fuller examination of this issue will be given in Part Four. Overall, regardless of the current strategy, it does represent the starting point for selection for the coming planning period.

Organizational objectives and strategic audit

In this area of consideration the major general principle is that the organizational strategy chosen should be the one that will be most effective in achieving the organizational objectives. While this may be true conceptually, in practice each possible combination of strategy alternatives cannot be tested to identify the one that is likely to be the most effective. Again, previous achievements in, say, reaching an objective of sales volume growth through, for example, product development, can be an indicator for aims of future growth. Using the criteria of a performance component of strategy, particularly relative to achieving profitability, has been cited by Carroll.[31] His claim is that many companies do not perceive the importance of linking strategy to performance, but merely use it as a positional component in order to match their positions to the environment. However, this criterion for selection is based on previous environmental conditions that may not be prevalent over the next planning period.

Another approach relative to organizational objectives is to utilize the well-documented method of performance gap analysis, as presented by many writers such as Higgins.[32] This involves comparing the desired levels of performance given in the quantitative objectives (such as sales volume and profits) with the probable levels of performance generated by the forecasts in the strategic audit, for the planning period. The probable level of performance is based upon the continuation of the current strategy, so that if the desired equates to the probable then the indications are that the current strategy should continue. However, if the desired exceeds the probable then there is a performance gap between the two levels, which is indicative of strategy modifications if the gap is to be closed. This closing of the gap would require growth beyond the current strategy, involving any of the alternatives from Ansoff's growth matrix as given in Fig. 5.3.

A further approach in organizational strategy selection, as suggested by Sheth and Frazier,[33] is to base the selection on two key organizational objectives, namely return on investment and net profit margin. This method uses a matrix approach based upon satisfactory and unsatisfactory return on investment (ROI) and satisfactory and unsatisfactory net profit margin, in which the company classifies itself into the matrix based upon its current objectives. The resultant quadrant classification within the matrix indicates the strategy to be pursued. For example, if both ROI and net profit margin are deemed satisfactory then the indicated strategy would be holding strategy (or entrenchment, using the terminology of Sheth and Frazier).

Another general principle is that strategy selection should be based upon the exploitation of environmental opportunities portrayed in the strategic audit. If industry life-cycles are expanding then a growth strategy of product development may be applicable, while an ending life-cycle may indicate harvesting or even liquidation. Similarly, opportunities within other industries are likely to warrant the consideration of participation in further product-market scopes. Finally, the strategic audit can also be helpful in highlighting the compatibility of organizational strategy alternatives with other stages within the overall corporate planning. Although backwards integration with other stages of strategic planning has been covered, forward integration into operational planning also needs to be considered. For marketing operational planning the ramifications of organizational strategy on marketing strategy can be considered. A treatment of the linkage of stages from strategic to operational planning has been given by Greenley.[34]

Selection techniques

This area concerns the range of techniques or models that have been presented within the literature to be used as aids for the selection of organizational strategy. A total of six techniques are given in Fig. 5.4. With the exception of the last technique, these are well documented in the major texts on strategic management already quoted, such as Harvey,[9] Glueck and Jauch,[10] Thompson and Strickland,[11] Higgins[12] and Byars,[13] so readers are referred to these texts for full details. The principles of these models in aiding the selection of organizational strategy are as follows:

Boston Consulting Group matrix This approach gives an indication of a strategy for each individual product-market scope or SBU, where the mix of scopes is referred to as the business portfolio. The method requires a classification of each scope or SBU based upon the criteria of business growth-rate and market share. The classification is based upon a matrix of high and low growth and market share, and the quadrant into which each scope falls indicates the likely suitable strategy. For example, high growth and high market share are indicative of a stability strategy, whereas low market share and growth suggest harvesting or even liquidation.

General Electric's planning grid A similar approach to that of BCG except that the criteria for the matrix are business strengths and industry attractiveness. However, both criteria are compounded from several variables, giving an added strength. Each criterion is rated as being low, medium or high for each product-market scope, and again the resultant classification for each scope within the matrix indicates whether growth, stability or defence is suitable.

Royal Dutch Shell's directional policy matrix This is based upon weak, average and strong competitive capabilities plus unattractive, average and attractive business sector prospects, where again several variables are used for each criterion. Again, each product-market scope is classified into the matrix and the resultant classification indicates the direction of growth, stability or defence.

Hofer's portfolio matrix In this approach, Hofer[35] has extended the BCG and GE approaches. He uses competitive advantage as one criterion and the stage of evolution of the particular product-market scope (ranging from decline to growth development) as the other. Again, location for each scope in the matrix is indicative of the strategy to be pursued.

Pearce's selection matrix Another matrix approach, suggested by Pearce,[36] uses the criteria of the purpose of the strategy, either to overcome weaknesses or to maximize strengths, together with the approach to be used to achieve this purpose, as either internal resources or external aquisition/merger/joint venture. Again, the resultant classification of each scope suggests the strategy to be pursued.

Market share models This approach is that market share has a major impact on profitability, so that to increase the latter a strategy needs to be selected to increase market share. This relationship was identified by the well-documented PIMS study carried out by the Marketing Sciences Institute and the Harvard Business School, reported by Buzzell.[37] Consequently, in this approach, the firm would adopt an organizational strategy that it anticipates would achieve the market share it desires. Writers such as Bloom and Kotler[38] have suggested strategies for high market share firms, while Woo and Cooper[39] have suggested implications for firms with low market share.

Timing considerations

In selecting an organizational strategy a major concern is that decisions are to be made today about long-term direction based upon an understanding derived from both historical performance and forecasts of the future. Although organizational strategy can be modified in subsequent years, it is still the case that current decisions represent commitment to future action and resource allocation. Consequently, there is the concept of change, with time affecting suitability of strategy. Additionally, there is the concept of timing relative to the point in time at which a strategy should be initiated. Therefore, overall, the concept of timing involves initiation of strategy, the period over which it should continue until environmental changes give rise to a modification, and finally the point in time when the strategy is no longer applicable.

A major contribution relative to timing is from the work of Abell.[40] This is based upon the concept of market evolution, where the principle to be followed is that changes in the level of demand within markets are normally experienced with changes in the life-cycle of the industry. Therefore the firm needs to monitor market evolution changes and adjust its strategies accordingly. For example, a major technological change may require strategy modification to product development, while improvements in channel efficiency may suggest a modification to market development. Therefore, as a market changes with time, there is likely to be only a particular period of time for which a particular organizational strategy is applicable. This period of time has been labelled the 'strategic window' by Abell, with the emphasis that these periods need to be identified so that a new strategy can be selected as a consequence of the market evolutionary change.

If such strategic windows are not identified then environmental changes may lead to forced strategy decisions, where immediacy of need to respond in itself places a time constraint on strategy change. A danger here is that strategy modifications may be made that are spontaneous and not systematically planned out.

Marketing orientation

Within each of the major areas of consideration for organizational strategy selection, the role of marketing orientation is evident.

In considering previous and current strategies the previous utilization of marketing by the firm can become evident, indicating whether the business approach has tended towards serving defined markets, or has tended towards product orientation of developing products and then looking for markets. Similarly, levels of marketing orientation achieved in setting the organizational objectives will also be transmitted into strategy through this selection process. The role of the strategic audit in giving a total understanding of the environment was described in the last chapter as being a major tool for achieving marketing orientation. Therefore its inclusion as part of the strategy selection process will also affect marketing orientation.

The whole range of reported selection techniques include criteria that require the firm to address marketing factors relative to their strategic planning. Consequently, all these models of selection encourage marketing within the organization. Finally, the area of timing considerations is, by its very nature, concerned with tackling changes within the market place. Again, the inclusion of this area as part of the selection process engages attention towards adapting to the market-place at the strategic level of planning.

SUMMARY

The chapter looked first at the origins of the word strategy, before moving on to explaining the major features of organizational strategy.

It then addressed the different approaches that are recommended to be adopted by companies in formulating organizational strategy. These approaches are based upon direction, components, competition, a hierarchy, and a typology. The approach for formulating organizational strategy as adopted in this book was presented as a four-stage process, which involves the development of different alternatives in its formulation. The first stage is concerned with product-market scope, while the second is concerned with determining growth, stability or defence. Stage three tackles competitive advantages and the fourth stage is concerned with the utilizing synergy effects.

The last section examined areas to be considered in the final selection of an organizational strategy. Four major areas of consideration were identified, the first being previous and current strategies. The second involves the organizational objectives and strategic audit, the third area is the range of specifically designed selection techniques, while the final area is that of timing.

CASE STUDY 8: GEORGE BASSETT HOLDINGS LTD*

Case outline

The subject of this study is a manufacturer of sugar confectionery products, which includes the famous Bassett's Liquorice Allsorts. Many organizational strategy issues are discussed in the study.

Illustration

The major organizational strategy issues have been extracted from the case and presented within the format of the four stages of strategy formulation, as presented in Fig. 5.2.

Stage 1 Product-market scopes

At the time the case study was written, the UK confectionery market was broadly split into chocolate products and sugar products. Of the two product-market scopes, Bassett had adopted the strategy of participation in only sugar products. Here they were very aware that the product life-cycle of many of its products is very long.

However other product-market scopes had been adopted as an extension of its strategy, being:

- Tobacco and confectionery wholesaling.
- Tobacco and confectionery retailing.
- Cake manufacturing.
- As a development from their own internal data processing, the development of a company in the business of data processing.

In looking to the future, Bassett were also considering other scopes. In particular there were indications of long-term market changes, with signs that savoury food snacks were becoming increasingly popular to the detriment of sugar confectionery. Possible causes were changes in consumer tastes and more awareness of health by the public. Such signs were indicative of considering the product-market scope of savoury snacks.

Stage 2 Growth, stability and defence

It is reported that, from the last war to the time of the case, Bassett have pursued a growth strategy. Just after the war a growth strategy of consolidation was adopted, but by 1956 they faced three alternatives. These were to accept a stability strategy due to market conditions, to pursue growth through market penetration, or to go for growth by diversification. The strategy alternative selected was the latter.

It appears that growth through market penetration has been continuously pursued by the firm. Growth through market development has been spearheaded by exporting, to Australia and Europe. Growth by product development is reported to have been pursued by the use of a wider range of materials in developing products within the existing product line. The pursuit of a growth strategy by diversification was through the entry to the additional product-market scopes of wholesaling, retailing, cake manufacture and data processing.

* Derived from R. M. P. Green, George Bassett Holdings Ltd. Copyright © 1976 R. M. P. Green.

Stage 3 Competitive advantage

A major approach to this area of organizational strategy was the achievement of domination by market share. At the time of the case study they were market leaders not only in liquorice confectionery, partly gained through buying market share by acquiring three manufacturers, but also in jelly babies, wine gums and children's soft confectionery. Similarly, they had also achieved domination in the sector of the market where children purchase their own sweets.

Bassetts had also used several marketing strengths in their competitive strategy. Well-known brand names such as Bassett and Barrett had a high level of consumer awareness. Also, a high-quality image had been developed. Another advantage was developed through vertical integration in the marketing channel, so that being manufacturer, wholesaler and retailer meant wide distribution coverage. The product benefit of a high quality standard had also been established in this area of its strategy.

Finally, research and development relative to production had revolutionized manufacturing, ensuring low costs relative to average sugar confectionery manufacture.

Stage 4 Synergy

It would appear that Bassett had achieved little synergy in their selling operations. Unusually for the industry, the salesforce was split by brand name and not retail outlet, so that there was duplication of calls to retailers, or a negative synergy. However, production and management organization synergy had been achieved. In the former there was flexibility within production plants to absorb any spare capacity. Management organization synergy had been achieved by rationalizing production in UK factories, integrating marketing operations, and standardizing accounting procedures.

REVIEW QUESTIONS

1. What do you consider to be the major features of organizational strategy?
2. Discuss the reasoning behind the different prescriptive approaches to organizational strategy.
3. 'Growth is central to the Western economies and therefore all firms must utilize a growth strategy.' Discuss.
4. Examine the proposition that a matrix/portfolio approach to selecting organizational strategy is totally inadequate.
5. Discuss the 'strategic window' concept, highlighting its significance to organizational strategy.
6. Explain how the formulation and selection of an organizational strategy can aid in achieving marketing orientation.

REFERENCES

1. R. Evered, 'So what is strategy?', *Long Range Planning*, **16**, 3, 57–72, 1983.
2. 'How Crompton took the strain', *Management Today*, March 1984.
3. Andrews, K. R., *The Concept of Corporate Strategy*, Irwin, Homewood, 1980.
4. 'Consolidated Food's new pack', *Management Today*, April 1984.
5. P. J. Hovell, 'The marketing concept and corporate strategy', *Management Decision*, **17**, 2, 157–67, 1979.
6. H. I. Ansoff, 'Strategy as a tool for coping with change', *Journal of Business Policy*, **1**, 4, 3–7, 1971.
7. Johnson, G., and K. Scholes, *Exploring Corporate Strategy*, Prentice-Hall, London, 1984.
8. Ansoff, H. I., *Corporate Strategy*, McGraw-Hill, New York, 1965.
9. Harvey, D. F., *Strategic Management*, Merrill, Columbus, 1982.
10. Glueck, W. F., and L. R. Jauch, *Business Policy and Strategic Management*, McGraw-Hill, New York, 1984.
11. Thompson, A. A., and A. J. Strickland, *Strategy Formulation and Implementation*, Business Publications, Plano, 1983.
12. Higgins, J. M., *Organizational Policy and Strategic Management*, Dryden Press, New York, 1983.
13. Byars, L. L., *Strategic Management*, Harper and Row, New York, 1984.
14. P. Spillard, 'Ansoff revisited: logic, commitment and strategies for change', *Quarterly Review of Marketing*, **6**, 2, 1–8, 1980.
15. 'Power complex at the CEGB', *Management Today*, May 1984.
16. 'BOC goes West', *Management Today*, January 1984.
17. R. D. Buzzell *et al.*, 'Market share—a key to profitability', *Harvard Business Review*, **53**, 1, 97–106, January-February 1975.
18. 'The fruits of Apple', *Management Today*, June 1984.
19. 'The King of Tires is discontented', *Fortune*, 28 May 1983.
20. 'Trouble at Procter and Gamble', *Fortune*, 5 March 1984.
21. 'International Harvester', *Business Week*, 11 February 1980.
22. 'Gould's golden gamble', *Management Today*, February 1984.
23. 'Ford's fragile recovery', *Fortune*, 2 April 1984.
24. 'Amstrad's personal ambitions', *Management Today*, June 1984.
25. Kollat, D. T., R. D. Blackwell and J. F. Robeson, *Strategic Marketing*, Holt, Rinehart and Winston, New York, 1972.
26. 'Black and Decker's gamble on globalization', *Fortune*, 14 May 1984.
27. 'The five-star management of Ball', *Management Today*, March 1984.
28. J. B. Quinn, 'Strategic change: logical incrementalism', *Sloan Management Review*, **20**, 1, 7–11, 1978.
29. C. D. Fogg, 'New business planning—the resource allocation process', *Industrial Marketing Management*, **5**, 3–11, 1976.
30. Chandler, A., *Strategy and Structure*, MIT Press, Cambridge, 1967.
31. P. J. Carroll, 'The link between performance and strategy', *Journal of Business Strategy*, **2**, 4, 3–20, 1982.
32. Higgins, J. C., *Strategic and Operational Planning Systems*, Prentice-Hall International, London, 1980.
33. J. N. Sheth, and G. L. Frazier, 'A margin-return model for strategic market planning', *Journal of Marketing*, **47**, 100–9, 1983.

34. G. E. Greenley, 'The integration of product decisions', *Management Decision*, **22**, 2, 36–44, 1984.
35. Hofer, C. W., *Conceptual Concepts for Formulating Corporate and Business Strategies*, Intercollegiate Case Clearing House, Boston, 1977.
36. J. A. Pearce, 'Selecting among alternative grand strategies', *California Management Review*, **14**, 3, 23–31, 1983.
37. R. D. Buzzell *et al.*, 'Market share—a key to profitability', *Harvard Business Review*, **53**, 1, 97–106, 1975.
38. P. N. Bloom and P. Kotler, 'Strategies for high market share companies', *Harvard Business Review*, **53**, 6, 63–72, 1975.
39. C. Y. Woo and A. C. Cooper, 'Strategies of effective low share businesses', *Strategic Management Journal*, **2**, 3, 301–18, 1981.
40. D. F. Abell, 'Strategic windows', *Journal of Marketing*, **42**, 3, 21–6, 1978.

6. Marketing objectives and environment
7. Marketing strategy
8. Marketing plan documents

OUTLINE

While the last part examined the role of the marketing process at the strategic level of planning, Part Three addresses the planning of marketing operations. This commences with an examination of marketing objectives in Chapter 6. This chapter also includes a discussion of the environment in which the marketing operations must be both planned and implemented. In Chapter 7 marketing strategy is explored as the long-range component of marketing operational planning. Part Three ends with an examination of marketing plan documents in Chapter 8, where the role of marketing tactics is particularly emphasized. While explaining the nature of marketing operational planning, this part of the book also aims to show how these planning stages relate to strategic planning.

MARKETING OBJECTIVES AND ENVIRONMENT

Learning objectives are to:

1. Understand the nature and roles of marketing objectives.
2. Obtain a detailed knowledge of the different types of marketing objectives.
3. Appreciate the importance of a knowledge of the marketing environment.
4. Be able to recognize the areas of analysis required for an understanding of the marketing environment.
5. Recognize major concepts that have been introduced.

This chapter tackles the first two stages of marketing operational planning, as developed in Part One. Here we are concerned with the aims to be pursued by the marketing operation, as well as the information needed for planning it.

Although there are certain similarities between this chapter and Chapter 4, which was concerned with organizational objectives and the strategic audit, the following sections will illustrate that the role of both objectives and information differ at the operational level of planning. Marketing objectives represent the contribution to be made by this area of company operations to its overall performance, while specific information is needed to make specific decisions on marketing action. Indeed, the first section of this chapter examines the role of marketing objectives within the total corporate planning framework. Emphasizing the role of marketing objectives is seen to be important, particularly when observers such as Cravens[1] claim that, despite their importance, little attention is given to marketing objectives and even when they are set they often do not fulfil the role required of them. The second section examines the range of marketing objectives to be considered when establishing those to be pursued.

The rest of the chapter is devoted to the information needs of marketing operational planning relative to the marketing environment. Again, there are links into strategic planning in that information generated from the strategic audit can be used here. Also, information gained for operational planning provides an input into the strategic audit.

ROLE OF MARKETING OBJECTIVES

In Chapter 4 we saw that establishing objectives is concerned with stating aims or levels of achievement for a particular period of time, and that as that period of time passes actual levels of achievement are measured against the planned levels given in the objectives.

The role to be played by objectives at the operational level differs from that at the strategic level. Whereas objectives in the latter relate to the overall aims, marketing objectives are seen to be a means of allowing the marketing operations to contribute to the accomplishment of overall aims, a principle well established in the literature, such as given by Kotler.[2] An example here comes from the UK-based pharmaceutical firm Glaxo, who recently entered the US market with a new product for ulcer treatment. With an organizational objective of extensive company growth in the US, a major marketing operational objective is the launching of a whole range of pharmaceutical products.[3] The link between these levels of objectives is via a hierarchy, as discussed in Chapter 4 and arising from the work of Granger,[4] while the overall process of management by objectives is just as applicable at the operational level as it is at the strategic level. Also, the establishment of marketing objectives needs to be related to the organizational structure of the firm. It is probable that a different set of operational objectives will be required for each product-market scope, SBU or division. However, the variations in organizational objectives for such organizational arrangements will also need to be taken into account.

Consequently, a major consideration in establishing the marketing objectives is the contribution or role they are able to play relative to the achievement of organizational objectives. Therefore, the first stage is to consider the range of organizational objectives to determine possibilities for contribution relative to the marketing operations. Writers such as Mali[5] have shown how, for a given range of organizational objectives, marketing objectives can be related, as illustrated in Fig. 6.1. In all cases the point is that guidance, direction, or a framework has been established for marketing objectives.

Organizational level	Marketing operational level
Growth	To increase product sales and to identify new markets
Profitability	To achieve higher price acceptance or increase volume
Market domination	To expand current market shares
Product leadership	To increase market share; to increase brand loyalty; or to develop market leadership
Public responsibility	To improve product quality; to improve efficiency of distribution; or to improve value for price

Figure 6.1 Relating organizational and marketing objectives

In the treatment of organizational objectives given in Chapter 4, effects of the personal influence of managers were examined, although it was also highlighted that a fuller treatment will be given in Part Four. However, it also needs to be emphasized that the personal influence of managers is just as likely to affect the formulation of objectives at the operational level as it is at the strategic. Again, the general principle applies that it is difficult for executives to separate their feelings, emotions and personal preferences from logical analysis and decision making. Expectations of marketing personnel, along with their individual personal objectives within the hierarchy, are likely to have an influence and to be reflected in the role that the marketing objectives will play within the overall corporate planning. Again, the general principle as a consequence of this situation is that marketing personnel need to strive to recognize any conflict between their personal aspirations and feasible levels of performance within the marketing operations.

Marketing objectives also need to relate horizontally within the hierarchy by being compatible with other operational objectives. Many writers, such as Cravens,[1] have emphasized that, in establishing marketing objectives, liaison with other company operations is essential in order to ensure horizontal consistency within the hierarchy.

The specific roles of organizational objectives were presented in Chapter 4. These roles or reasons for can also be related to marketing objectives in that they can be considered to relate to objectives *per se*. However, perhaps the most important specific roles of marketing objectives are to:

- Measure and judge the performance of marketing operations. Here there are claims in the literature, such as by Latham and Yukl,[6] that specificity in objectives tends to lead to improved performance.
- Relate marketing plans to organizational objectives.
- Serve as a control for the marketing operations.
- Clarify expectations of the individual marketing functions, such as advertising and pricing.
- Enhance communications among marketing personnel.
- Stimulate the motivation of marketing personnel.

The literature also contains reports on the nature of the presentation of objectives. Eilon[7] considers that objectives should be measureable, quantified, time-based, and feasible. As will be seen later, some marketing objectives need to be quantifiable whereas other do not, while all are time-based relative to the corporate planning structure. Reif and Bassford[8] offer additional guidelines on the presentation of objectives, stating that they should:

- be clear and concise;
- state what to achieve and not how to achieve it;
- be a challenge to marketing personnel;
- be mutually agreed by all marketing personnel.

The final consideration in the role of marketing objectives is the time period to which they apply. Within the corporate planning framework established in Part One, marketing strategy appertains to the long-term whereas marketing tactics appertain to the short-term. But, as will be seen in Chapter 8, marketing operational planning in companies tends to be orientated to the annual marketing plan and therefore there is a tendency to set marketing objectives on an annual basis. However, they can be for a longer period. In 1980 it was predicted that the US automobile industry would not be able to significantly increase the production output of small-engined cars until 1985. Consequently, the setting of market share objectives at the time would have required a long-term planning element.[9] Therefore, the general principle is that although certain objectives may be applicable, they need to be scheduled into suitable time periods.

TYPES OF MARKETING OBJECTIVES

Several formats are given in the literature for the type of marketing objectives that can be established. Migliore and Stevens[10] consider that they should relate to sales, profits and specific consumer objectives. Jain[11] has suggested profits, market share, sales and unique objectives, the latter relating to the firm's current operational situation. Writers such as Bluell[12] and Cravens[1] purport that marketing objectives should be based upon sales, market share, marketing costs, profits and objectives relating directly to the elements of the marketing mix. Indeed, this is the approach adopted within the book, with the major areas in which marketing objectives can be established being given in Fig. 6.2. Consequently, the rest of this section is concerned with a detailed examination of each of these five areas.

Sales volume
Presented by: market sales
product sales
geographical sales
quota sales

Market share
Presented by: individual markets
individual products

Marketing costs
Related to: marketing research
product management
selling and distribution
advertising and promotion

Profit
Presented by: individual markets
individual products

Marketing mix
Related to: product management
pricing
selling and distribution
advertising and promotion

Figure 6.2 Major areas for establishing marketing objectives

Sales volume objectives

From the framework of organizational objectives concerned with performance and particularly growth, a range of sales volume objectives can be established. These may start with an overall sales objective for each particular product-market scope or SBU, but most firms are likely to require the type of breakdown given in Fig. 6.2. Indeed, a more specific breakdown could include specific market segments and individual salesmen's territories. As will be seen in the next section this is, by necessity, the most common marketing objective and there are many company examples to be found. Consequently, the gearing of the total organization to the level of revenue to be earned over the next planning period is a fundamental job of the marketing department. In a recent report on Jaguar Cars, setting a sales volume objective proved to be difficult in that, although it was possible to set the objective to a certain level based upon market demand, the firm was not able to produce at that level. Such a situation means that a realistically lower level of sales volume would need to be included in the objective.[13]

An example of market sales volume objectives is provided by tyre manufacturers Goodyear, who, unlike other tyre companies, aim to achieve sales from a wide-range market beyond the traditional US tyre market.[14] An example of an emphasis on product sales comes from the previous example of drugs for ulcer treatment. Here the two major suppliers, Glaxo and Smith-Kline, concentrate their efforts towards a sales volume objective for each of their respective products primarily due to their duopoly type competitive situation.[3]

Market share objectives

The setting of market share objectives for the next planning period needs to be based upon both organizational objectives and organizational strategy. In the former a directional objective of market leadership needs to be considered, while a growth strategy may also affect the formulation of market share objectives.

Research by Buzzell et al.[15] through the PIMS study has claimed that high market share leads to high levels of profitability. Although this view is supported by writers such as Catry and Chevalier,[16] other writers do not agree, for example James[17] and Woo and Cooper.[18] The general principle is that, although such an end result may be achieved through aiming for and achieving higher market share, it is perhaps necessary to assess the importance of market share within the particular industry relative to competitors. In industries where the norm is that it is important to the companies, such as in passenger cars, this needs to be taken into account relative to both market leadership at the strategic level and market share at the operational level. In the competitive battle between Smith-Kline and Glaxo within the market for ulcer treatment, market share between the two companies has developed as an important objective.[3] Although Procter and Gamble have previously maintained high market shares in many of their markets, a recent report has outlined that many of these high levels have been lost. Consequently, the company will no doubt be reviewing the importance of market share objectives in their future marketing operations.[19]

Marketing cost objectives

This area for the setting of marketing objectives links back to the group of internal organizational objectives. The setting of objectives relative to costs is a standard inclusion in MbO for the purpose of reducing and controlling costs. Therefore this is equally applicable to marketing operations, although the utilization of a budget in the marketing plan may reduce the importance of such objectives. This issue will be pursued further in the next chapter.

However, objectives can be set for the reduction of costs within the individual elements of the marketing mix, or to achieve a different allocation of costs across the mix. Additionally, costs can be related to sales volume, such as a ratio of advertising expenditure to sales volume, so that objectives can be set to achieve certain levels within such ratios. The whole system of the utilization of ratios will be examined relative to the control of the implementation of plans in Part Five.

Profit objectives

Although profit was included within organizational performance objectives, it is frequently also advocated within the set of marketing objectives. This is based upon the logic that the marketing operation affects both sales volume and price, which are key elements in the achievement of profits, as for example, discussed by Christopher.[20] However, all the other business operations also affect profit, so that writers such as Christopher[20] and Piercy[21] suggest that the marketing department should not be responsible for profit. However, responsibility does need to be identified within the organizational structure and if this is not to be at director level from the point of view of control, then it may be decided that the marketing department is a logical and convenient location for responsibility.

An alternative is to set objectives relative not to profit but to a marketing contribution, the latter being the difference between sales revenue and marketing costs. Whichever approach is taken, a breakdown can be by products and markets.

Marketing mix objectives

Writers such as Bell[22] see objectives within the elements of the marketing mix as being a separate level within a company's hierarchy of objectives. Regardless of their level, objectives within each of the elements can be considered as follows:

Product management The major organizational objectives that have an effect here are the directional objectives of market spread and customer service. An early approach to classifying product objectives was from Pessemier;[23] this was based upon a matrix using the parameters of increasing technological newness and increasing marketing newness. Examples of product objectives have been suggested by Bell,[22] some of which are discussed below:

- Introduction of new products to achieve growth. General Electric and Campbell Soup in the USA have pursued such an objective by introducing new products.[24]
- Introduction of modified products. For example, the machinery manufacturer Wadkin have an objective to modernize and redesign their products.[25]
- Finding new uses for existing products.
- Aiming for the development of product differentiation. In 1980 this was reported as being the basis of the US car manufacturers' marketing, through a wide array of highly visible buyer options, such as interior finishes.[9]
- Improvements in the quality of both existing and future products. This objective is central to the marketing of Jaguar cars, being a major requirement within the range of their customers' needs.[13]
- Developing a full product line aimed at all customer requirements. For example, AT and T are reported to be aiming to supply a broad range of products associated with computing facilities, except for mainframes.[26]
- Aiming for cost reductions to current products, but in relation to customer requirements.
- Utilization of excess production capacity.

Pricing objectives The areas of organizational objectives that are applicable here are performance and social responsibility. Price is a unique element of the mix in that changes directly affect sales volume and profit. Indirectly, the price level can affect issues such as image and resource utilization, hence its relevance to social responsibility. Types of pricing objectives have been suggested as follows by Hisrich and Peters,[27] developed from an article by Oxenfeldt:[28]

- The achievement of maximum profits.
- The achievement of a particular rate of return on investment.
- Survival of a particular product by aiming for a minimum level of profit.
- Increasing sales volume and/or market share.
- Discouragement of competitors and new market entrants.
- Following price leads by competitors.
- Conforming with product line pricing.
- The promotion of corporate and brand/product image.
- Phasing out obsolete products.
- Creaming particular market segments.

Selling and distribution objectives Within this group, objectives are relative to efficiency in supplying the market place, being affected by the organizational objectives of market spread, growth and internal efficiency. Jackson and Aldag[29] have suggested the types of objectives that can be established relative to selling efficiency:

- Achieving higher gross margins of products sold.
- Concentration on higher margin products.

– Balancing number of calls per unit time with customer service.
– Improving order-call ratios.
– Rate of new-account generation.
– Improving efficiency of selling expenses.

Objectives relative to distribution efficiency have been suggested by Guirdham:[30]

– Ability of channels to reach target audience.
– Product flow within the channel.
– Adequate stocking of products.
– Elimination of unnecessary costs.
– Provision of market information.

Advertising and promotion Here the framework is provided by organizational objectives from the areas of market leadership, market spread, growth and social responsibility. Writers such as Aaker and Myers[31] give these objectives as being concerned with aiming either directly to increase sales or at the behaviour of the target audience. In the latter case the early work of Colley[32] has provided a basis for these objectives, as follows:

– Giving an understanding, such as introducing new products. An example here is the US drug firm Searle, who have used advertising with the aim of introducing 'Nutra Sweet', a low-calorie sweetener, that will be included in many US and European food manufacturers' products.[33]
– Changing attitudes, such as product identification and image building.
– Affecting customer action, such as achieving brand loyalty. For example, American Airlines have been reported as having created brand loyalty in the commodity business of air travel.[24]

   An illustration of the applicability of marketing objectives relative to a reported company situation is given in Case Study 9 (page 103).

EVIDENCE OF MARKETING OBJECTIVES

The nature of marketing objectives established by firms has been reported by Greenley[34] relative to UK firms, Hopkins[35] relative to US firms and Shipley[36] who gives a UK–US comparison. As a general comment, Hopkins reports that 'marketing planners are united' in agreeing that objectives should be realistically achievable, should be quantifiable in terms of units, and should allow for measurement.

   All three sources report the frequency of firms adopting the different types of objectives. These results are summarized relative to the major areas for establishing marketing objectives, as given in Fig. 6.2.

Sales volume

Greenley found that nearly all his respondents establish sales volume objectives, whereas with the US firms cited by Hopkins the frequency was given at 60 per cent. The Shipley comparison identified that in both countries sales volume objectives are considered to be of less importance than those relating to profit. However, Greenley found lower numbers of firms setting objectives relative to individual product and market sales, although these were not reported in the other two surveys.

Market share

Here Greenley found that about 60 per cent of his samples declared using market share objectives, whereas Shipley found that his firms rated them as being less important than profits and sales revenue. Certainly there does not appear to be as much attention given to market share as the attention given in the literature, as discussed in the last section, might suggest.

Marketing costs

Only Greenley reported the incidence of these objectives, with less than half the firms claiming to use them. Although this result is not significant in itself, it is perhaps indicative of a low level of utilization of a full MbO system. Evidence of the use of other approaches to the control of costs will be examined in Part Four.

Profits

Despite the split in the difference of opinion within the prescriptive methodology relative to the inclusion of profit within marketing objectives, all researchers found a high frequency of firms setting marketing profit objectives. This is probably indicative of a common incidence of allocating profit responsibility to the marketing function, although the importance of profit to commercially orientated firms is likely to have affected the eagerness of respondents to declare a profit objective at the operational level.

Marketing mix

Both Greenley and Hopkins found low levels of firms declaring objectives within the elements of the mix, with a maximum of just over half in the former and just over 60 per cent in the latter. However, within this response both found product management and selling effectiveness to be the most common, although the low level of response needs to be taken into account in understanding this result.

APPROACHING THE MARKETING ENVIRONMENT

In Chapter 4 we examined the strategic audit and its dual role of the collection of information for strategic planning as well as an information input into operational planning. The information need relative to the marketing environment, for the purpose of operational planning, differs from that generated through a strategic audit, as will be illustrated later in this chapter. However, there are many parallels between these two stages of planning, which will be emphasized where appropriate.

The major difference between the two sets of information is simply that one is for long-term direction, whereas information for marketing operational planning is for current planning needs. Whereas organizational objectives contribute to the plotting of this direction, marketing objectives are concerned with immediate performance and aims. Consequently, they are very much affected by the current marketing environment, so that the role of information extracted from the marketing environment is concerned with planning decisions to affect the current performance.

The marketing environment understanding is also very necessary for the control of the implementation of plans, which will become fully apparent in Part Five. Here the information serves to allow for the monitoring of plan information and for taking corrective action. Therefore an understanding of the marketing environment can also be seen as having two roles: providing information to allow for operational planning, and allowing for the control of the implementation of plans. A third role of such understanding is providing an information input into the strategic audit, which then becomes part of the data base for strategic planning, as outlined in Part Two. Indeed, in Chapter 4 part of the specific external environment was seen as requiring an input of information from the marketing environment.

This stage of planning is also concerned with identifying opportunities in marketing that the firm is potentially able to pursue. Here the theme developed is that these can be relative to both current operations, identifying, say, an opportunity for increased market penetration, but can also give indications of long-term directional opportunities, such as potential diversification. The importance of identifying such opportunities relative to business success has recently been highlighted by the US-based electronics firm Motorola. Historically the firm had been mediocre in consumer electrical products, but has achieved success through the identification and exploitation of opportunities in semiconductors, communications equipment and computer technologies.[37]

Finally, the marketing environment can also represent a number of threats to the company. As will be seen in the following sections, threats can take different forms; however, the general principle is that the understanding of the marketing environment needs to include the identification of threats as well as opportunities.

The rest of this chapter is concerned with the areas of information required to provide an understanding of the marketing environment. Several approaches to this understanding have been given in the literature. That suggested by Jain[11] comprises of three areas of consideration: an internal appraisal, an external appraisal and a product/market appraisal. This lead is to be followed so that the next three sections correspond to these three areas.

INTERNAL APPRAISAL

The major role of the internal appraisal is to provide a base for developing the current marketing operational plans, although the appraisal also provides an input for the strategic audit. There are three major considerations pertinent to these roles: the framework set in the strategic planning, the previous performance of the marketing operations and ramifications from other operational planning.

Strategic planning framework

Consideration of all stages as presented in Part Two gives the expectations of the overall company performance. Consequently, their nature will allow for the identification of contributions from the marketing operations, as well as pointing to levels of achievement to be established in marketing objectives, plus areas to be established within the marketing strategy. The nature of these considerations will vary according to the planning processes to be used. Although the latter is to be tackled in Part Five there is a general comment worthy of mention here. Where the overall process can be described as having been top-down, there is likely to be a need for deliberations in assessing contributions. However, where the marketing personnel have been involved in strategic planning then integration of the two levels of planning is likely to be more apparent.

Marketing operations

Here the appraisal is concerned with the previous planning period, where the appropriateness of the previous planning needs to be assessed as well as the success of the individual marketing functions. Success in achieving objectives can be appraised and where there has been failure the reasons can be observed for consideration in the next planning period. Again, this relates to the control function which will be pursued further in Part Five. Following on from this, the suitability of the previous marketing strategy can also be appraised, and a critical look taken at the tactics within the marketing plan.

An appraisal of the individual marketing functions has already been emphasized in Chapter 4 on the strategic audit, the criteria being set out in Fig. 4.6. However, at the operational level this appraisal is concerned with assessing suitability for the attainment of operational objectives. A full appraisal is normally achieved through the use of a marketing audit. This is also a method to be used for control, so that again full treatment will be given in Part Five. However, the point is that information generated in the audit is applicable to this appraisal.

Other operational planning

Running parallel with marketing operational planning is, obviously, the planning of other business operations, which also contribute to the achievement of strategic plans. Obviously, marketing operations need to take into account constraints imposed by the other operations and indeed the latter also need to consider marketing implications. Here a further example comes from Smith Kline: the pharmaceutical industry features extensive research and development in order to generate marketing opportunities and Smith Kline are no exception, with R and D having expanded, so that their marketing operations had to be planned alongside technical research and development.[3]

EXTERNAL APPRAISAL

As markets are to be included in the next appraisal, this section is restricted to the general external environment and competitors. The former was adequately covered in the strategic audit. Indeed, information collected here can also be used as an input to operational planning. Consequently, the major areas of (1) economic variables, (2) technical developments and (3) political–legal influences and social developments represent the general environment within which the marketing operations must be implemented. They also represent a source of both opportunities and threats. Another previously quoted example is also applicable here, that of the US car industry in 1980. A major threat was increased competitors' market share, although the cause was from the general external environment, namely an accelerating increase in gasoline prices, itself partly caused by the revolution in Iran, which was expected to continue within the prevailing economic conditions. Small-engined, fuel-efficient cars from abroad were gaining market share, as they were obviously cheaper for customers to run, while the inefficient, large-engined American cars were losing market owing to their higher running costs.[9] Therefore the general principle is that firms need to be aware of developing trends within the areas of the general external environment for operational as well as strategic planning.

An appraisal of competitors is labelled the competitive audit by many writers, such as Cannon.[38] Although the share of a market's sales between the competing companies is important, the competitive audit is concerned with specific details of the nature and activities of competitive companies. An approach to such an appraisal has been given by Rothschild,[39] where the following areas of assessment are given:

- Nature of competitors and any potential change.
- Objectives and strategies they appear to be pursuing.
- Industrial competitor commitment to the industry, particular markets and specific segments.
- Key strengths and weaknesses of each, particularly marketing and management capability.
- The effects of competitors on own company marketing operations.

Within such a framework the aim is again to identify threats and opportunities. In a recent report a perceived opportunity over a competitor turned into a threat. In developing a particular home computer, Texas Instruments assumed that its costs were in line with its major competitor without making a proper investigation. Consequently when TI and Commodore started to compete through price reductions, Commodore had larger margins and was able to reduce prices lower than TI. Such price reductions eventually led to TI experiencing high financial losses from the home computer market.[40]

PRODUCT/MARKET APPRAISAL

Within this particular part of the examination of the marketing environment, three areas of appraisal are suggested. Again, there are links back to the strategic audit, while the appraisal also provides inputs into the strategic audit, as emphasized in Chapter 4. The three areas of appraisal are product performance, market trends and market opportunities.

Product performance

This appraisal involves analysing the previous performance of each product or product line relative to the criteria given in Fig. 6.3. In fact, this is the same set of criteria as adopted for the strategic audit and illustrated in Fig. 4.5. The outcome of such an appraisal is the establishment of trends relative to these major indicators of performance. The value is to identify the causes of these trends so that they can be incorporated into the next planning round. These trends can also be used as part of the forecasting procedures to be utilized within the marketing operational plan, which will be covered in the next chapter. Consequently, the results will give a basis for product decision-making relative to both strategy and tactics.

Market criteria
Total market size
Market share

Product criteria
Price per product
Variable cost per unit
Contribution per unit
Fixed cost per unit
Profit per unit

Financial criteria
Sales value
Variable costs
Contribution
Fixed costs
Total profit

Figure 6.3 Product performance appraisal

Market trends

Information for the appraisal of market trends should normally be available from the marketing research function. The latter represents a mammoth body of knowledge within the literature, with major texts by writers such as Tull and Hawkins.[41] Here the aim is to identify both trends in markets over previous years, plus forecasts of future market trends. This would require both monitoring and specific research surveys relative to the criteria given in Fig. 6.4.

Current market size

Trends in market size

Market shares

Market structure

Assessment of competitors

Figure 6.4 Criteria for identifying market trends

The first and second criteria are concerned with the current potential for sales volume over the next planning period and the trend of any change in that volume. The importance of identifying such trends was recently realized by Atari when the market for video games suddenly matured; this had not been forecast within the industry, and the result was unexpected losses for Atari.[40] Trends in changes in market share also need to be monitored, as even though current market share may be acceptable the trend may be indicative of a change. The previously cited example of the decline of Procter and Gamble's share of many of the markets in which they participate serves to illustrate this appraisal.[19] Market structure is concerned with an appraisal of the behavioural aspects of customers relative to the buying situation, including an understanding of market segmentation, consumer motivation and attitudes, plus buyer awareness of available products. A recent survey by German car manufacturers Porsche identified particular aspects of buyer behaviour—it is perhaps surprising that such an understanding was not already available to them. The survey revealed that Porsche owners are not the impulse buyers that their dealers had made them out to be, but that they carefully compare products and regard the purchase of a Porsche as an investment.[42]

The final criterion given in Fig. 6.4 is the assessment of competitors. As this has already been examined as part of the external appraisal, further consideration is obviously not necessary.

Market opportunities

Overall direction with regard to the level of growth that the firm strives to take has already been established in Chapter 5, being part of the organizational strategy. At the operational level an aim of marketing is to identify opportunities within various markets that will allow for the pursuit of this particular component of organizational strategy. The range of opportunities for growth that can be identified from markets has been listed by Kotler,[43] and can be classified as follows:

Intensive growth Opportunities here are to be derived from existing markets and products, covering Ansoff's matrix components of market penetration, market development and product development, examples of which were given in Chapter 4.

Integrative growth Here the total industry in which the firm participates exhibits growth potential. The opportunities could be to develop participation either backwards, forwards or horizontally within the manufacturing/distribution chain. An example here comes from Alcoa of the USA, producers of aluminium ingots: they have achieved forward integration by moving from not only producing the raw material to also manufacturing aluminium products through the processes of extruding, casting, forging and rolling.[44]

Diversification Here the opportunities lie outside the scope of current markets and products, as described in Chapter 4, where examples were also given.

An illustration of internal and external appraisals was given in Case Study 7 in Chapter 4 (page 63), which also serves as an illustration at this stage of this chapter.

EVIDENCE OF ENVIRONMENTAL APPRAISALS

Hopkins[35] observed that the marketing plans of most of his respondents start with a review of current markets and products, with the focus being on product offerings. However, he also claims that there is a tendency towards brevity, although some companies did highlight the problem of such brevity, which is that emerging trends can be easily overlooked. From here he goes on to list the items that he found to be most common in such appraisals, the major ones being:

– Product sales.
– Market situation and competitive environment.
– Problems and opportunities.
– Planning assumptions and constraints.

In the surveys by Greenley,[34] the respondents were asked to indicate the areas of information used in the planning of their marketing. The following areas were given by more than 70 per cent of the respondent firms:

– Past market trends.
– Market forecasts.
– Product performance.
– Competitive appraisal.
– Customer buying behaviour.
– Economic changes.
– Corporate requirements.

The writer also observed a tendency towards emphasis being placed upon product-market appraisals, with the external environmental appraisal receiving a lower rating of importance.

During an investigation carried out by Cossé and Swan[45] the following areas were found to have the greatest frequency of appraisal within the sample used:

– Long-term forecasts of own product sales.
– Estimates of direct product costs.
– Long-term projections of product contribution.
– Forecasts of industry sales.
– Projections of market share of own products.
– Product profitability projections.

The first three areas were declared by more than 70 per cent of the responding firms, while the other three areas were declared by more than half. Again, the emphasis is towards product appraisal, with individual product performance being the concern of the two most important areas.

A different approach to investigating the marketing environment was taken by Hooley, West and Lynch.[46] Almost all their respondent firms were able to give a prediction of the long-term future of their major market. Almost half anticipated a mature/stable market, whereas the rest were split between predicting either a general decline or growth. This result was set within the context of a declaration concerning the affects of the economic recession of the early eighties upon the companys' businesses. Indeed, only a third of the firms stated that the economic recession had caused major difficulties within their marketing operations.

SUMMARY

In this chapter we have been concerned with marketing objectives and the total environment in which marketing operational planning is set. The chapter first addressed the roles of marketing objectives and their links with organizational objectives. The next section examined the types of marketing objectives that can be established, these being within the areas of sales volume, market share, marketing costs, profit and the elements of the marketing mix.

The chapter then focused on the marketing environment. Information from the environment was seen as being important to allow for decision making in operational planning, as well as providing an input to strategic planning. However, the need to look at the environment as a source of both opportunities and threats was also highlighted. Three areas of appraisal were given as being necessary to examine the marketing environment, these being an internal appraisal, an external appraisal, and a product/market appraisal. The internal appraisal was concerned with the strategic planning framework, the marketing operations, and other areas of operational planning. The external appraisal was concerned with the general external environment as well as with competitors. Finally, the product/market appraisal was concerned with product performance, market trends and market opportunities.

CASE STUDY 9: LEVI STRAUSS AND COMPANY*

Case outline

By 1981 Levi Strauss and Company were the world's largest manufacturer of jeans. Although marketing objectives are not explicitly given, the case allows for the illustration of the applicability of objectives as described in the chapter.

Illustration

By utilizing the information given in the case study brief, marketing objectives are applicable to Levi Strauss within the major areas from Fig. 6.2.

Sales volume

The company's growth is reported to have been strong despite extreme competition and the cyclical nature of the business, indicating the pursuit of sales volume objectives. Company acquisitions by LS (as well as other large manufacturers) have led to market concentration, which will allow them to exploit market sales objectives. Growth in other segments of the apparel market in which they participate was reported, such as activewear and womenswear, allowing for the setting of further market sales objectives. However the segment of activewear was selected as requiring particular emphasis for the pursuit of sales volume development.

Relative to product sales objectives, LS USA is split into product divisions based upon jeanswear, youthwear, sports and activewear, womenswear, and accessories, allowing for a structuring of product sales objectives.

Relative to geographical sales objectives, LS International is split into geographical areas based upon Europe, Canada, Latin America and Asia/Pacific. Here the divisionalization allows for the setting of geographical sales objectives. Additionally, a major aim was given as being the expansion of international sales, exploiting the trend of expanding US apparel exports.

Market share

By 1981 LS was the world's largest manufacturer of jeans, commanding a market share of about 33 per cent. Such a situation is indicative of market share objectives having been pursued, and of a dominant position for future market share objectives. Within the general apparel industry in the USA it was reported that there were 15 000 manufacturers at the time, but with a trend of concentration towards a smaller number of companies. Given the previous strategy of LS of acquisition relative to this trend, a basis had been established for future market share objectives.

Marketing costs

Little evidence is given in the case study to illustrate the applicability of marketing cost objectives. However, intense competition was reported, putting pressure on market price levels. Therefore, a general situation is reported of there having been a need to control all cost inputs, so that objectives relative to marketing cost control would have been pertinent.

* Derived from N. H. Snyder, Levi Strauss & Co. Copyright © 1981 Neil H. Snyder.

Profit

There is little evidence in the case study to illustrate the setting of profit objectives at the operational level. However, it was reported that owing to their growth rate and marketing expertise the company was in a strong position to aim for increased profits within individual product lines.

Marketing mix

There are several indications of objectives having been established relative to product management, such as:

– Aiming for products in every product line.
– Aiming to make products import resistant.
– Developing new products with a long product life-cycle in the different market segments.
– Developing products for the 20 to 39 age-group market segment.

Similarly, there are several indications of pricing objectives, such as:

– Discouraging competition through product exclusivity to ease pressure on price caused by market saturation.
– Promoting product image through the use of reasonable prices.
– Aiming to counteract retail price discounting through product image.

Finally within this area there is evidence of the company having established advertising and promotion objectives, such as:

– Pursuing a high level of exceptance of the Levis brand name and trademark.
– Pursuing wide customer acceptance of their brand image based upon quality and style.
– Aiming to achieve effectiveness in product display at the point of sale.

REVIEW QUESTIONS

1. How do the roles of objectives differ between the operational and strategic levels of planning?
2. Discuss the necessity of including marketing objectives within a firm's operational planning.
3. 'Having multiple marketing objectives is likely to cause more confusion than a complete absence.' Discuss.
4. Highlight the many links between the strategic audit and an understanding of the marketing environment.
5. 'Perhaps only a product/market appraisal is really necessary.' Discuss.

REFERENCES

1. Cravens, D. W., *Strategic Marketing*, Irwin, Homewood, 1982.
2. Kotler, P., *Marketing Management: Analysis, Planning and Control*, 5th edn, Prentice-Hall, Englewood Cliffs, 1984.
3. 'Smith Kline's ulcer medicine holy war', *Fortune*, 19 September 1983.
4. C. H. Granger, 'The hierarchy of objectives', *Harvard Business Review* **43**, 3, 63–74, 1964.
5. Mali, P., *Managing Objectives*, Wiley, New York, 1972.
6. G. P. Latham and G. A. Yukl, 'A review of research on the application of goal setting in organizations', *Academy of Management Journal*, **18**, 4, 824–45, 1975.
7. Eilon, S., *Aspects of Management*, Pergamon, Oxford, 1979.
8. W. E. Reif, and G. Bassford, 'What MBO really is', *Business Horizons*, **16**, 23–30, 1973.
9. 'Losing a big segment of the market—forever?', *Business Week*, 24 March 1980.
10. R. H. Migliore and R. E. Stevens, 'A marketing view of management by objectives', *Managerial Planning*, **29**, 16–19, 1980.
11. Jain, S. C., *Marketing Planning and Strategy*, South-Western, Cincinnati, 1981.
12. Bluell, V. P., *Marketing Management in Action*, McGraw-Hill, New York, 1966.
13. 'How Jaguar lost its spots', *Management Today*, April 1984.
14. 'The king of tyres is discontented', *Fortune*, 28 May, 1984.
15. R. D. Buzzell, B. T. Gale and R. G. M. Sultan, 'Market share—a key to profitability', *Harvard Business Review*, **53**, 1, 97–106, 1975.
16. B. Catry and M. Chevalier, 'Market share strategy and the product life cycle', *Journal of Marketing*, **38**, 29–34, 1974.
17. B. James, 'Market share strategy and corporate profitability', *Management Decision*, **10**, 243–52, 1972.
18. C. Y. Y., Woo, and A. C. Cooper, 'Strategies of effective low share businesses', *Strategic Management Journal*, **2**, 3, 301–18, 1981.
19. 'Trouble at Procter and Gamble', *Fortune*, 5 March, 1984.
20. W. F. Christopher, 'Marketing achievement reporting: a profitability approach', *Industrial Marketing Management*, **6**, 149–62, 1977.
21. N. Piercy, 'Cost and profit myopia in marketing', *Quarterly Review of Marketing*, **7**, 4, 1–12, 1982.
22. Bell, M. L., *Marketing Concepts and Strategy*, Houghton Mifflin, Boston, 1979.
23. Pessemier, E. A., *New Product Decisions: An Analytical Approach*, McGraw-Hill, New York, 1966.
24. 'Eight big masters of innovation', *Fortune*, 15 October, 1984.
25. 'How Wadkin worked clear', *Management Today*, May 1984.
26. 'IBM's move into communications', *Fortune*, 15 October 1984.
27. Hisrich, R. D., and M. P. Peters, *Marketing Decisions for New and Mature Products*, Merrill, Columbus, 1984.
28. A. R. Oxenfeldt, 'A decision-making structure for price decisions', *Journal of Marketing*, **37**, 1, 1973.
29. D. W. Jackson and R. J. Aldag, 'Managing the sales force by objectives', *MSU Business Topics*, **22**, 2, 53–9, 1974.
30. Guirdham, M., *Marketing: the Management of Distribution Channels*, Pergamon, Oxford, 1972.
31. Aaker, D. A., and J. G. Myers, *Advertising Management*, Prentice-Hall, Englewood-Cliffs, 1975.
32. Colley, R. H., *Defining Advertising Goals for Measured Advertising Results*, Association of National Advertisers, New York, 1961.
33. 'Searle's big pitch for a tiny ingredient', *Fortune*, 3 September 1984.
34. G. E. Greenley, 'An overview of marketing planning in UK manufacturing companies', *European Journal of Marketing*, **16**, 7, 3–15, 1982.
   'Where Marketing Planning Fails', *Long Range Planning*, **16**, 1, 106–16, 1983.
   'An overview of marketing planning in UK service companies', *Journal of Marketing Intelligence and Planning*, **1**, 3, 55–68, 1983.

35. Hopkins, D. S., *The Marketing Plan*, The Conference Board, Research Report Number 801, 1981.
36. D. D. Shipley, 'Marketing objectives in UK and US manufacturing companies', *European Journal of Marketing*, **19**, 3, 48–56, 1985.
37. 'Motorola's leading edge', *Management Today*, November 1983.
38. Cannon, J. T., 'Auditing the competitive environment', in Bonge, J. W., and B. P. Coleman, *Concepts of Corporate Strategy*, Macmillan, New York, 1972.
39. W. E. Rothschild, 'Competition analysis: the missing link in strategy', *McKinsey Quarterly*, 42–53, Autumn 1979.
40. 'High-speed management for the high-tech age', *Fortune*, 5 March 1984.
41. Tull, D. S., and D. I. Hawkins, *Marketing Research: Measurement and Method*, Macmillan, New York, 1984.
42. 'Porsche's civil war with its dealers', *Fortune*, 16 April, 1984.
43. Kotler, P., *Marketing Management: Analysis, Planning and Control*, 3rd edn, Prentice-Hall, Englewood Cliffs, 1976.
44. 'Alcoa rolls the dice once more', *Fortune*, 6 August 1984.
45. T. J. Cossé, and J. E. Swan, 'Strategic marketing planning by product managers', *Journal of Marketing*, **47**, 92–102, 1983.
46. Hooley, G. J., C. J. West and J. E. Lynch, *Marketing in the UK*, the Institute of Marketing, Maidenhead, 1984.

SEVEN

MARKETING STRATEGY

Learning objectives are to:

1. Appreciate the overall meaning of marketing strategy.
2. Understand the various approaches taken in explaining the nature of marketing strategy issues.
3. Gain an understanding of the adopted component parts of marketing strategy and the reasons for their inclusion.
4. Realize the position of marketing strategy within the planning framework.
5. Recognize major concepts that have been introduced.

The aim of this chapter is to examine the nature of marketing strategy relative to its role within the planning framework as developed in Chapter 2. It is also intended that the outcome of the preliminary discussions should provide a logical progression to, and justification of, the guidance given towards the end of the chapter for the preparation of marketing strategy.

The variation in the usage of planning terminology both within the literature and in organizations has already been noted. However, this variation is perhaps more apparent relative to the treatment of strategy developed for marketing than to other areas of the planning of marketing. In addition, the word strategy tends to have been used widely, as well as being used within a context to which it is not applicable, as observed by writers such as Wind and Robertson[1] and Carroll.[2] The latter writer also notes the abuse of the word strategic in that it is often used as a synonym for the word important. Many examples are apparent where books and journal articles include strategic or strategy in their titles only to impart a degree of importance. A similar situation can also be observed in organizations, where the word strategy is used when the importance of a particular issue is to be emphasized, despite the inappropriateness of the context.

In explaining marketing strategy reference needs to be made to organizational strategy, examined in Chapter 5, as organizational strategy provides a framework for the preparation of marketing strategy. In addition, reference also needs to be made to other areas of the operational planning of marketing, as marketing strategy provides a framework for these areas.

MARKETING STRATEGY IN THE PLANNING FRAMEWORK

The first consideration is the location of marketing strategy within the planning framework as developed in Chapter 2. Although this particular aspect will be considered again later in the chapter, a clarification is necessary before we examine the nature of marketing strategy.

The logic of the planning framework indicates that strategic planning should take place before operational planning. The former provides the long-term continuity of the organization into which the shorter-term periods of operational planning must fit. In addition, strategic planning establishes the overall direction to which the individual operations must contribute. Also, the strategic planning consolidates the overall organization and dictates the role required by each of the operations. In the case of marketing strategy, this role is specifically dictated to by the established organizational mission and organizational strategy, as previously examined in Chapters 3 and 5 respectively. Within the planning framework, as developed in Chapter 2, the difference between long-run and short-run operational planning was identified. Marketing strategy is classified as being the marketing component of long-run operational planning in that it is normally established for a period of time in excess of the annual marketing plan, being enduring in nature. Although individual components of marketing strategy are obviously changed after periods of time, the point is that this is done within an overall framework of consistency. For example, German sports car manufacturers Porsche recently planned a major change to their marketing strategy in the USA, although the plan resulted in considerable opposition to the point of abandonment. They planned to change, from supplying their products to the markets through distributors, to using agents, who would sell cars but not buy them first for resale, as well as to opening their own retail outlets in competition with the agents.[3] However, such decisions are obviously enduring in nature, far exceeding the period of the annual marketing plan. This principle will again be pursued later in this chapter.

Despite this logic within the planning framework of the sequence of plan preparation, the results of recent research by Greenley[4-6] indicate that many organizations do not follow such an approach. An outcome of this research is that less than 45 per cent of organizations prepare their strategic plan before their marketing planning. Therefore in such a situation the strategic framework is not available for the development of a marketing strategy. Indeed, in many organizations the strategic plan is merely a compilation of the annual marketing plan and other operational plans. The consequences of such a situation are twofold. First, it means that there is no overall integrating framework for relating the marketing strategy to the overall thrust of the organization's efforts. Second, it means that greater reliance is placed upon the marketing strategy giving the company direction, and often the role and functions of strategic planning in general and organizational strategy in particular are subsumed within the role of marketing strategy.

Another approach is that marketing and organizational strategies are prepared as a cyclical process, as, for example, suggested in a proposal by Greenley.[7] Here both strategies are formed in conjunction with each other and each provides an input to the other. For example, the potentials to be developed from marketing strategy give an indication of the product-market scope to be defined in the organizational strategy. Similarly, the establishment of the product-market scope will affect the finalization of the detail of the marketing strategy.

Having considered the location of marketing strategy within the planning framework plus application problems, we now direct our attention to the nature of marketing strategy. However, further consideration will be given to these aspects later in the chapter.

APPROACHES TO MARKETING STRATEGY

The aim of this section is to examine approaches taken within the literature to explain the nature of marketing strategy, as well as to outline approaches taken by companies.

Most writers on the subject of marketing strategy start with a broad encompassing statement of what they consider it to be. For example, Chang and Campo-Flores[8] refer to marketing strategy as being a crucial and central issue to the use of the marketing function. Similarly, Baker[9] sees it as being a broad means of achieving given aims, Luck and Ferrell[10] as being fundamental means or schemes and Kotler[11] as being the grand design to achieve objectives. Several writers also draw parallels between strategy in business and strategy in military practice, for example Kotler and Singh[12] and Evered,[13] as mentioned in Chapter 5. Evered also notes that military strategy has become to mean the deployment of forces over wide spaces and long times, with large movements of forces, all at a time before contact with the enemy, while tactics deal with the actual action on the battle field. Similarly, marketing strategy is concerned with the deployment of marketing forces at a time before the commencement of the operational plan, whereas marketing tactics are the actions to be implemented during the period of this plan.

Similar broad statements were also given by the companies participating in the research reported by Greenley.[4-6] Several companies claimed that their marketing strategy was long-term activity, others that it provided for the overall achievement of objectives and others still that it provided a broad plan of action. A summary of encompassing statements is given in Fig. 7.1.

1. Crucial and central issues to the use of marketing

2. The broad means of achieving given aims

3. Fundamental means or schemes within marketing

4. The grand design to achieve objectives

5. Deployment of marketing forces before the commencement of plans

6. Long-term marketing activity

7. A broad plan of action

Figure 7.1   Broad explanations of marketing strategy

Having made such a statement, most writers then move on to explain the detailed issues, means or schemes which they prescribe as constituting a marketing strategy. Here there are four major bases used in the literature to explain the detail of marketing strategy. These are the marketing mix, the product life-cycle, market share and competition, and positoning. In addition, some writers also advocate special marketing strategies for both international and industrial markets. Each of these bases will be examined in turn.

The marketing mix base

A common approach in the literature is to simply link these issues to the elements of the marketing mix. For example, Foxall[14] defines marketing strategy as being an indication of how each element of the marketing mix will be used to achieve the marketing objectives. This definition gives a complete reliance on the mix and therefore the utilization of the elements is the strategy. This is, however, a very restricted approach to marketing strategy, as will be illustrated later in the chapter. Chang and Campo-Flores[8] also develop this theme, suggesting a range of marketing component strategies which constitute the total marketing strategy. These they give as strategies relating to products, distribution, sales promotion and pricing. This approach is also followed by Jain,[15] who gives the same breakdown, again following a simple approach of relating marketing strategy merely to the mix elements. Modifications to this approach are also evident. For example, Udell[16] splits the issues into price and non-price strategies.

Several examples of a marketing mix strategy can be found. Amstrad, manufacturers of electrical home entertainment products, have a reported marketing strategy for audio equipment and TVs of attractive products at a relatively low price.[17]

The PLC base

Other writers extend this theme of the marketing mix to the concept of the product life-cycle (PLC). For example Kotler,[18] Baker[9] and Doyle[19] state that the marketing strategy for a particular product needs to be modified as the product moves through the various stages of its PLC. This is based upon a change of the mix at different stages, so that a change is made in the relative degree of reliance of each element, giving a different mix, and hence a different marketing strategy, at each stage. This treatment is extended by other writers, such as Scheuing,[20] who defines a specific strategy for each stage of the PLC, labelling them life-cycle marketing strategies. However, there are two major and well-documented problems associated with this approach. The first is that it is difficult for the company to be able, at a particular point in time, to identify the stage at which a product is within its life-cycle. The other problem is that the specific strategies for each stage do not always allow for application to all products, given the wide variation experienced by companies in market and product conditions.

The market share base

Another approach used in the literature to explain the issues involved in marketing strategy is to link the latter to market share and competition. A major example here comes from the work of Bloom and Kotler.[21] Their approach is first to explain how a company can identify its optimal market share, given a particular set of conditions. Having identified this level the company needs a marketing strategy to achieve the optimum. The second stage is to select a strategy from a range of strategies that are designed to build, maintain or even reduce market share. However, within each of these share-linked marketing strategies they also advocate a range of further strategies, again based upon the elements of the marketing mix. A similar approach is also advocated by Buzzell, Gale and Sultan,[22] although they label the alternatives as being building, holding and harvesting strategies. The approach taken by Doyle[23] is to simply equate one strategy as the pursual of market share and another as its non-pursual. The Ball Corporation of the USA, producers of containers, have recently claimed that their marketing strategy is the pursual of market share growth.[24] However, overall this approach of linking marketing strategy to market share appears to be merely the utilization of the elements of the marketing mix, linked with an objective or aim (and therefore not a strategy), as discussed in Chapter 6, which is concerned with a predetermined level of achievement (being market share).

In addition to the market share link, competitive marketing strategies have also been described by Kotler,[18] with a revision in a later publication.[25] In the earlier work he prescribed a range of nine competitive marketing strategies, from which the company should choose, at a particular point in time, that which relates directly to the activities of its competitors. In the latter work he advocates an approach in which the company has a range of competitive marketing strategies from which to choose, depending upon which of the four strategy ranges its market share places it in. Here there is a liberal use of the word strategy; there are strategies within strategies and the application of the approach into specific company situations is perhaps not likely to be immediately apparent to managers.

The positioning base

Another approach in the explanation of marketing strategy is to utilize the concept of positioning. The major overall problem here is the variation given in the literature as to the meaning of positioning. For example, Wind and Claycamp[26] explain a product's position as its overall situation in the market relative to its sales, market share and profitability. Cravens,[27] however, sees positioning as being the selection of a marketing strategy from a range of alternatives, although the latter can be considered to be component parts of organizational strategy, as discussed in Chapter 5. Yet another variation of the interpretation of product positioning is reflected in the articles of Alpert and Gatty[28] and Holmes.[29] Here a product's position is related to its customers, in that it explains the user profile and how they perceive the image of the product.

The concept of positioning can also be explained in terms of both market and product positions, as illustrated, for example, by Kotler.[11] Here the company investigates the segmentation of a particular market and then decides which segment or segments to participate in. This selection is referred to as market positioning. For each segment the company requires a product, or products, and the number of products developed, plus their overall nature, is referred to as product positioning. Again the example of the Ball Corporation is applicable. Their broad approach to marketing has been to select particular 'niches' of container markets in which to participate, and, unlike competitors, supply low-priced containers, such as two-piece beverage cans in only two standard sizes.[24] Similarly, product positioning for a range of products is given in an article by Warwick and Sands,[30] while the application of market segmentation in the marketing strategy of UK building societies is illustrated by Doyle and Newbould.[31]

International markets

Although several references are made in the literature to international marketing strategies, these tend to relate to the elements of the marketing mix. The fundamental tenet here is that these need to be varied for different countries, on the basis of variations in market conditions in these countries. For example, for a particular overseas market Keegan[32] gives a range of five alternative marketing strategies, based upon the elements of the product and communications. This range allows for variation in the product and the communications mix, but is nevertheless based on the marketing mix. Similarly, Halfill,[33] in reporting the results of a survey, uses the phrase multinational marketing strategy, but again bases this on the marketing mix, with the emphasis on advertising. In a survey to investigate the nature of international marketing strategies in American companies, Samli[34] also illustrates this emphasis on the marketing mix, but identifies an orientation of the mix towards competitors within each market.

In contrast, the international advertising agency Saatchi and Saatchi advocate a common global marketing strategy for many of their client companies. This they claim is due to the 'homogenization' of world-wide customer requirements in many markets.[35]

Industrial markets

In the case of industrial marketing strategies described in the literature, a similar situation exists. Copulsky[36] describes industrial marketing strategies as also being based upon the marketing mix, but with an emphasis on the product and price. ICI has developed a clear plastic for drinks bottles, such as Coca-Cola, to replace glass. ICI's marketing strategy has been based upon specific product development for individual drink manufacturers, to produce bottles for their specific requirements.[37] A similar emphasis on products was also reported from the investigations of Cunningham and Hammouda.[38] Two other articles on industrial marketing strategy also emphasize the orientation to the marketing mix, but broaden their base to utilize the concept of positioning. In the article by Forbis and Mehta[39] the use of market segmentation is advocated and hence market positioning is included in their industrial marketing strategy. Similarly, Corey[40] utilizes market segmentation, but advocates both market and product positioning within industrial marketing strategies.

Evidence of company marketing strategies

The major feature of the marketing strategies adopted by many companies is that of a wide variation in nature, plus confusion on the part of personnel. Such a situation is reported in the results of research by Greenley,[4–6] Hopkins[41] and McDonald.[42] In the case of the last it was reported that the lack of ability to be able to determine strategies was a major weakness of the sample.

The term strategy, relative to marketing, was identified by Hopkins as having two different meanings, being a grand strategy for a product, or group of products, plus a range of strategies that are necessary within the marketing operation. In the former Hopkins identifies certain key issues that constitute the grand strategy, with 80 per cent of companies relating to market share and just over half relating to market segmentation. However, in the case of the former, confusion is apparent as to whether this is indeed part of the strategy or whether it is included within organizational objectives as a major aim, as opposed to a means to an end. The usage of market segmentation was more apparent, as the majority considered the selection of and participation in market segments as being a major part of marketing strategy. The range of strategies was reported to be directly related to the marketing objectives and developed as the approach to the individual elements of the marketing mix.

In the surveys by Greenley[4–6] nearly 90 per cent of firms claimed to have a marketing strategy although almost all respondents exhibited great difficulty in explaining its nature. In relation to components of strategy, a similar response to that of Hopkins was obtained relative to market segmentation, with most firms choosing a strategy of concentrating on a range of market segments. An excess of 70 per cent also gave consideration to marketing mix elements and their range and number of products. However, common to all these responses was a lack of clarity as to whether or not these components are perceived as being integral components of marketing strategy, or merely aspects of the marketing function that are utilized. The result that there are wide variations in open-ended definitions is suggestive that they are not perceived as being integral parts, although this is far from being conclusive.

In differentiating between marketing strategy and tactics, the results of Hopkins show further confusion on the part of respondent firms. In the Greenley surveys almost 70 per cent claimed that they are able to make such a differentiation. Indeed, the author concludes that they were adequately able to explain marketing tactics, relative to definitions given in the literature, even though confusion is apparent as regards marketing strategy.

THE COMPONENTS OF MARKETING STRATEGY

This section is concerned with defining the components of marketing strategy to be adopted within the book. This approach develops logically from the discussions presented in the last section. In defining these components there are two major aims. The first is that the resultant marketing strategy should be consistent with the logic of the planning framework, despite the apparent confusion both within the literature and in practice. The second is that the nature of the components should be such that they can be readily applied directly into company situations. This means that they need to be comprehensive in covering major issues central to the marketing function, that they should be applicable to all company situations, and that they should provide a practical framework for the development of the specific action of the marketing tactics.

The approach adopted in the book is to define marketing strategy as being composed of five major components, which is similar to the approach taken by Greenley the author elsewhere.[43] The first three components are extracted from the previous discussion, being market positioning, product positioning and the marketing mix. The other two components are taken to be market entry and timing.

Market positioning

This part of the strategy is concerned with deciding which approach to adopt relative to segmentation of the market and the selection of the segments in which the company is to participate. Depending upon the range of product-market scopes, or strategic business units (SBUs) adopted, each scope may require a different approach to segmentation within the market. In selecting the segments for participation the company has the alternatives of pursuing all segments, only one segment, or several. For example, Patek Phillippe, Swiss manufacturers of expensive and exclusive watches, participate only in the segment featuring such product requirements.[44] However, tyre manufacturers Goodyear position in many segments, such as new cars, replacement tyres, high-performance tyres, light-truck tyres, and 'all-season' tyres.[45] The choice here could well be affected by the rate of growth required, the nature of competitors within the segments and the corporate approach to them, plus the synergy developed by the relative strengths and weaknesses. This component is seen as being, logically, the first decision to be made in establishing a marketing strategy, in that all consequential marketing activity is based upon the nature of the segments and the requirements of their customers. In other words, the logic relates directly to marketing orientation, as discussed in Chapter 1.

Product positioning

Having selected the market segments for each product-market scope, the number of products the firm is to offer to each segment must be determined and their overall nature must be specified. Jaguar cars had been previously positioned in the executive car market segment. However Jaguar have recently modified its product positioning strategy by increasing the number of products to two basic saloons, two higher specification Sovereigns, and two ultra-expensive, luxury Daimlers.[46] Again, this decision area can be affected by the organizational strategy components of growth, competition and synergy. However, the major consideration is obviously the market requirements within each segment. The understanding of these requirements obviously provides a basis for deciding whether each segment of participation requires one or several products, as well as determining the overall nature of each product. However, exact details of product specifications are not considered to be part of the marketing strategy, but are considered to be decisions relative to the tactical planning of marketing. Rather, the product positioning contribution to the overall nature of the product stems from the overall market need of the segment, epitomizing the major product USP. Further clarification of the difference between product positioning and the product specification of tactical planning is given in the next chapter, although further reference can be made to an article by Greenley.[47]

Marketing mix

Having determined the range of segments in which the company will participate, plus the nature and number of products to be offered, the next decision in formulating the marketing strategy is to determine the utilization of the individual elements of the mix, plus the relative degree of reliance to be placed upon each. For Goodyear, an unglamorous product like tyres requires a mix based on low price.[45] For electronic equipment manufacturers Motorola, a special marketing mix strategy is needed for police communications equipment in the USA. This is based on product quality, quality image and a large sales-and-service team.[48]

Again, the distinction needs to be made between the role of the marketing mix within marketing strategy and its role within marketing tactics. In the former, decisions are required to determine which of the elements are to be used in order to market the selected products, as well as deciding the relative degree of importance or reliance to be placed on each in order to satisfy the market requirements. Here there are numerous alternatives in developing this component of marketing strategy. One alternative is considerable reliance on the sales force, with perhaps little or no reliance on advertising and promotional activities. Complex engineering products may require a strategy based upon the technical excellence of the product, presented through representative negotiations and not requiring any advertising. Alternatively, mass-produced consumer food products are likely to be based upon a strategy of heavy reliance on advertising, sales promotion and efficient distribution, with telephone order-taking within the trade. One extreme within this component would be a production-orientated company using only the selling element, the other an organization using all the elements based upon the roles for which they are intended. Further examples of the utilization of the marketing mix can be found in the text by McCarthy.[49]

However, the role of the marketing mix within marketing tactics is in the specification of details, such as product features, brand name and image, price structure, copy platform and selling techniques. Again, consideration of such detail will be taken further in the next chapter.

Once more, the finalization of this component is affected by market requirements, so that the marketing strategy may need to vary with product-market scope. In addition, the corporate approach to competitors may also affect decisions, in that the mix may need to be varied on the basis of the effects of competitors' mixes. Similarly, the corporate approach to growth may dictate a greater reliance on certain mix elements, although this is likely to vary with product-market scope, as may the effective synergy developed within the organization.

Market entry

This component is concerned with how the company intends to enter, re-enter, position itself, or reposition itself within each of the selected market segments. Here Kotler[11] gives the alternatives of acquisition, collaboration and internal development, although similar presentations are well documented in the literature. In the former the approach of acquiring an existing product(s) or company is well documented, as, for example, given by Fogg.[50] Several examples of collaboration and acquisition are evident. In order to launch its new product into the USA, Glaxo required a large sales force in order to sell and promote directly to the tens of thousands of doctors, this being a requirement of the market. Their strategy of market entry was to collaborate with Hoffman-La Roche in a joint venture, utilizing their sales force to augment Glaxo's and so give the required coverage.[51] The US corporation Exxon entered the high-tech industry by firstly establishing a division, Exxon Enterprises. This firm then acquired a number of small firms to achieve entry, such as Zilog (microprocessors), Vydec (graphic terminals), and Qyx (electronic typewriters).[52]

The selection of this strategy component would be affected by the overall direction of the company as specified within the organizational mission. Further, the organizational strategy components of growth, competitive advantage and synergy would also relate to such a decision.

Collaboration with another company that can provide expertise in marketing, or indeed any other business area, can be similarly affected by organizational strategy. The purpose element of the organizational mission would provide the guideline for such a strategy, but the overall level of synergy within the company would give a major indication of the need to adopt a collaborative strategy. Finally, internal development means that the company does not need to involve other companies, so that the marketing operations are developed by the company through its own resources. Adoption of such a strategy would again be affected by the purpose elements of the organizational mission, the level of synergy and also the stipulated rates of growth.

The inclusion of such a component is based upon its being a broad issue appertaining to the marketing function. As a component it is obviously secondary to the component of market positioning, in that the nature of such selected segments, relative to the company's resources, will dictate how the company is able to enter the market. However, this component can also affect decisions on the previous three components. If entry means an internal development for which resources are not available then an extension of market positioning may not be possible. Similarly, collaboration with another company may allow for an extension of product positioning, but may place additional reliance on certain elements of the marketing mix. This illustrates the cyclical relationship of the components of marketing strategy, this being of a type similar to the relationship between marketing strategy and organizational strategy.

Timing

Here the component relates to the point in time at which the other components of the marketing strategy are to be implemented, plus the points in time when particular tactics within the marketing mix are to be implemented. One approach here is to link the strategy to competitors' activity, as, for example, outlined by Jain.[15] Here the strategy can be to be first to implement, or to be early but following the first company, or to take a laggard position and be one of the last companies to implement. Again the example of Amstrad is applicable here. It is reported that they were the first company to offer a stacking stereo system into the lower-priced market segment, establishing a competitive lead that they have maintained.[17] Here the competitive advantage component of organizational strategy is likely to have a bearing, as is the purpose element of the organizational mission. Another approach of selecting times is to follow relevant indicators from the external environment. These can range from economic indicators, through industry trends and seasonal trends, to trade exhibitions. Timing has been important to the US company Intel, manufacturers of microprocessors. Intensive international competition and continuous and fast changes in technology have been reported as having the potential of rendering Intel's product 'obsolete overnight'.[53] Here there is probably less effect from the organizational mission and strategy, although the immediacy of required growth would need to be considered.

The timing component of marketing strategy also relates to selecting the optimum time to exploit a particular market or market segment. Abell[54] has identified the importance of recognizing the time period associated with a particular opportunity within a market, which he labels the 'strategic window'; he offers an approach in the decision-making process to determine when the particular implementation of strategy or tactics should take place. Here there can be consideration of the organizational strategy (in relation to the immediacy of required growth) and of the impact on such a strategic window of the corporate approach to competitors, and of the level of synergy within the company.

The component of timing is, perhaps, different in nature from the other four components. Although it is classified as being a component in that it is an issue relative to how the marketing effort is to be utilized, the decision making is concerned with when it is to be utilized. Therefore the role of the component within marketing strategy differs, as the other components are concerned with decision making that relates directly to the development of action itself. The five components of marketing strategy are summarized in Fig. 7.2, while their application to a specific company situation is illustrated in Case Study 10 (page 120).

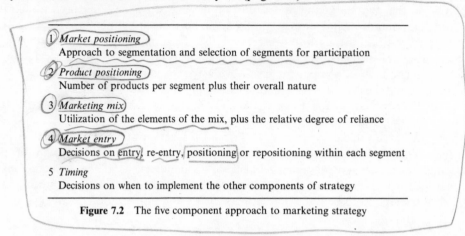

1 *Market positioning*
Approach to segmentation and selection of segments for participation

2 *Product positioning*
Number of products per segment plus their overall nature

3 *Marketing mix*
Utilization of the elements of the mix, plus the relative degree of reliance

4 *Market entry*
Decisions on entry, re-entry, positioning or repositioning within each segment

5 *Timing*
Decisions on when to implement the other components of strategy

Figure 7.2 The five component approach to marketing strategy

The result of the consideration of these five component parts is indicative of a large number of potential alternatives. While this is theoretically possible, in practice it is likely that the individual company situation will in fact shape the resultant strategy. First, the effects of the strategic planning, as already discussed, are likely to dictate the market segments, reduce the number of products, outline the role of the marketing mix, and give guidance to both market entry and timing. In particular, company resources are likely to place restrictions on positioning, unless the company is aiming for increased growth. Alternatives within the mix elements are likely to be affected by the traditional approaches expected within the markets, as well as the nature of the products, such as consumer products *per se* being dependent upon advertising, and industrial products *per se* being based upon their technical excellence and technical negotiations in their selling.

However, the range of alternatives increases where a number of SBUs or product-market scopes are to be perused. In effect, it is likely that a different marketing strategy will be required for each SBU and product-market scope. Each will exhibit its own market segmentation, requiring decision making relative to participation. In addition, each will require a decision on product positioning, while the nature of market requirements will affect the marketing mix, so that a range of marketing mixes is likely to result. Similarly, the timing of the implementation of the components will be a result of the nature of market requirements.

The final consideration in this section is the justification of the composition of marketing strategy relative to the five components. The rationale for finalizing marketing strategy as being composed of these five components is that they represent the central issues of the marketing operation. These vary from the framework for activities to be carried out within each of the elements of the marketing mix to marketing strategies concerned with positioning, plus the issues of market entry and timing. The PLC base is rejected due to its inherent weaknesses, which make it unsuitable as a basis for strategy, although it is recognized that at the tactical level adjustments to the mix are valid relative to the PLC. The market share base is rejected, as it is considered to be an objective at which to aim strategy performance, as opposed to being a marketing strategy basis itself. Also, particular attention to competitors as a marketing strategy base is rejected. This is because full consideration of competitors is, by necessity, given in the formulation of the five selected component parts. In addition, more direct consideration is given to competitors in both the planning and implementation of marketing tactics. Consequently it is seen to affect strategy rather than being part of it. Finally, the international and industrial market bases are also rejected, as the principle established is that the five components of marketing strategy can be applied as a general rule. Therefore all can be applied in any market situation, regardless of the nature of the market profile and regardless of the particular market requirements. However, what is obviously important in formalizing the five components for any market situation is a full understanding of the total environment in which the company operates, which gives variation in the application of the five components within any specific market, as opposed to a stereotyped market *per se*.

RECAPITULATION OF PLANNING FRAMEWORK

Having established the components of marketing strategy, this section is concerned with a further examination of the position and role of marketing strategy within the planning framework, as an extension of the treatment given earlier in the chapter.

The model for the development of marketing strategy proposed by Greenley[43] is based upon three levels of consideration, as follows:

Level 1—organizational mission
Level 2—organizational strategy
Level 3—the five marketing strategy components

This locates marketing strategy in a position relative to strategic planning, following the planning framework as developed in Chapter 2.

As the organizational mission provides an encompassing understanding of the company's purpose and overall direction, as discussed in Chapter 3, it is considered as being level one of the process in developing marketing strategy. By providing the broad scope of the business in terms of customers, products and markets, it is the starting point for making decisions on marketing strategy, in that the central issues of the total marketing operation must follow the company's central theme. Within this scope the framework is prescribed in the form of the classes of customers the firm wishes to serve, giving the scope for market positioning and examining suitability of variations in the marketing mix. Similarly, the scope of products provides a framework for product positioning as well as giving ramifications within the marketing mix. The scope of business domains also gives a framework to market positioning, in that the supply of products to different areas (such as industrial, consumer, or international business areas) will each have different ramifications on the decisions to be made on marketing strategy. The theme of purpose also needs to be reflected in the marketing strategy. This may vary from company to company as it could be based upon the development of a particular technology, a particular raw material, a particular section of society, or indeed on any other similar theme. However, whatever the specification of the purpose, the components of the marketing strategy must support it.

Level two in the development of marketing strategy is the established organizational strategy. The product-market scope component is itself an extension of the mission, as it gives more detail in specifying the scope of the business. Although this component is narrower in its definition of scope than the mission, it still allows for decision making within marketing strategy, in the selection of markets, market segments, product lines and individual products. However, the point is that the product-market scope component defines the framework for these decisions, giving the range to be pursued. The choice of a growth, stability or defence strategy will also affect marketing strategy. Stability and defence will each dictate different resultant marketing strategies, depending upon the alternatives chosen. Each growth alternative will affect decisions on product positioning, while the very nature of the market within each growth alternative will require a different approach to market positioning and the marketing mix. The component of competitive advantage will dictate the approach to be taken in each element of the marketing mix and indeed will affect their inter-relationship. Overall approaches to competitors may also necessitate making decisions on both market and product positioning. Finally, the organizational strategy component of synergy will affect marketing strategy in that identified company strengths and weaknesses, in relation to the approaches the company is to take towards these, may provide either restrictions to the development of marketing strategy, or indeed may provide an improvement to its effectiveness. The position of marketing within the planning framework is illustrated in Fig. 7.3.

The role of marketing strategy within the planning framework can be considered to be due to its enduring nature. Each of the five component parts is enduring in nature, with the result that marketing strategy is classified as being an integral part of long-range operational planning. Alternatively, marketing tactics are considered to be transient in nature and are therefore considered to be the marketing element of short-range operational planning. Hence the tactics relate to the annual marketing plan, within the framework of marketing strategy, and can be adjusted throughout the annual plan relative to market conditions. The outcome of such a classification is that the marketing tactics are the prime means of achieving the annual marketing objectives, even though they are developed within the framework of marketing strategy. However, the marketing strategy is seen as being a means of achieving the organizational objectives, but with a contribution to the marketing objectives by providing the framework for the marketing tactics. However, this does not mean to say that marketing strategy should be subsumed within strategic planning, as tends to be suggested by writers such as Abel and Hammond.[55] Indeed, its nature as described above locates its role within long-range operational planning, which is summarized in Fig. 7.4.

SUMMARY

The chapter examined the nature of marketing strategy relative to its role in the planning framework. The first consideration was a brief examination of the logic of completing strategic planning before the development of marketing strategy, as a prelude to the rest of the chapter.

The overall understanding of marketing strategy was given as being broad issues that are central to the utilization of marketing. The nature of these issues as presented in the literature was examined, and they were found to be derived from six different bases, namely marketing mix, product life-cycle, market share, positioning, international markets and industrial markets. Research into adopted company marketing strategies showed a wide variation and confusion on the part of managers in being able to adequately explain it.

The approach taken in the chapter was to adopt five component parts as constituting the nature of marketing strategy, these being market positioning, product positioning, marketing mix, market entry and timing. However, the bases of market share, product life-cycle, international markets and industrial markets were rejected. The overall justification for this adoption is that they represent central issues, while being consistent with the planning framework and capable of being applied directly into company situations.

The position of marketing strategy within the planning framework was then re-examined,

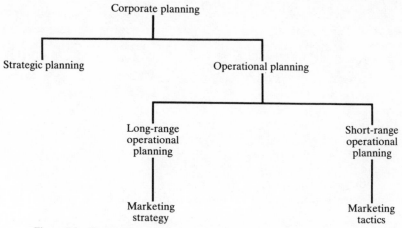

Figure 7.3 The position of marketing strategy in the planning framework

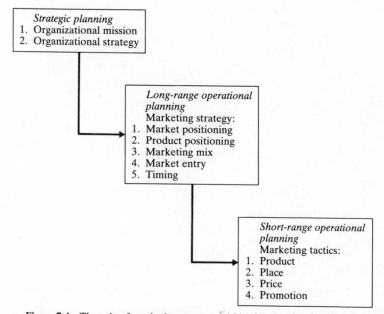

Figure 7.4 The role of marketing strategy within the planning framework

relative to strategic planning, with its development being concerned with three levels of treatment.

Finally, the role of marketing strategy was identified as being part of long-range operational planning, arising from its enduring nature and the commitment required to decisions that are made. In contrast, marketing tactics were given as being transient in nature, being part of short-range operational planning.

CASE STUDY 10: FISHER PRICE CO. LTD (B)*

Case outline

This case is based upon the formation of the Fisher Price Toy Co. Ltd, to provide a European business base for Fisher Price Inc. of the United States.

Illustration

Information is given within the case study which can be used to apply the components of marketing strategy developed in Chapter 7. However, although the case is orientated to the problems facing the new managing director in formulating a marketing strategy, that adopted by the company is not specifically given in the case.

The five components of marketing strategy can be applied to the company as follows:

Market positioning

A major feature of this component is that Fisher Price perceive the toy market to be segmented upon age, and at the time their positioning strategy was within the preschool market segment. However, they had also investigated segmentation based upon the requirements of parents within the different socio-economic groups. Although the implication is that previously they had aimed to be positioned in the higher groups, they had some information (although limited) that they could be positioned within most of the segments based on socio-economic groups. A particular market need identified was that of the educational value of the toys, although this was linked to socio-economic groups in that it appeared to be more applicable to the A, B and C groups. The company had also utilized geographical segmentation of the world toy market, having already positioned in several European countries. However, they aimed to consolidate this positioning, and indeed to expand by positioning in additional country segments.

A major restriction on Fisher Price's UK marketing strategy at the time was that they were limited to the product range of Fisher Price Inc., developed for the United States. Consequently, the approach to the marketing strategy was to find markets to fit the products, as opposed to identifying market segments and matching products to the requirements of these segments.

Product positioning

Preschool children feature rapid development in their early years with rapidly changing playing patterns, so that a wide range of products is required in this segment. Additionally, they spend long periods of time at play which requires product variety, again indicative of the need for a wide product range. Retailers reported that parents, as customers, tend to specify product type and not brand name in their buying behaviour. Therefore both situations are indicative of a product positioning strategy of many products, particularly as none of the competitors featured such a strategy.

However, other factors also needed to be considered. The willingness of retailers to promote a wide range at the point of sale would affect product positioning, while in opposition a policy of Fisher Price Inc. appeared to be to offer an extensive product range. Finally, the product positioning strategy was restricted in that the available products had been designed for market needs in the USA, while there were also production capacity limitations.

* Derived from T. E. Milne, Fisher Price Co. Ltd (B), Copyright © 1973 The Scottish Business School.

Marketing mix

The previous UK marketing mix strategy, before the formation of Fisher Price Ltd, had been based upon selective distribution and high prices. However, the case study emphasizes that such decisions were being seen as major problems by the new managing director. With respect to distribution, the main retail outlets were known, but they were having difficulty in defining an appropriate distribution spread. Similarly, they had the opportunity of utilizing the sales force and distribution channels of a major UK toy company, although the MD was uncertain as to its appropriateness for their new mix.

The role of price in the mix was also a problem. In the United States success had been achieved with prices relatively lower than currently in the United Kingdom, although it appears that price sensitivity in the United Kingdom had not been researched. Similarly, they were also uncertain about the role of discounts to the trade within their future mix, although there was little retail price cutting at the time.

The MD was also uncertain of the role to be played in their mix by advertising and had received conflicting reports from retailers as to its effectiveness. In the United States the products had a high reputation and had established brand awareness, and it was hoped that such an image would become an important element of the mix in the United Kingdom.

Market entry

The formation of Fisher Price Co. Ltd had been through an agreement between the US parent company and Britoy Ltd, a leading UK toy manufacturer. With the establishment of the new company the MD was also perplexed about the formulation of a market entry strategy. He had three alternatives. The first was to utilize both the sales force and distribution channels of Britoy, the availability of which had been previously negotiated. The second alternative was to continue and extend the services of the previously appointed agents, while the third was to establish their own sales force and distribution channels. Again this component of marketing strategy had not been finalized at the time the case was written.

Timing

There were two major issues to be considered in the timing component of the marketing strategy to be developed for Fisher Price. The first was that Christmas is obviously an important time for purchases and indeed the company recognized that this time caused considerable anxiety to many parents in their toy purchases. Consequently, the marketing mix could be utilized accordingly. The second timing issue is that purchases of gifts are also continuous throughout the year, while they considered that there are more gift-giving occasions for pre-school children than for other age groups. Thus, the timing strategy would need to respond to the yearly constant demand as well as the special peak at Christmas, with both purchasing situations being different.

REVIEW QUESTIONS

1. Why do you think there should be so much confusion surrounding marketing strategy?
2. Discuss the implications of different approaches to the sequence of plan preparation.
3. Discuss the various approaches taken to explain the nature of marketing strategy. What considerations would you recommend to a firm when determining this strategy?
4. Do you agree with the five-component approach to marketing strategy? Explain your reasoning.
5. 'The range of alternative marketing strategies is excessive.' Discuss.
6. Examine the advantages and disadvantages of preparing a marketing strategy in isolation from other plans.

REFERENCES

1. Y. Wind, and T. S. Robertson, 'Marketing strategy: new directions for theory and research', *Journal of Marketing*, **47**, 12–25, Spring 1983.
2. P. J. Carroll, 'The link between performance and strategy', *Journal of Business Strategy*, **2**, 4, 3–20, Spring 1982.
3. 'Porche's civil war with its dealers', *Fortune*, 16 April 1984.
4. G. E. Greenley, 'An overview of marketing planning in UK manufacturing companies', *European Journal of Marketing*, **16**, 7, 3–15, 1982.
5. G. E. Greenley, 'Where marketing planning fails', *Long Range Planning*, **16**, 1, 106–15, February 1983.
6. G. E. Greenley, 'An overview of marketing planning in UK service companies', *Marketing Intelligence and Planning*, **1**, 3, 55–68, 1983.
7. G. E. Greenley, 'The relationship of marketing planning to corporate planning', *West Midlands Regional Management Centre Review*, **1**, 1, 40–6, Autumn 1981.
8. Chang, Y. N., and F. Campo-Flores, *Business Policy and Strategy*, Goodyear Publishing, Santa Monica, 1980.
9. Baker, M. J., 'Limited options for marketing strategies', *Marketing*, 23–7, June 1978.
10. Luck, D. J., and O. C. Ferrell, *Marketing Strategy and Plans*, Prentice-Hall, Englewood Cliffs, 1979.
11. Kotler, P., *Marketing Management: Analysis, Planning and Control*, 3rd edn, Prentice-Hall, Englewood Cliffs, 1976.
12. P. Kotler, and R. Singh, 'Marketing warfare—1980's', *The Journal of Business Strategy*, **3**, 30–41, Winter 1981.
13. R. Evered, 'So what is strategy?', *Long Range Planning*, **16**, 3, 57–72, June 1983.
14. Foxall, G. R., *Strategic Marketing Management*, Croom Helm, London, 1981.
15. Jain, S. C., *Marketing Planning and Strategy*, South-Western Publishing, Cincinnati, 1981.
16. J. G. Udell, 'The perceived importance of the elements of strategy', *Journal of Marketing*, **32**, 34–40, January 1968.
17. 'Amstrad's personal ambitions', *Management Today*, June 1984.
18. P. Kotler, 'Competitive strategies for new product marketing over the life cycle', *Management Science*, **12**, 4, 104–19, December 1965.
19. P. Doyle, 'The realities of the product life cycle', *Quarterly Review of Marketing*, 1–6, summer 1976.
20. E. E. Scheuing, 'The product life cycle as an aid to strategy decisions', *Management International Review*, **4**, 5, 111–25, 1969.
21. P. N. Bloom, and P. Kotler, 'Strategies for high market-share companies', *Harvard Business Review*, **53**, 6, 63–72, November-December 1975.
22. R. D. Buzzell, B. T. Gale and R. G. M. Sultan, 'Market share—a key to profitability', *Harvard Business Review*, **53**, 1, 97–106, January-February 1975.
23. Doyle, P. 'Market share and marketing strategy', *Quarterly Review of marketing*, 1–3, Autumn 1975.
24. 'The five-star management of Ball', *Management Today*, March 1984.
25. P. Kotler, *Marketing Management: Analysis, Planning and Control*, 4th edn, Prentice-Hall, Englewood Cliffs, 1980.
26. Y. Wind, and H. J. Claycamp, 'Planning product line strategy: a matrix approach', *Journal of Marketing*, **40**, 2–9, January 1976.
27. D. W. Cravens, 'Marketing strategy positioning', *Business Horizons*, **18**, 53–61, December 1975.
28. L. Alpert, and R. Gatty, 'Product positioning by behavioural life-styles', *Journal of Marketing*, **33**, 65–9, April 1969.
29. J. H. Holmes, 'Profitable product positioning', *MSU Business Topics*, **21**, 2, 27–32, Spring 1973.
30. K. M. Warwick, and S. Sands, 'Product positioning: problems and promises', *University of Michigan Business Review*, 17–20, November 1975.
31. P. Doyle, and G. D. Newbould, 'Marketing strategies for building societies', *Management Decision*, **13**, 1, 41–50, 1975.

32. W. J. Keegan, 'Multinational product planning: strategic alternatives', *Journal of Marketing*, **33**, 58–62, January 1969.
33. D. S. Halfill, 'Multinational marketing strategy: implications of attitudes towards country of origin', *Management International Review*, **20**, 4, 26–9, 1980.
34. A. C. Samli, 'International marketing strategy decisions and the growth rate of major American firms', *European Journal of Marketing*, **8**, 2, 108–18, 1974.
35. 'What makes Saatchi and Saatchi grow?', *Fortune*, 19 March 1984.
36. W. Copulsky, 'Strategies in industrial marketing', *Industrial Marketing Management*, **5**, 23–7, 1976.
37. 'ICI's new yarn', *Management Today*, February 1984.
38. M. T. Cunningham, and M. A. A. Hammouda, 'Product strategy for industrial goods', *Journal of Management Studies*, **6**, 2, 223–42, May 1969.
39. J. L. Forbis, and T. Mehta, 'Value based strategies for industrial products', *Business Horizons*, **24**, 3, 32–42, May/June 1981.
40. E. R. Corey, 'Key options in market selection and product planning', *Harvard Business Review*, **53**, 5, 119–28, September/October 1975.
41. D. W. Hopkins, 'The marketing plan', *The Conference Board, Research Report Number 801*, 1981.
42. M. H. B. McDonald, 'International marketing planning', *European Journal of Marketing*, **16**, 2, 3–32, 1982.
43. Greenley, G. E., 'An understanding of marketing strategy', *European Journal of Marketing*, **18**, 6, 90–103, 1984.
44. 'Patek Philippe's better time', *Management Today*, February 1984.
45. 'The King of Tyres is discontented', *Fortune*, 28 May 1984.
46. 'How Jaguar Lost Its Spots', *Management Today*, April 1984.
47. G. E. Greenley, 'The integration of product decisions', *Management Decision*, **22**, 2, 36–44, 1984.
48. 'Motorola's leading edge', *Management Today*, November 1983.
49. McCarthy, E. J., *Basic Marketing*, 7th edn, Irwin, Homewood, 1981.
50. C. D. Fogg, 'New Business Planning', *Industrial Marketing Management*, **5**, 3–11, 95–113, 179–95, 1976.
51. 'Smith Kline's ulcer medicine holy war', *Fortune*, 19 September 1983.
52. 'High speed management for the high-tech age', *Fortune*, 5 March 1984.
53. 'Eight big masters of innovation', *Fortune*, 15 October 1984.
54. D. F. Abell, 'Strategic windows', *Journal of Marketing*, **42**, 3, 21–6, July 1978.
55. Abell, D. F., and J. S. Hammond, *Strategic Market Planning: Problems and Analytical Approaches*, Prentice-Hall, Englewood Cliffs, 1979.

EIGHT

MARKETING PLAN DOCUMENTS

Learning objectives are to:

1. Understand the role of the marketing plan in operational planning.
2. Appreciate the contents of a marketing plan and their relationship to previous chapters in the books.
3. Gain an understanding of the nature of marketing tactics within each of the elements of the marketing mix.
4. Appreciate programming methods and approaches to marketing budgets.
5. Recognize major concepts that have been introduced.

In the planning framework established in Chapter 2 the marketing plan document was located as the final component part within operational planning. Indeed, this sequence has been followed in Part Three on operational planning. However, the major role of the plan document is the unification of the areas of marketing operational planning, including marketing objectives, environment and strategy, as previously discussed in the other chapters of Part Three.

Also in Chapter 2, a distinction was made between long- and short-range operational planning. While it is apparent that there is a tendency for companies to orientate their plan documents to the annual marketing plan, the approach taken in this book is that the marketing plan document should contain both long- and short-range elements. Consequently, the long-range operational planning is represented not only by the framework established in the strategic planning, but also by the marketing strategy. The other elements of the marketing plan would be short-term elements. Of particular importance, and again as already established in Chapter 2, are the marketing tactics applicable for the next annual planning period. These represent the detailed activities for each of the elements of the marketing mix, as previously established in the marketing strategy. Other short-range elements applicable to the annual planning period will also be examined in the chapter.

CONTENT OF MARKETING PLANS

Although it has already been stated that the major roles of the marketing plan are unification and a basis for commitment, Luck and Ferrell[1] have identified four major functions of the marketing plan:

– The specification of results to be expected.
– The identification of resources needed to carry out the plans.

- The description of actions, leading to the delegation of responsibilities.
- The provision of monitoring to allow for control.

Here the implication is that these functions or roles of the plan need to be considered when formulating its content, which will be examined again later in the chapter.

Although the approach advocated in this book is to combine long- and short-range operational planning in the same document, writers such as Walker[2] suggest that two plans could be produced, or indeed that long-range operational planning should be combined into the strategic plan. This approach is also suggested by writers such as Jain[3] and Abell and Hammond.[4] Indeed, the latter suggest that major marketing issues should be included in the strategic planning, with the shorter-term activities being directly related into a sales plan. However, the reason for taking the approach advocated in the book should be apparent to the reader, being based upon the split between strategic and operational planning, as given in the planning framework in Chapter 2.

Additionally, the framework of a single document provides a vehicle for the integration of the long-range marketing strategy and the short-range marketing tactics for the next year. For example, the performance of General Motors' Vauxhall cars in the UK during 1983 started with established market and product positioning strategies, including the launch of the Nova in the small-car segment, while promotion featured as part of their marketing mix strategy. However, their marketing tactics for 1983 included an aggressive campaign of sales to the public, although exact details of the tactics were not reported, plus sales incentives to retailers in the form of bonuses and other incentives, with again the exact details not revealed. Similarly, any detailed changes in product specifications (again not reported), such as modernizing radiator grills, light clusters, bumpers and logo design, or internal design changes such as instrument panels, cloth trim, improved legroom and an added cassette player, would all be changes in marketing tactics concerning the product component of the marketing mix.[5]

The content of the marketing plan can also be affected by the organizational structure of the company. Although the work of major writers such as Chandler[6] and Channon[7] in the area of organizational affects on planning will be examined in Part Four, a brief mention is pertinent here. The practise of many firms in organizing their marketing operations around product or brand groups can lead to separate marketing plans for each group. Alternatively, where the operations are organized around the different marketing functions, then there may be separate plans for, say, advertising, selling and product development. Additionally, the overall organization into a number of SBUs or divisions is likely to result in a separate marketing plan for each.

The different sections to be included within the content of a marketing plan document have been presented in the literature from two sources. The first is that prescribed by various writers within the literature, while the second is based upon empirical evidence from the marketing plans adopted by companies. Both these sources are examined in the following two sections.

Prescribed marketing plan contents

After having examined the recommendations of a number of writers, the approach to be adopted in this book was finalized and is given in Fig. 8.1.

Although writers such as Cravens[10] suggest that such a format could be applied to any company situation, others, such as Bell,[8] suggest that no hard and fast rules should apply. Indeed, examples of marketing plans developed for particular company requirements will be discussed in the next section.

Also to be considered is the sequence of preparation of each stage and the sequence to be presented within the plan document. Again, there are 'no hard and fast rules', although by necessity the environmental analysis needs early consideration and the marketing strategy, being subserviant to the organizational strategy, also needs early consideration. As the marketing tactics are aimed at the achievement of the marketing objectives, then it follows that they must be formulated after the latter. However, this point again illustrates the cyclical nature of the stages of planning and that each stage is not discrete, being one of the themes of the book.

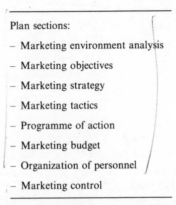

Plan sections:

– Marketing environment analysis

– Marketing objectives

– Marketing strategy

– Marketing tactics

– Programme of action

– Marketing budget

– Organization of personnel

– Marketing control

Figure 8.1 Adopted marketing plan content. Writers referred to: Bell,[8] Christopher,[9] Cravens,[10] Higgins,[11] Hussey,[12] Kollat, Blackwell and Robeson,[13] Kotler,[14] Luck and Ferrell,[1] McDonald,[15] Staudt and Taylor,[16] Walker,[2] Winkler,[17] and Wilson[18]

The sections of the marketing plan also provide links into the longer-term planning of the strategic plan. Analysis carried out as part of control in last year's plan will provide inputs to the marketing environment for this year, plus inputs to the strategic audit. The marketing strategy provides a link to organizational strategy, but also provides an on-going framework for the marketing operations. This framework is also applicable to marketing objectives, so that their role is keyed into both the organizational strategy and the objectives. Within such an interrelated system the marketing tactics can also be endowed with consistency from year to year, although particular emphasis is likely to change from year to year within the mix, depending upon the particular tasks to be pursued, such as a new product launch or brand image modification. Readers interested in the model-building approach to relationships in planning should refer to writers such as Morris[19] and Kotler.[20]

Within the sections given in Fig. 8.1, the marketing environment and objectives have already been examined in Chapter 6, while a treatment of marketing strategy was given in Chapter 7. As organization is to be discussed in Part Four and control in Part Five they will not be considered further in this chapter. Consequently, the major sections which will be addressed later in the chapter are on marketing tactics, the programme of action and the marketing budget.

Empirical evidence of marketing plans

The content of marketing plans formulated by companies has been researched by Greenley,[21] Hooley, West and Lynch[22] and Hopkins.[23] Greenley found that, although 70 per cent of his respondent companies prepare an annual marketing plan, only a quarter have a plan that can be considered to be comprehensive when compared with a standard, such as that given in Fig. 8.1.

Hooley, West and Lynch obtained a similar result relative to the overall incidence of a marketing plan, although only 20 per cent of firms separated this plan from long-range plans. Similarly, Hopkins found that 40 per cent do not separate a marketing plan from their long-range plan, although the remaining 60 per cent of the sample did have an annual marketing plan.

In the Greenley surveys the companies were asked to give the headings of the major sections normally incorporated into their annual marketing plans. The results gave an almost unique response for each company, although a form of commonality was observed in that plan formats could be classified into three different types of groups, by comparing them with a standard such as that given in Fig. 8.1. The three groups were:

Comprehensive format In this group the content of the marketing plan was considered to be comprehensive in that it contained sections appropriate to a full range of planning activities. Only a quarter of the respondents were classified into this group.

Company's own format In this group there was little evidence of commonality of content, but there was a commonality of approach in that firms appeared to have their own formats. Here nearly a third of the respondents were classified into this group.

Sales plans In this final group the declared plans can probably be best described as sales plans as opposed to marketing plans. For each company classified into this group, the content of their plans was orientated almost entirely to the selling function, with little attention to other marketing areas. Just over a tenth of the respondent firms were classified into this group.

The surveys of both Hopkins and Hooley, West and Lynch took a different approach, in that they investigated the importance of major marketing issues that are taken into account in formulating the marketing plan. Of the list of issues investigated by Hopkins, only five showed a relatively high degree of utilization by the sample, being:

- forecasts of demand;
- own and competitors' market share;
- competitive strengths and weaknesses;
- market segmentation;
- customer needs.

All but the last of these issues were also found to be utilized by a relatively high sample proportion in the investigation of Hooley, West and Lynch. The results obviously show an orientation to the external environment, with market forces being important, and all require forecasting in their utilization with a marketing plan. However, the overall conclusion to these two surveys is that the results cannot be used to determine the content of the marketing plan of these firms, but that they merely give issues that are seen by many companies to be important in preparing these plans.

MARKETING TACTICS

At various stages, in the previous chapters of the book, explanations have been made of the nature of tactics as well as how they differ from marketing strategy. Earlier in this chapter it was stated that tactics are the details of each element of the marketing mix and an illustration of the marketing strategy and tactics of Vauxhall cars was given.

In Chapter 2, tactics were identified as being the short-range element of marketing operational planning, while in Chapter 7 several differences between strategy and tactics were given. In the military context, tactics are actions on the battlefield, which correspond to actions of the marketing plan. They were also shown to be transient in nature, as opposed to strategy which is enduring. Finally, in Chapter 7 tactics were described as being the prime means of achieving the annual marketing objectives, whereas marketing strategy is a prime means of achieving organizational objectives. These differences are summarized in Fig. 8.2.

Marketing strategy	*Marketing tactics*
Utilization of the marketing mix	Details of the marketing mix
Long-range operational planning	Short-range operational planning
Deployment of resources	Specific actions
Enduring in nature	Transient in nature
Organizational objective achievement	Marketing objective achievement

Figure 8.2 Differences between marketing strategy and tactics

The actions of marketing tactics are concerned with the operation of the mix elements. Readers of this book will be well acquainted with the plethora of attention to the marketing mix within the literature, which appears to have been pioneered by McCarthy[24] in 1960 with his 'four *ps*' approach, continued in the eighth edition of that text by McCarthy and Perreault.[25] A further role of marketing tactics is described in Bell.[8] In addition to the determination of specific actions for each element of the mix, he also sees the outcome of this stage of planning as providing the basis for the remaining stages of the marketing plan. Consequently, it provides a basis for scheduling a programme of activity for the coming year, for finalizing a marketing budget, and for the organization of personnel.

The remainder of this section is concerned with an examination of the major issues to be considered in the tactical planning of the four major components of product, place, promotion and price that constitute the marketing mix. Readers of this book will be familiar with general marketing texts that cover these components, such as McCarthy and Perreault,[25] Kotler,[26] and Cannon.[27]

Product

Product tactics relate to the nature of individual products together with changes within the current product line. The nature of an individual product has been well explained by Kotler[28] as being concerned with three levels: the core product, the tangible product and the augmented product.

Core product This is the fundamental nature of the product, that is, in marketing terms, the benefits offered to consumers to satisfy the identified needs. For example, Apple is claiming that the benefits of its Macintosh personal computer mean that it is a simple, instantly usable appliance like a telephone or TV. Other personal computers do not have such benefits, but require the consumer to master and remember many tasks and codes.[29]

Tangible product This level represents the make-up of the product, comprising features, quality, styling, branding, packaging and labelling. In developing their Tower stereo system, Amstrad included every 'imaginable special feature' (such as remote control and double cassettes), while the overall styling was to produce attractive units within the system, but featuring the Amstrad brand.[30]

Augmented product These are additional services to the product such as after-sales service, product trials, delivery, technical advice, credit facilities and a complaints procedure. Here Apple have recognized that a customer requirement relative to personal computers is a low incidence of appliance breakdown. Therefore, although a repair service is still needed, reliability of each unit of product is a tactical approach to augmenting the product to meet this requirement.[29]

Within the product line, tactics can involve product modification, product elimination, new product introduction, or indeed no change to the current line. Writers such as Greenley[31] and Littler[32] have suggested approaches to such changes, while Greenley[33] has reported how such decisions are made by a sample of companies. For example, Black & Decker recognized that there was little difference between the products that all companies offer into the small domestic appliance market in the United States. All manufacturers' toasters were similar, as were coffeemakers. Consequently, modifications were made to their products by introducing product group banding but still emphasizing the Black & Decker logo.[34]

Place

After the marketing strategy decision on channels of distribution, tactical decisions are needed to determine actions within the channels. In managing channels of distribution, Kotler[28] has identified three major decision-making areas, being the selection of individual middlemen, their motivation and their evaluation.

In selecting individual middlemen several factors can be considered, such as reputation, services offered, efficiency and geographical coverage. In motivating the middlemen, Kotler suggests co-operation through incentives, partnership through agreement on key issues such as market coverage, and distribution programming by establishing personnel within the company who are responsible for middlemen liasion. Some of these tactical arrangements are illustrated with the Swiss Company Patek Philippe, manufacturers of exclusive watches, already referred to in earlier chapters. Given an overall marketing strategy of limited retail outlets, the company tactically selected only 500 retailers worldwide to sell their watches, in order to reflect exclusivity. Additionally, they are able to achieve 'partnership' with 'control' of 60 per cent of these outlets. However, they have recently used tactics to increase from only one exclusvie retailer in each major city to several selected ones. Although many of their established retailers objected, Philippe's motivation for acceptance was that additional spread would result in more overall business for all retailers.[35]

Promotion

Tactical planning within this component of the mix can be split between promotion through personal selling and that concerned with advertising and other forms of sales promotion. Major tactics to be included in personal selling can be considered to be concerned with the management of sales personnel. Again, such tactics are well documented in books on general marketing, and again those suggested by Kotler[28] are suitable here. The first group of tactics are directed at recruiting and selecting sales personnel who exhibit attributes compatible with both the company and the product range. The second group are concerned with training personnel to carry out their job functions, with particular emphasis laid on the principles of personal selling. Of central importance here is the orientation of sales people to the benefits that the company's products feature in relation to customer needs. Again, the previous example of the Apple Macintosh personal computer is appropriate, where simplicity of operation is the major benefit to the consumer.[29] Other tactics in selling include the direction or supervision of personnel within their job performance, motivation of efforts given that sales people often work in isolation to other company personnel, and evaluating their performance relative to norms and standards.

Tactics concerned with advertising and sales promotion originate with those involving the nature of the message to be communicated. Here the tactics involve determining the message that will be communicated and the way in which it will be put across. Despite the exclusiveness of their products, Patek Philippe have communicated messages through advertising to establish brand identification within the market-place.[35] Advertising and promotion tactics also need to be established in deciding upon the mix of media to use to communicate these messages. Such tactical planning normally involves an examination of the effectiveness of each medium in reaching a certain number of people, the frequencies with which the message needs to be repeated, and the impact they have in achieving communication to the target audience.

Price

As with the other elements of the mix, tactics are well described by the general marketing texts, in particular that by Kotler.[28] At this stage the overall role of pricing should be established within the marketing strategy, as well as the method to be used to determine price. In the case of the former, most writers list a range of pricing objectives, while a range of methods for determining price is also given.

From here tactical planning can be developed. The first range of tactics concerns modifications to prices for several reasons. One alternative is to have different prices for different countries or indeed different regions of the same country. Another alternative is to offer price discounts or allowances, such as a fixed sum to consumers or a quantity discount to middlemen. In entering the UK home computer market, Amstrad avoided price-cutting tactics following the 'blood-bath' of price-cutting wars that had materialized in the United States.[30] Another approach is to modify price as a tactic in sales promotion, such as followed by Goodyear in the overall reliance on price in the marketing strategy of their tyres, this approach of promotional pricing being dictated by the unglamorous nature of the product.[36] Another reason for modification is to offer different prices to different groups of customers, such as in different retail outlets, although the products may be basically the same. Similarly, the firm may modify price through a product's life-cycle, although the nature of the product may vary little. Finally, price modification may be based upon other elements of the mix. Product-line pricing is a common tactic, where a progression of quality in individual products across the line is reflected in individual product prices. Exclusive Swiss watch manufacturers Patek Phillipe use this tactic, rising from a base price of around £2000 for a watch with a leather strap to £5000 with a gold strap and £15 000 for gold, jewels, and intricate enamelling with intricate gold engraving.[35]

The other range of tactics is concerned with responding to price changes. Tactical planning must include the buyers' reactions to price changes, as well as the likely affect to be expected on competitors' pricing tactics. Also to be included are plans of how the firm will react to price changes initiated by competitors. Such tactical decisions can range from no reaction, to following competitors' price changes, or to counter-action through other marketing-mix tactics.

In Case Study 11 (page 136), the utilization of an annual marketing plan is illustrated along with both marketing tactics and strategy.

Contingency tactics

The final area of consideration in developing marketing tactics is to prepare a range of contingency plans. This is a planning stage, involving making preparations to take certain actions should a particular situation suddenly arise. Anticipating changes to pricing tactics as a result of competitive price changes, as discussed above, is an example of contingency planning.

Clay[37] has claimed that contingency planning also has its roots in military terminology. Here he identifies two types of contingency situations that may unexpectedly arise during the planning period to which a company may need to react. The first is defensive reaction to a threat which had not been anticipated at the time the plan was prepared. The second is offensive reaction to opportunities that had not been identified at the time the plan had been prepared. Defensive contingency tactics could be triggered by many situations, such as unfavourable advertising effects, sudden product obsolescence, unfavourable publicity, or a price war. Offensive contingency tactics could also be initiated by many situations, such as a sudden new product launch by a major competitor, a failed advertising campaign of a competitor, sudden market expansion, favourable legislation such as credit availability, or a sudden breakthrough in research and development.

Within the contingency planning it is perhaps possible to differentiate between contingencies that have a high probability of occurring and those likely to occur only by chance. In the former category, changes that competitors make to their pricing tactics are likely to be classified. In such a situation it may be that the firm will have a number of alternative courses of action, depending upon the level of such a price reduction. Below 5 per cent may be indicative of no change, between 5 and $7\frac{1}{2}$ per cent may mean the same reduction, whereas about $7\frac{1}{2}$ per cent may trigger several tactical changes across the mix. For contingencies likely to occur only by chance, their very nature obviously means that their anticipation is unlikely and that therefore planned reaction is inappropriate. Perhaps the ultimate risk in business is of an event occurring for which little anticipation was possible. Here the contingency tactics become immediate actions to the given situation, without the advantage of advanced planning.

Central to the use of contingency tactics is obviously the identification of contingency situations as they develop. Constant monitoring of the environment is the process required for such identification, within the full range of areas described in Chapter 6. Methods to be used in such monitoring are part of the overall control of plan implementation, which is to be examined in Part Five.

PROGRAMME OF ACTION

This stage of the marketing plan is concerned with determining the time periods at which the various tactics are to take place within the overall period of the plan. The aim is to co-ordinate the full range of activities by arranging their timing to achieve an effective sequence of events, relative to the interrelationship of each event with the others. For example, sales literature and advertising need to be scheduled in relation to a predetermined date for a new product launch. The US company Osborne Computers recently announced to the market its second generation of portable computer, to replace the first generation, too early before its launch date. Dealers stopped buying the current model to wait for the new product, so that the company lost sales in the period up to the launch.[38]

The full range of tactics across the elements of the mix can be extensive and their interrelationships can be complex. Methods within the literature which can be utilized to programme the action of a marketing plan tend to be based upon network analysis. This is defined by Wilson[39] as problem solving based upon systematic and logical analysis of the relationships and time factors involved in carrying out a particular project, namely the full content of the marketing plan. Here Allen[40] suggests that network analysis can be applied to tactics such as in new product launches, advertising campaigns, distribution problems, market research surveys and new market exploitation.

Full details of the utilization of network analysis is considered to be outside the scope of this book, although interested readers should refer to specialist texts such as that by Weist and Levy.[41] However, there are two major methods that show the relationships between the activities that must be performed in terms of time in completing a particular project: critical path analysis (CPA) and the programme evaluation and review technique (PERT). Both techniques produce charts that show the relationships among all the activities that must be performed in terms of time. A major problem can be, however, that the resultant chart becomes very detailed and complex, so that the overall aim of communicating the sequence and coordination of events tends to break down. This can be avoided by using several charts. The first would include the major overall events of the annual marketing plan, and the others would each cover a specific area of marketing tactics, such as advertising or product development.

Another approach to programming is to use a flowchart for the period of the plan. This approach simply lists the events to be carried out and uses a horizontal line to represent the period of time which the event spans. This gives an overall visual communication of the period of time for each event, and 'slippage' on particular events can be easily adjusted on the chart. However, the disadvantage of the flowchart method compared with CPA and PERT is that the interrelationship of events is not included, so that co-ordination can suffer as a consequence; also, although 'slippage' can be accommodated immediately on the chart, it is not always obvious how it is likely to affect the other events.

MARKETING BUDGET

This is the stage of quantifying the content of the marketing plan document, usually in the form of financial statements. The importance of budgets within marketing is seen by Wilson[18] to be related to co-ordination, control, and the acquisition and utilization of resources over a given period of time. This leads on to the establishment of centres of responsibility on the basis of budgeted levels of expenditure, which will include an attempt to isolate the performance of these centres by relating the actual expenditure to that in the budget. This section of the chapter is concerned with the nature and preparation of the marketing budget. Its utilization as a method for control will be examined in Part Five, as will its role in the delegation of responsibility.

Writers such as Welsch[42] and Hartley[43] identify three different types of budgets within organizations, as follows:

– Operating budgets showing planned operations for a coming period of time.
– Capital budgets detailing planned changes in fixed assets.
– Financial budgets dealing with anticipated sources and uses of funds.

The nature of a budget within the marketing plan is clearly classified as being an operational budget. As an operational budget, many writers claim, the marketing budget should include revenue, costs and profits. However, the inclusion of the last item relates back to the discussion already covered in Chapter 6 within the context of marketing objectives. If the company decides that the marketing department is to be responsible for net profit (and indeed a profit objective is included in the set of marketing objectives) then it follows that it needs to be included in the marketing budget. If the marketing department is not so responsible, then a suitable breakdown would be to a gross margin or level of contribution, but in a format to allow for marketing decisions to be made relative to individual products and markets. Writers such as Clay[37] have also emphasized the importance of flexibility in order to allow for contingencies that may arise, as reflected in any contingency tactics within the plan. Although it can be argued that flexibility within the figures weakens the value of the budget as a means of control, the figures are nevertheless assessments as to anticipated levels in a future period of time, so that some flexibility is appropriate.

Content of marketing budgets

A simple approach to the content of marketing budgets is to present sales revenue less costs to give profits, for each market and product, for each month of the period of the plan. Here the approach is often followed, of determining a gross margin before marketing costs, the gross margin then being reduced to net profit by the subtraction of the marketing costs. However, the problem of relating marketing costs to this gross margin is that fixed costs have been removed, and, as the allocation of the latter is arbitrary, a reliable comparison is not made. To overcome this, many writers prescribe a contribution method where only variable costs are removed to leave a contribution to profits and fixed costs. Such an approach, adapted for Fig. 8.3, is given by Doyle;[44] it too can be presented by different markets and products. After the deduction of non-marketing costs, the margin or gross contribution gives a contribution to both profit and overheads, before the removal of arbitrary fixed costs. It is therefore claimed that, by relating either level of contribution to total sales as ratio, a more feasible assessment of the contribution being earned by each product or market is made.

	£
Sales value	
Less: Non-marketing variable costs	————
Contribution	
Less: Marketing costs:	
marketing research	
product development	
selling	
distribution	
advertising	
sales promotion	————
Adjusted contribution	
Less: Fixed costs	————
Net profit	

Figure 8.3   Contribution approach to the marketing budget. Adapted from Doyle[44] by permission of Elsevier Science Publishing Co. Inc.

An example of an extension of this approach has been given by Beik and Buzby.[45] Again, variable costs are deducted from sales revenue to arrive at contribution, but here the marketing variable costs are split into two types as follows:

– Assignable costs that can be directly related to particular products or markets.
– Non-assignable costs that cannot be directly related to particular products or markets.

This type of approach is illustrated in Fig. 8.4. Here three levels of contribution are evident, all of which can be related to sales ratios. The first level is the manufacturing contribution and any reductions in these costs will be reflected in an increased ratio. The second level is labelled product/market contribution, which represents that earned directly by the product or market, as only directly attributable costs are included. Again a reduction in these costs will be reflected in an increased ratio, and such an increase will identify the extra contribution being made by that product or market. Finally, the marketing contribution is after the deduction of total marketing costs that are allocated between all products and markets. This ratio will also reflect changes in levels of costs, and hence net contribution, but will identify such changes as being due to general marketing costs, as opposed to costs directly related to a particular product or market. As already indicated, further implications of marketing budgets will be considered relative to control in Part Five.

	£
Sales value	
Less: Variable manufacturing costs	————
Manufacturing contribution	
Less: Assignable marketing costs	————
Product/market contribution	
Less: Non-assignable marketing costs	————
Marketing contribution	
Less: Fixed costs	————
Net profit	

Figure 8.4 An extended contribution approach to the marketing budget

In his surveys of UK manufacturing companies, Greenley[21] investigated the marketing budgets of his respondent firms. These results showed that nearly 40 per cent declared that they do not have a separate marketing budget specifically for the purpose of a marketing plan. Only just over 20 per cent include a full breakdown of revenue and costs to give profits, while the remaining companies consider the marketing budget to be only costs incurred in operating the marketing function.

Marketing expenditure

The final area of consideration in this section is the allocation of a budgeted level of expenditure to the marketing operations for the period of the plan. Writers such as Hartley[43] have epitomized the major problem in determining future expenditure; this is that the future effects of such marketing expenditure will be difficult to determine, because the many variables to be found in the marketing environment can affect the future effectiveness of levels of expenditure, as well as planned increases in expenditure. The approach taken in the discipline of economics, as illustrated for example by Wilson,[46] is that costs should be increased as long as they are producing extra revenue, up to the point at which this marginal cost equals marginal revenue. However in practice this is difficult, as it relates to a period of time in the future, and the effects that external variables can have on the effectiveness of these marginal costs are difficult to assess. Consequently, a number of methods for determining marketing expenditure are suggested in the literature, as follows:

Affordable or given-sum method Here the company decides 'what it can afford' relative to other company costs and profit levels required. This can be with or without consultation with marketing personnel, but the resultant level of expenditure is a given fixed sum for expenditure on the marketing operations.

Percentage of sales method Here a fixed percentage is used, based upon sales in previous years and the level of expenditure used to generate such sales. However, the problem is that conditions prevailing in the past may not be applicable in the future, rendering a fixed ratio inappropriate. Alternatively, a percentage can be based upon forecast sales. The problem here, though, is that as sales increase or decrease the level of expenditure will do the same, whereas the opposite may need to be the case.

Following competitors This means determining expenditure for the marketing plan directly from that of competitors. However, this is likely to be difficult to assess, while the objectives to be achieved by their marketing expenditure are likely to be different.

Objective and task method This is a logical approach which comprises establishing the marketing objectives, determining the marketing tactics to achieve these, specifying the tasks of the tactics, and costing out the tasks to give a resultant level of required expenditure. As this method provides a logical progression within the plan and starts with the objectives, it tends to be favoured by many writers.

Sales response function This method has been well described by Kotler.[28] The approach is to graph changes in levels of expenditure on the elements of the marketing mix, relative to the effect or response that these levels will impart to the sales revenue. However, the approach tends to be theoretical, as again the relationships are in the future and are difficult to assess within the environment of many variables and their potential influences.

SUMMARY

As the final area of study in Part Three, Chapter 8 has been concerned with marketing plan documents. The initial consideration was of the various roles that the plan document plays within operational planning. Although there are variations within the literature concerning the recommended content of a marketing plan, examination of a number of formats led to an adopted range of contents for this book. Therefore, the content of a marketing plan was suggested as being an environmental analysis, marketing objectives, marketing strategy, marketing tactics, programme of action, marketing budget, organization of personnel, and marketing control.

As many of these areas are considered in the various chapters of the book, Chapter 8 has concentrated on tactics, programming and the marketing budget. Attention was then given to differentiating between marketing strategy and tactics before emphasizing tactics within the elements of the marketing mix. This covered the product, place, promotion and price, but concluded with a consideration of contingency tactics.

Methods of programming the content of the plan were given, with network analysis methods and flowcharts being outlined.

The final section addressed the marketing budget. Different approaches to the budget were examined, while various approaches to content were considered, with particular attention to contribution methods. The section concluded with methods that can be used to determine expenditure on marketing operations for the duration of the plan.

CASE STUDY 11: POLAROID FRANCE (SA)*

Case outline

This case is concerned primarily with the marketing of Polaroid still cameras in France, as a major effort of this United States-based company to expand international business. The main product feature of Polaroid cameras is that they provide instant still photographs that are processed in the camera.

Illustration

In late 1965 Polaroid introduced a new product, named the Swinger, to be part of its strategy for expanding international business. This allowed for entry into the inexpensive segment of the still-camera market, while such a market positioning strategy allowed for access to a large-volume market.

At the same time, the parent company introduced a new planning and control system for marketing operations. Consequently, Polaroid France was required to prepare an annual marketing plan based on the following format:

1. Review of market conditions and trends
2. Marketing objectives for the year
3. Marketing activities of:
   – sales force;
   – advertising;
   – publicity;
   – market research;
   – customer service.
4. Budgeted operating results for each major product of:
   – sales revenue;
   – operating expenses;
   – profits;
   – cash flow.
5. Monthly control reports of:
   – actual results compared with plan;
   – significant discrepancies;
   – explanations of discrepancies.

From the information given within the case study both the marketing strategy and tactics adopted at the time can be highlighted. During 1966 the mix component of marketing strategy was re-emphasized, with the launch of the Swinger, as follows:

– Product line expansion.
– More reliance on advertising and promotions.
– Expansion of retail distribution.
– Expansion of marketing personnel.

Within each of the elements of the mix, strategy and tactics were:

---

* Derived from Robert Buzzell, Polaroid France (SA), Case 9-513-119. Boston: Harvard Business School. Copyright © the President and Fellows of Harvard College and the Institut Européen d'Administration des Affaires (INSEAD).

Product

A strategy of three products in the line, with the Swinger aimed at the inexpensive market segment. Tactics within this component included the benefit of only a 15-second development time, styling and colour to relate to its brand image, and availability of the special films for this camera.

Place

Given the overall strategy of expanding retail distribution, tactics included the selection and utilization of many additional retailers, resulting in a doubling of retailers from 1965 to 1967. Selling tactics were related to distribution by Polaroid. Here tactics included the recruitment of an additional 12 salesmen to give a salesforce of 22, as well as determining call rates and job specifications.

Promotion

Here the advertising strategy included devoting half the 1966 advertising expenditure to the launch of the Swinger. Tactics included media selection, promoting consumer awareness, projecting the youthful and exciting brand image of the Swinger, and carrying out in-store demonstrations.

Price

Pricing strategy included co-ordinated prices on an international level, while in France the gross margin on the Swinger was less than on other models. Pricing tactics were based upon discounts to dealers based upon quantities purchased. This allowed for an average gross profit for retailers of 33 per cent based upon the full recommended retail price.

REVIEW QUESTIONS

1. Why do you think that it is important to formualize marketing operations into a plan document?
2. Suggest a typical format for a marketing plan and justify the sections that have been included.
3. 'In formulating a marketing mix there is little point in differentiating between strategy and tactics.' Discuss.
4. Select a particular product and examine the range of marketing tactics that could be developed for that product.
5. Discuss the advantages of using a contribution approach to the marketing budget. Does such an approach remove the responsibility for profits from the marketing plan?

REFERENCES

1. Luck, D. J., and O. C. Ferrell, *Marketing Strategy and Plans*, Prentice-Hall, Englewood Cliffs, 1979.
2. K. R. Walker, 'How to draw up a marketing plan that will keep you on track', *Industrial Marketing*, 126–8, September 1976.
3. Jain, S. C., *Marketing Planning and Strategy*, South-Western Publishing, Cincinnati, 1981.
4. Abell, D. F., and J. S. Hammond, *Strategic Market Planning: Problems and Analytical Approaches*, Prentice-Hall, Englewood Cliffs, 1979.
5. 'Germany's medium-sized miracle', *Management Today*, June 1984.
6. Chandler, A. D., *Strategy and Structure*, MIT Press, Cambridge, 1962.
7. Channon, D. F., *The Strategy and Structure of British Enterprise*, Macmillan, London, 1973.
8. Bell, M. L., *Marketing Concepts and Strategy*, Houghton Mifflin, Boston, 1979.
9. W. F. Christopher, 'Marketing planning that gets things done', *Harvard Business Review*, **48**, 5, 56–64, 1970.
10. Cravens, D. W., *Strategic Marketing*, Irwin, Homewood, 1982.
11. Higgins, J. C., *Strategic and Operational Planning Systems*, Prentice-Hall, London, 1980.
12. Hussey, D. E., *Corporate Planning*, Pergamon, Oxford, 1976.
13. Kollat, D. T., R. D. Blackwell and J. F. Robeson, *Strategic Marketing*, Holt, Rinehart and Winston, New York, 1972.
14. Kotler, P., *Marketing Management*, 4th edn, Prentice-Hall, Englewood Cliffs, 1980.
15. McDonald, M. H. B., *Marketing Plans*, Heinemann, London, 1984.
16. Staudt, T. A., and D. A. Taylor, *A Managerial Introduction to Marketing*, Prentice-Hall, Englewood Cliffs, 1970.
17. Winkler, J., *Winkler on Marketing Planning*, Cassell, London, 1972.
18. Wilson, R. M. S., *Management Controls and Marketing Planning*, Heinemann, London, 1979.
19. G. D. Morris, 'Models, computers: why should I use them in corporate planning?' *European Business*, 60–9, Winter/Spring 1974.
20. P. Kotler, 'Corporate models: better marketing plans', *Harvard Business Review*, **48**, 4, 135–49, July-August 1970.
21. G. E. Greenley, 'Where marketing planning fails', *Long Range Planning*, **16**, 1, 106–16, 1983.
22. Hooley, G. J., C. J. West, and J. E. Lynch, *Marketing in the UK*, Institute of Marketing, Maidenhead, 1984.
23. Hopkins, D. S., *The Marketing Plan*, The Conference Board, Research Report Number 801, 1981.
24. McCarthy, E. J., *Basic Marketing*, 1st edn, Irwin, Homewood, 1960.
25. McCarthy, E. J., and W. D. Perreault, *Basic Marketing*, Irwin, Homewood, 1984.
26. Kotler, P., *Principles of Marketing*, 2nd edn, Prentice-Hall, Englewood Cliffs, 1983.
27. Cannon, T., *Basic Marketing: Principles and Practice*, Holt, Rinehart and Wilson, Eastbourne, 1980.
28. Kotler, P., *Marketing Management*, 5th edn, Prentice-Hall, Englewood Cliffs, 1984.
29. 'The fruits of Apple', *Management Today*, June 1984.
30. 'Amstrad's personal ambitions', *Management Today*, June 1984.
31. G. E. Greenley, 'Tactical product decisions, *Industrial Marketing Management*, **12**, 1, 13–18, 1983.
32. Littler, D., *Marketing and Product Development*, Philip Allan, Oxford, 1984.
33. G. E. Greenley, 'An investigation of company product decision making', *Omega: the International Journal of Management Science*, **13**, 3, 175–180, 1985.
34. 'Black and Decker's gamble on "globalization"', *Fortune*, 14 May 1984.
35. 'Patek Philippe's better time', *Management Today*, February 1984.
36. 'The King of Tires is discontented', *Fortune*, 28 May 1984.

37. M. J. Clay, 'Contingency planning', *Long-Range Planning*, **3**, 3, 70–3, 1971.
38. 'High-speed management for the high-tech Age', *Fortune*, 5 March 1984.
39. Wilson, M. T., *The Management of Marketing*, Gower, Aldershot, 1980.
40. Allen, P., *Marketing Techniques for Analysis and Control*, Macdonald and Evans, Plymouth, 1977.
41. Weist, J. D., and F. K. Levy, *A Management Guide to PERT/CPM*, Prentice-Hall, Englewood Cliffs, 1977.
42. Welsch, G. A., *Budgeting: Profit, Planning and Control*, Prentice-Hall, Englewood Cliffs, 1976.
43. Hartley, R. F., *Sales Management*, Houghton Mifflin, Boston, 1979.
44. P. Doyle, 'Market planning in the multiproduct firm', *Industrial Marketing Management*, **4**, 183–92, 1975.
45. L. L. Beik and S. L. Buzby, 'Profitability analysis by market segment', *Journal of Marketing*, **37**, 48–53, 1973.
46. Wilson, J. H., *Microeconomics: Concepts and Applications*, Harper and Row, New York, 1981.

PART
FOUR
THE PLANNING PROCESS

9. Managerial influences on planning
10. Organization and planning
11. Planning effectiveness

OUTLINE

Part Four is devoted to the planning process, as opposed to considering details of individual stages of planning, which has been the approach taken in Parts Two and Three. In Chapter 9 attention is given to the influences of managers within the stages of planning, as caused by their own personal dispositions. These influences are consolidated in this chapter, although several instances of managerial influences have already been included in previous chapters. Chapter 10 examines the role of the managerial organizational structure within the planning process. Although the structure is seen to be affected by planning, the latter can also be influenced by the structure. In the final chapter of Part Four the effectiveness of planning is addressed. This is a relatively new area of consideration within the literature. Currently available methods for assessing effectiveness are examined, all presenting problems in their application.

MANAGERIAL INFLUENCES ON PLANNING

Learning objectives are to:

1. Appreciate the nature of managerial influence on the planning of marketing.
2. Understand the concepts of both values and attitudes.
3. Become aware of some of the problems that are likely to be experienced in planning.
4. Understand the importance of managerial capabilities within the context of planning.
5. Appreciate the likely affects of potential change to be caused by planning.
6. Recognize major concepts that have been introduced.

Throughout the preceding chapters the issue of the influence of managers on the planning of marketing, due to their personal dispositions, has been discussed. Indeed, this issue has been emphasized as a major theme of the book. The aim of this chapter is to develop a consolidated and structured understanding of these influences, drawing upon the issues raised in Parts Two and Three.

Consequently, the chapter starts with a recapitulation of these previous influences, consolidating the principles already presented, as a basis for the rest of the chapter. Attention is then given to the managerial job functions to be involved in the planning of marketing, as a prelude to an examination of five major considerations in the understanding of managerial influences.

The first consideration is the values of managers in relation to those established as being adopted by the organization. The second is the attitudes of managers towards planning within the marketing context, while the third is an examination of problems in planning. The fourth consideration is the influence of managerial capability on planning, while the last is managerial reactions to change as a consequence of both the need for planning and the changes likely to occur as a result of the implementation of the plans.

These five major considerations are illustrated in Fig. 9.1. As the major thrust of this chapter is these five areas, five corresponding sections represent the bulk of the chapter.

RECAPITULATION

The concept of the influence of managers on the planning of marketing, due to their personal dispositions, was established initially in Chapter 3 within the context of stakeholders, with these managers being obviously classified as decision makers within the range of internal stakeholders.

The initial basic principle established was that the personal benefits that they seek to receive from the firm may have a direct affect on the planning. If situations arise where there is a difference between managers' expectations and company capability, then conflict may result. However, such conflict will also be affected by the nature of the participation of each manager in the planning. Here the nature of such participation was related to the concept of management style, which can be explained in terms of criteria such as decision-making ability, commitment, need for achievement and the need for power.

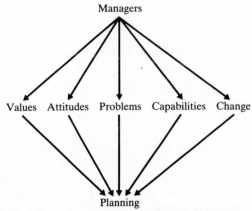

Figure 9.1 Major managerial influences on planning

Chapter 3 also advanced the principle that managers have difficulty in separating their values, expectations, feelings, emotions and personal preferences from logical analysis and decision making. Although stages of planning may be set out in logical stages, planning is a process carried out by people, and the ramifications of human behaviour are apparent in planning just as they are in other human activities. Values and expectations were outlined as being central to these influences, with the former being affected by both the values of society and other values established within the company. Expectations are the result of desired achievements from the working environment and beliefs about the likelihood that such outcomes will be realized. However, just as conflict is likely between managers and the company, conflict of values between individual managers is also likely.

The final area of consideration in Chapter 3 was the formalization of some values and expectations. This was in the form of guidelines that the board of directors establish within which all planning must be carried out, being labelled business policy, but also being reflected in the philosophical aim of organizational mission.

In Chapters 4 and 6 objectives were discussed and here the personal objectives of managers were illustrated, along with both the organizational and the marketing operational objectives. Again, conflict can arise between personal objectives and those formally set within the firm. However, in order to help to avoid such conflict the company can establish certain aims that directly affect the welfare of personnel, including the managers responsible for the planning of marketing. These chapters also looked at internal and external environmental affects on planning. Of particular importance was an internal capability analysis, which included the responsiveness of management to change and their competence to tackle responses. Also included was an assessment of managerial strengths and weaknesses, being very much the concern of a study of behavioural aspects. Within operational planning the whole framework of

probably fall into this second set, in that he was recently named as entrepreneur of the year by both the Harvard Business School and the Stanford Graduate School of Business.[5]

In a survey by Guth and Tagiuri,[8] a range of value orientations of managers were identified that are likely to affect preference or choice of behaviour in planning. These value orientations are likely to have been shaped by the full range of personal experiences, including the cultural environment. The range of value orientations is:

- a theoretical orientation towards truth and knowledge;
- an economic orientation toward what is useful and powerful;
- A political orientation towards power;
- an aesthetic orientation towards form and harmony;
- a social orientation towards the love of people;
- a religious orientation towards unity in the universe.

At a more specific level, England[9] investigated the values of managers in five different countries. Although many variations were identified, as could be expected, pragmatism, high achievement, competence, and a high value on traditional organizational goals were identified. The value of pragmatism is perhaps exhibited by the chairman of Amstrad, Alan Sugar, who avoids theoretical management principles, basing the planning of the company on basic and practical rules, such as only entering high-profit potential markets, and aiming to keep overheads low.[10] Values of achievement, competence and traditional organizational goals are illustrated in a report concerning Pepsi, in that these values were promoted in their managers in their battle against Coca-Cola, by changing their culture from passivity to aggressiveness. The Pepsi company developed a 'creative tension' and job rotation to nurture achievement, developed a competitive environment so that only competent managers would survive, and demanded continued improvements in market share, product volume, and profits.[11]

Personal objectives

As an end result of the value set of each manager involved in the planning of marketing, a range of personal objectives is likely to be formed. Where the company practices management by objectives, then each manager will be forced into either writing them down or into giving greater consideration to them, as the performance objectives relative to this job function are formulated.

In 1958, March and Simon[12] wrote that managers obviously devote a lot of their time and efforts to the pursual of their personal self-interests, which may or may not be compatible with those of the organization. Also to be considered are the interests of the department of the company in which the manager works, which again may or may not be consistent with his personal objectives. Saunders[13] claims that the higher the manager is within the hierarchy, then the easier it will be for him to pursue self interests, even to the detriment of the firm. However, where both sets of interests are compatible then the influence of the manager on the planning is likely to be of benefit to both and the manager will be satisfied in his work, while his participation in planning will be constructive to the overall corporate planning. An objective of Robert W. Woodruff, who was chief executive of Coca-Cola for 32 years, was to market Coca-Cola throughout the world. This personal objective was obviously consistent with the company's interests, and has been cited as being a major influence in the worldwide success of the company.[11] We have already seen in Chapter 3 that the expectations of managers to be able to actually achieve their objectives will also affect their formulation. Where such expectations are a belief that personal objectives have the potential to be realized then motivation within planning is likely to be high. Motivation is considered in Part Five and therefore expectancy theory is given more attention there.

In Chapter 4 personal objectives within the planning framework were broadly classified into those of performance and achievement. The former can relate not only to an individual manager's performance within the total marketing effort but also to the performance of the unit or department in which he works, such as the advertising function at one level and the total marketing department at another level. Achievement can relate to personal achievement, such as promotion within a career structure, status within both the company and society, and self-actualization. Additionally, achievement can also be a personal objective in relation to the manager's unit or department. Success in identifying a new marketing opportunity followed by successful exploitation would be an achievement not only by the marketing team but also by the individuals concerned.

In addition to these personal objectives, Hicks and Gullett[14] have cited those concerning both economic and psychological security of individual managers. The former obviously relates to total remuneration and its ability to be able to provide the standard of living required by each manager. However, it is likely that for most managers achievements in planning will not be linked to financial rewards, but may be linked to short-term gains such as sales or contribution margins. Objectives related to psychological security were given as including job security, belonging to an organization, sickness and retirement security, and rewarding work. Where planning is not seen to be part of management it may be that it will not be included in the job-satisfaction objective, so that the planning requirements of the firm could result in conflict. Further consideration of the values of managers relative to their motivation towards planning will be considered in Part Five.

Levinson[15] sees the pursual of personal objectives as being a mutual task. First, the company needs to assess the individual needs fo managers, which should then be compared with the needs of the firm. Such a comparison may be indicative of a change of job function, a reappraisal of certain marketing objectives, or the inclusion of additional objectives to allow individual managers further scope for additional performance or achievement.

This treatment of values is illustrated in Fig. 9.2.

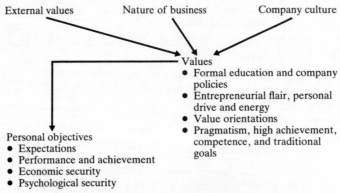

Figure 9.2 Summary of values of managers

ATTITUDES TOWARDS PLANNING

Most writers addressing the concept of attitudes admit to problems both in defining them and in the major differences to be found between definitions. Within the context of this book the definition of attitudes by Baron and Byrne[16] has been adopted, as follows: 'relatively enduring organizations of feelings, beliefs, and behaviour tendencies towards other persons, groups, ideas, or objects'. While values were defined in terms of influences on behaviour, attitudes are overall predispositions or tendencies of managers towards planning, representing their behaviour when they were required to be involved in the planning process.

In an investigation by Higgins and Finn,[17] the companies with the most experience of planning were found to be more favourably predisposed towards it. Although all managers within the hierarchy were supportive of strategic planning, senior managers were found to be more enthusiastic. Similarly, Ames[18] found a tendency for successful companies to have managers whose attitudes are favourably disposed towards marketing planning. Such support and enthusiasm has recently been reported in the planning carried out by Tandem Computers. Senior executives are supportive of their broad strategic planning, while the total commitment of the chief executive to planning the firm's future is featured throughout its short history.[5] Studies by Grinyer and Norburn[19] and Leontiades and Tezel[20] have identified that the chief executive officers within their respondent companies consider the function of planning to be very important. Total company commitment by Kim Woo-Choong, founder and chairman of the Korean Daewoo Group, extends to 15-hour days, never taking a holiday, and adopting the philosophy of self-sacrifice for the next generation.[21]

Investigations by Ames[18] and by Kudla[22] have identified managerial attitudes towards support from senior managers, plus individual participation within the planning process, where both conditions are seen to be vital to planning success. Additionally, Ames proposes four major attitudes that are likely to be common:

– Managers seek guidance in at least the setting of overall objectives.
– Attitudes towards the organizational structure can affect attitudes towards planning.
– Liaison within the business functions is essential.
– The attitudes of senior managers towards planning are of major importance.

These issues lead on to a consideration of commitment to planning. Hopkins[23] received comments from his respondents that actual commitment is not always consistent with purported attitudes of senior managers. In such situations these managers may claim that they consider planning to be important, but they also affect behaviour that is indicative of a lack of commitment, such as showing that they do not really understand the planning process, or taking decisions outside the plan. Brown[24] has suggested several reasons for a lack of commitment towards planning:

– A lack of understanding of planning.
– A lack of ability to measure results.
– Complacency due to previous successes without planning.
– Reluctance to make long-term commitments.
– Tendency to focus on the short term which is more identifiable.

McDonald[25] has identified a tendency for managers to be evaluated and rewarded on the basis of current operations as opposed to future plans, with the implication that such a situation is likely to affect commitment.

Two examples of commitment are applicable here. A report on the Quaker Oats Co. in the United States in 1980 included a commitment by the president towards more aggressive marketing, following failures both in diversification and in increasing its share of retail shelf space.[26] Wadkin, the UK manufacturer of woodworking machinery, also features commitment from the top, by chairman Michael Goddard. Here the chairman uses visual aids to communicate the major points of company plans within the company. Additionally, the board are prepared to be committed to high-risk product innovations and capital investment in order to plan successful opportunity exploitation and growth, despite significant Japanese competition.[27]

Subjects of an investigation by Taylor and Irving[28] included the reasons why strategic planning was initially introduced into the respondent companies. Here a wide range of reasons were given, reflecting little commonality across the sample. However, a major cause in about a third of the companies was a change in attitude at director level towards giving a directive on the utilization of planning. Changes in external variables, such as competitors and economic conditions, were also cited by many firms. Also, nearly one-fifth of the companies claimed that there was no specific reason or event that instigated the utilization of strategic planning. Planning played an initial role in the launch of Tandem Computers. Start-up plans were prepared in 1974, including initial objectives, and a market positioning strategy of being only in a small segment of the computer market. However, the start-up also included long-range planning to become a large company participating in many segments of the general all-purpose computer market.[5]

Writers such as Higgins and Finn[17] and Al-Bazzaz and Grinyer[29] have put forward several attitudes towards the advantages of planning, particularly at the strategic level, examples of which are that it:

– promotes awareness of problems, strengths and weaknesses;
– initiates the utilization of information and communication;
– provides a system for the allocation of resources;
– provides a system for co-ordination and control;
– fosters a disciplining to explore alternative courses of action;
– promotes confidence in the future.

Consequently, at this stage of the chapter, two of the major considerations in the understanding of managerial influences on planning have been examined. The first is the values or preferences of managers, including their personal objectives, while the second consideration is that of the attitudes of managers towards planning. The next three sections of the chapter address the other three major considerations concerning managerial influences.

An illustration of some major values and attitudes within a UK company is given in Case Study 12 (page 158).

PROBLEMS IN PLANNING

The problems faced by managers in their planning are also taken to be a consideration in the understanding of managerial influences, in that the nature and severity of such problems will affect how they will react to both current and future planning. If such a problem was, say, not being able to accurately forecast market trends, then the setting of specific marketing objectives might be seen to be of limited value.

Most of the investigations into attitudes cited in the last section also investigated the planning problems of their respondent firms. Although a wide range of problems were identified, they can be classified into three groups, these being based upon people, the planning process itself, and externally caused problems. Each of these classifications is considered in turn, on the basis of these previously cited investigations.

People-based problems

Much of the research has indicated that the majority of the problems in planning are due to the people involved. Many reports were given of the difficulty in getting managers to actually do planning, as it is often seen as being an additional task to bear and not a part of the job of management. This could be a problem of the personal deficiencies in managers, i.e., of their either being unable or unwilling to develop plans. The former could be due to a deficiency in education, training or planning experience, whereas unwillingness was cited many times as being due to insufficient time for planning given the multiplicity of tasks demanded of executives. Again the example of Tandem Computers is applicable. Having established ambitious marketing objectives to facilitate their organizational strategy of growth, they then faced problems of a lack of managerial skills and the necessity of developing an organizational structure to plan and achieve the attainment of these objectives.[5] Additionally, the complexity of some large organizations was given as being the cause of many communication breakdowns, including the integration of many separate planning efforts.

Many managers also reported problems in applying planning procedures to their specific market situations. A reluctance to think beyond the current tactical planning period can cause problems in developing overall strategies, particularly an operational marketing strategy. One of the investigations also found that a major problem was in the setting of marketing objectives, where many were merely extrapolations of past trends without a full consideration of applicable objectives within an integrated planning framework.

An over-emphasis of the short term to the detriment of long-range planning also appears to be a common problem. This could be partly due to the rewarding of managers on the basis of short-term results, as mentioned in the last section. However, other firms reported that a problem with planning is that it requires large amounts of executive time that could be employed in other activities.

Planning process problems

An initial problem here is that of the organizational arrangements for the preparation of plans at both strategic and operational levels. This was due partly to confusion on the part of personnel as to the difference between the roles of the two forms of planning, but for many firms there also appears to be a problem of integrating the levels of planning into an overall framework. This difficulty is perhaps exacerbated further in that the confusion within both the literature and firms, relative to the nature of the individual components of planning, raises inherent obstacles within the process of, for example, marketing strategy formulation. An additional problem lies in formulating specific stages of planning. Such a difficulty has been reported as having been applicable to IBM in the United States. The status of the company is that they have a huge customer base and highly reputable products compared with those of their competitors. However, the problem of such a status is that they have a high potential for incurring losses in devising their organizational strategy. Consequently, they have been reported as 'walking a fine line' between pursuing growth through product development and pursuing stability through harvesting by price adjustments for increased profits.[30]

Lack of control within planning was also cited by several respondent companies. Here evaluative procedures, such as a strategic audit, were not utilized, while in large organizations, with divisional structures and dispersed sites, control problems can occur within the system as a result of these structures.

Externally caused problems

Probably the greatest problem identified is that of being able to realistically forecast trends within the external environment as a basis for planning. This problem is considered to be in three parts.

First there is the problem of obtaining reliable data as a basis of forecasting, whether primary data collected by the firm, or secondary data from one of the many sources. Second there is the problem of anticipating changes within the external variables that have the potential of affecting the company's marketing, with, not surprisingly, economic variables being cited as being important. Finally, many firms consider actual forecasting methods to be both difficult to handle and unreliable in their results, so that the actual forecasting itself is seen as being a major problem. Such a situation also gave rise to the problem of effectively monitoring performance against the plan, in that the basis for comparison is seen to be inadequate.

Several examples are applicable here. The CEGB in the United Kingdom has a problem of forecasting the demand for electricity to over 50 million consumers, who consume at the flick of a switch a product that cannot be stored, but must be instantly generated.[31] ICI Fibres also have a problem, owing to the derived nature of the demand for their products. Consequently, they make fibres that are demanded by the manufacturers of fabrics, the latter being demanded by clothing manufacturers whose products are demanded by the general public. Here there are three levels of demand to be considered by ICI, each one of which could cause forecasting problems.[32]

A range of planning problems experienced by a UK firm is given in Case Study 13 (page 160).

MANAGERIAL CAPABILITY

In this section attention is given to managers' capabilities of performing planning duties, which in themselves will be an influence on the resultant planning. Another influence will be the overall capabilities of managers in carrying out the full range of managerial duties; this is due partly to the location of planning as being but one of the range of integrated managerial duties, but also partly to individual ability, initiative and acceptance of risk, which will influence creativity in planning alternative objectives, strategies and tactics. By 1980 the tremendous expansion in competition for grocery products through product proliferation had challenged the capabilities of the Quaker Oats Co. Capabilities were stretched by a 'hectic drive' to diversify, which in itself has been reported as having sapped managerial capabilities. Additionally, a reported study revealed serious deficiencies within the marketing operations at that time, especially in planning tactics for shelf space and product presentation at the point of sale.[26] Consequently, it could be expected that higher levels of capability would be reflected within resultant planning, constituting an influence similar to the three major considerations already examined.

Within the various stages of planning, at both the strategic and operational levels, the establishment of the individual stages can be considered to be a series of decisions. Depending upon the organizational structure and the arrangements for participation within each of the planning stages, these decisions will be made either by single managers or by managerial groups of various sizes. Although organizations will also include a system for approval and official company acceptance of decisions, which is likely to include modifications of plans, initial decisions still need to be made within the planning stages. Therefore, in this section, the first concern is that of the nature of decision making, followed by an examination of decision making within managerial groups, and concluding with assessing capabilities.

Decision-making models

Many books addressing the principles of management discuss models that explain the decision-making process, while writers such as Higgins[33] present a model within the context of decision making at the strategic planning level. Such an approach is applicable here, but can also be generalized to any level within the framework of corporate planning.

The model is based upon four stages. The first is a recognition of the need to make a decision, followed by a second stage of identification to specify the nature of the decision. The third stage involves a search and evaluation of alternative courses that can be pursued, while the final stage is the choice and implementation of the preferred alternative.

The recognition stage, within the context of planning, includes the realization of the need to prepare the various stages within both the strategic and the operational planning of marketing, such as operational marketing objectives and a marketing strategy. The stage of identification, in specifying the nature of the decision, refers to the nature of each of the individual planning stages. Additionally, there seems to be a tendency for writers to orientate this stage to problems and opportunities, with the former being, say, a decline in market share, and the latter being, say, potential for extending a market positioning strategy.

The third stage of the establishment of alternative courses to be pursued could again be in relation to the marketing strategy. Here there could be many alternative combinations of market and product positioning and marketing mix, with the potential value of each combination representing their evaluation. Implementation is given by Higgins as being based upon authority: first there is a requirement for authority to make the choice of alternatives to be pursued, which is then followed by the authority needed to be able to actually pursue, for example, participation within additional market segments.

Group decision making

Where decisions are to be made by a group of managers then this will be within an environment of not only the planning framework but also the full range of values, attitudes and capabilities of each person within the group.

An initial stage within this decision-making process is to identify the preferences of each person concerned, relative to the range of alternatives applicable to the decision making necessary in, for example, the establishment of a marketing strategy. From here it may be that there are major differences of preference, some managers may have dominant opinions, there may be some grouping of agreement to form some kind of coalition, or indeed there may be total agreement, forming an overall coalition within the group. If the decision is to be made by this group without any outside intervention then any disagreements must obviously be overcome until a coalition is reached. Major texts concerned with organizational behaviour give in-depth treatments to group decision making, but the text by Kast and Rosenzweig[34] outlines the ways in which decisions can be arrived at, as follows:

- By the authority of the senior member in declaring the decision.
- As a result of a minority rule due to the dominance of the proceedings by a small number of group members.
- As a result of a majority by voting on the alternatives.
- Through a consensus of opinion as the most acceptable across the group.
- Through unanimity of agreement as to the most appropriate alternative.

Leadership in decision making is illustrated in previous modifications to the organizational strategy of the US electronics firm Gould Inc. The chairman and chief executive, William T. Ylvisaker, had pioneered the planning of a major restructuring of the company's portfolio of product-market scopes. However, despite the decisions of direction and subsequent acquisitions that he pursued, many members of the board of directors did not agree with the decisions that followed. Consequently, this domination of decision making led many executives to leave the company.[35]

Assessing capabilities

The concept of organizational capability has been developed within a major and recent text by Ansoff.[36] It consists of the capability within each of the major business functions or operations, plus the capabilities of managers. The functional capabilities were discussed in Chapters 4 and 6 within the context of assessing the environment for both strategic and operational planning; the approach taken by Ansoff to assess managerial capabilities is within a framework of three major capability attributes, being:

- the climate of managerial will to respond to planning decisions;
- the competence of managers to be able to respond to the requirements of effective planning;
- the capacity of volume of work that the managers can handle in order to be able to contribute to planning activities.

These three capability attributes are then developed into a capability profile to be used to assess individual managers' capabilities, which is adapted and summarized in Fig. 9.3. As will be seen, this profile is in three parts, the first being concerned with specific characteristics of individual managers. The success of new product launches by ICI Fibres Division, and their subsequent marketing, have been partly due to the capabilities of the chairman, John Lister. These included developing additional strategies, open-mindedness to alternatives, and competence to reorganize the board of directors as a consequence of newly adopted strategies.[32]

This consists of the components of capability, listed in three groups

1   *Managers*
1.1 Mentality: preoccupation with problems, time orientation, propensity for risk, success factors, values, norms and personal goals
1.2 Power: power position and drive to use power
1.3 Competence: talents, problem-solving skills, leadership ability, and business knowledge
1.4 Capacity: personal work habits and capacity

2   *Climate*
2.1 Culture: attitudes towards change, propensity for risk, time perspectives, action perspectives, triggers for change, and shared models of the world
2.2 Power: distribution of power, stability of power structure, and militancy in the structure

3   *Competence*
Organizational problem solving skills, management systems, information systems, organizational structure, rewards and incentives, job definitions, technological aids for managers, and organizational capacity

---

Figure 9.3   Ansoff's management capability profile. Reproduced by permission of Prentice-Hall International (UK) Ltd

The second part of this profile covers the overall climate within the firm in which the manager operates. A comparison here is between Tandem Computers and Pepsi Cola. As stated earlier, in the former a major objective has been given as being the generation of superior management quality, while the company is a 'good place to work'. Alternatively, at Pepsi a 'creative tension' was created to put pressure on managers to show continuous improvements in performance.[5, 11]

The final part of the profile addresses more fundamental issues about the structure of the firm within which individual competences must be developed.

REACTIONS TO CHANGE

These are the last of the five major considerations in the understanding of managerial influences on change. In Chapter 5 the general human trait of resistance to change was raised within the specific context of considerations for the selection of organizational strategy. Where previous strategy is seen to have been successful, a change of strategy may be interpreted as a high-risk option, particularly where the current organizational strategy is the result of a process of logical incrementalism over a number of years, producing a sophisticated and comprehensive strategy. This principle can be extended throughout both strategic and operational planning. Indeed, by its very nature, planning is concerned with the consideration of alternative objectives, strategies and tactics that will affect changes for both the company and the people that it employs. Consequently, the way managers react to such potential changes will influence the planning decisions they make.

Types of change

Two approaches have been given by Gray and Starke[37] to classify the types of change to be found in companies. The first is based upon the level within the organization at which the change takes place, while the second is based upon the degree or extent of the change.

At the individual level, change may have little impact on the company as a whole, even though it may have a major effect on individuals. Proposed changes in marketing tactics, such as approaches to advertising, may mean increased workloads for certain individuals, leading to resistance and a consequential influence on such planning. In planning their competitive actions against Coca-Cola, Pepsi made many changes, including some at the individual level. Severe pressure was put on individual managers to show continued improvements in market share, product volume and profits, to the point where, if improvements were not made, individual jobs were in jeopardy.[11] At the group level, changes affect either formal or informal groups, both of which can be applicable in relation to planning. Proposed changes in either marketing objectives or strategy are likely to affect all members involved in the operational planning of marketing. However, plans to extend market positioning are likely to affect an informal group that have been advocating such a change for some time. At the organizational level, change will affect the total firm, with plans for major changes in organizational strategy falling into this classification.

The classification based upon the degree or extent of change is also applicable at the three major levels, being broadly classified as either minor or major changes. Here Gray and Starke have suggested that minor changes, such as to budgets and communication systems, generally cause only minor changes in patterns of interaction between organizational members. However, in areas of greater behavioural change, such as reorganization as a consequence of a major change in organizational strategy, greater emotional reaction is likely. Resistance is likely to result as people tend to be reluctant to give up behavioral patterns that are comfortable, psychologically satisfying and provide security. The degree of change at Pepsi, as described above, is perhaps obvious. Similarly, in the last section, the example of a major restructuring of Gould's portfolio of product-market scopes was given, which obviously also represented a major change, but at the organizational level.[35]

Resistance to change

Again, Gray and Starke[37] have provided a valuable contribution to understanding resistance to change. A major point is that, although resistance is a common phenomenon, not all change will be met by it. However, it is likely that minor changes will result in little resistance, while major changes are likely to result in more, although they point out that there is little empirical evidence that resistance is widespread. These authors, though, give some common reasons why employees are likely to resist change, which are also pertinent where managers are resisting changes proposed in both strategic and operational planning. These reasons can be simplified as follows:

- A threat to personal economic wellbeing and security.
- Social factors, such as group disruption, an example being the autonomy of the marketing department.
- Consequential changes in status, such as the comparative status of marketing executives within the firm.
- General security, covering all aspects of personal and family security.
- A reduced company need for specific skills and competences. Withdrawal from a particular product-market scope may be seen by some managers as a threat, resulting in resistance.
- The 'path of least resistance' reason. Given as a general reason where change is merely resisted for its own sake, with a preference for the retention of the status quo.

The ability of managers to resist change will be based upon their power to affect the finalized planning. Power can be considered to be an individual's ability to be able to pursuade or induce others to follow certain lines of thought or behaviour, or, within the context of planning, to favour particular objectives, strategies, or tactics. Power can obviously be through a manager's position in the organizational structure, such as that available to the marketing director. However, acquired power can also be through situations such as personal skills of leadership, for example in co-ordinating the planned launch of new products, or through specific knowledge, such as a detailed understanding of a particular product-market scope. Further consideration will be given to power in Part Five. Again, the example of US manufacturers Gould, as given in the last section, is useful here. Although many of the senior executives resisted the chief executive's planned restructuring of the organizational strategy, they were not able to overcome his power and determination to implement these plans. Consequently, about half the senior executives left the company.[35]

Managing change

As a consequence of the above discussions, a central principle in the management of change is perhaps obvious. This is that the nature of the changes likely to result from the various alternatives developed in both strategic and operational planning need first to be classified and then to be assessed for likely resistance.

In assessing resistance there are two pertinent aspects. The first is given by Gray and Starke,[37] which is that people have a natural instinct to adapt to their environment. Here the implication is that, even though resistance may be initially exhibited where planning is to cause change, such changes are likely to be eventually accepted. Consequently, despite the severe pressure introduced at Pepsi, many managers were able to adjust to the changed level of expected personal performance, and indeed it was reported that some managers thrive under such conditions.[11] However, the achievement of the acceptance of change leads on to the second aspect, as described by Ansoff,[36] which is that a supportive climate should be established in order to promote the acceptance of planned change and to reduce resistance.

Developing such a climate may require many considerations. Probably the most important is that of participation within the various stages of planning, so that managers are involved in the planning of change initially, which has the effect of increasing their commitment to these planned changes. Another consideration is improvements in communication within the hierarchy, particularly in progressive improvements down the hierarchy to make managers aware of planning decisions already made, in which they did not participate. Reassurances of the likely outcome of planned change can also contribute to the supportive climate, particularly for major change in, say, company direction. Other considerations can include reassessment of individual abilities in relation to their job functions, training programmes to improve capabilities to adapt to change, redeployment of available personnel, and the requirement to appoint additional personnel with skills not currently available but which will be needed when the planned changes materialize. In 1980 the American Telephone and Telegraph Company were planning major changes in strategies and plans. Several actions were taken to provide a supportive climate, including written details of new requirements from employees, acknowledgement of a lack of skills including marketing, and internal promotion for managers with innovative ideas and advanced degrees in business administration.[11]

SUMMARY

Chapter 9 has addressed the influences of managers on the planning of marketing, by drawing upon references to such influence in previous chapters to develop a consolidated and structured understanding. Five major considerations were examined to develop this understanding, being values, attitudes, problems, capabilities, and relations to change. However these considerations were preceded by a recapitulation of managerial influences plus the nature of personnel involved in the planning of marketing.

The section addressing values looked at explanations of different types, before concentrating on the personal objectives of managers as part of their value set. The examination of attitudes to planning was based largely upon the results of previous research. These investigations have produced a range of results and the consequences of each were discussed.

Similarly, problems in planning were also examined within the context of previous research results. Here there was some commonality in that identified problems could be classified into people-based problems, planning process problems, and those externally caused.

Managerial capabilities were explained as being based upon a range of decisions to be made throughout the planning framework. This included both decision-making models and group decision making. Finally, this section looked at approaches to assessing capabilities, including a management capability profile.

The final major consideration in the understanding of managerial influence was the way in which the reactions of managers to change actually constitute potential consequences of planning. Here different types of change were classified, the likely resistance of managers to change was examined and the management of change was also considered.

CASE STUDY 12: LEX SERVICES GROUP (D)*

Case outline

This British company has developed as a major distributor and importer of vehicles, including Volvo, BL, Rolls-Royce and heavy trucks. The company had also developed businesses in hotels and transportation and vehicle hire.

Illustration

The group had encompassed the overall values of the company in several business policy statements. These values are summarized as follows:

- Development in the superiority of services supplied.
- Achieving managerial attitudes of high personal motivation and close management of services supplied.
- Utilization of strategic planning to identify the right organizational structure and personnel skills.
- Specific definitions of business strategies and personnel skills needed to achieve superiority through product (service) differentiation.

Within this framework the case study describes the planning, implementation of plans, and major strategic and operational issues of the group's performance. Within this description managerial values and attitudes are discussed as follows:

Values

The case study emphasizes that the managing director, Mr Trevor Chinn, infused his personal values into the Lex Group of companies. These included publicly declared commitment to the highest standards of honesty and morality towards all its shareholders. He also linked the delivery of high-quality service with company personnel, so that their personnel policy assured good working conditions, good benefits and job security. The MD's personal objectives also had an influence. He wanted to head a large company so that growth was the 'general goal'. This was achieved from 1968 to 1972 with a fourfold increase in sales and a sevenfold increase in profits. During this period Mr Chinn provided entrepreneurial spirit and intense energy, and set a rigorous pace for the group's direction.

This set of personal values provided the basis for the company culture, although there were other aspects that created a further set of values. Business policy statements were established, including criteria for assessing potential new industries to pursue for growth, plus a comprehensive customer service manual to instil the attitude of supplying high-quality services. The culture was enhanced with management training programmes to develop professional skills.

Attitudes

Overall, the managing director had been favourably predisposed to the utilization of a formal planning system within the company. Planning the overall direction was mentioned above, and here his attitude was that of confidence in the ability of the management team to follow the direction and achieve the specified growth. During the early seventies a planning manager was

---

* Derived from Dean Berry, Lex Services Group (D). Copyright © 1978 by the London Business School.

included in the organizational structure, while systematic strategic and operational planning were introduced. By 1975 the structure included a corporate strategy manager in addition to the planning manager.

There are several aspects to the approach taken to obtain managerial commitment to planning. Overall, there was an official directive of a general company commitment to improve the level of customer satisfaction, measured by complaints, repeat business, and customer market research interviews. Managers within the different divisions were required to prepare and submit their own one-year operational plans, while head-office planners prepared strategic plans for long-run growth. Within this system was the encouragement of the MD, including his sense of fairness, decency and generosity.

However, there were some negative aspects of managerial attitudes that reduced commitment to planning. One head-office manager claimed that he had little authority to develop his own ideas, and that the bulk of decisions were made by the MD. Achievements were seen as being only possible through a close relationship with the MD. Another manager reported frustration caused by the MD's autocratic style, although he claimed that this had changed after a financial crisis in 1976, in that he then delegated more, listened more to the opinions of his managers, and allowed a shift of influence to line managers.

CASE STUDY 13: ENGLISH GLASS CO. LTD (ENGLASS)*

Case outline

This company manufactures a range of industrial glass products, manufactures a range of dispensers under licence, and markets, as an agent, a range of industrial ceramic component parts. Although many aspects of the company are featured in the case study, some planning problems are also evident.

Illustration

These problems have been extracted from the case study brief, and have been classified within the three different groups of planning problems as given in the chapter. These are discussed as follows:

1 People-based problems

A major concern is the apparent lack of marketing orientation within Englass, as reflected by the given organizational structure and the experience and qualifications of executives within this structure. The board of directors does not feature a marketing director, while the function of marketing does not appear within the list of responsibilities given for each director. Although a sales director was employed, his responsibilities did not extend beyond selling into other marketing functions. Indeed, the only marketing role was given as that of a marketing assistant. This position was in the managing director's department, was at a low level, and indeed was a staff position, being out of the line of responsibility.

Additionally, the details of experience of the directors shows an absence of marketing experience and qualifications. The MD is an engineer, all his experience is in engineering and he was originally appointed to the board as technical director. Similarly, the sales director is also an engineer, his major experience being in technical sales, but excluding other marketing functions. Although a member of the Institute of Marketing, he did not become it by examination, which again shows a lack of marketing knowledge.

2 Planning process problems

Several problems were evident within this classification. At the start of the eighties the firm was experiencing financial constraints. A similar situation had existed in the sixties, and had been overcome by diversification. A similar strategy was now to be pursued, although the problem of such planning was a lack of research to identify such opportunities.

Although the firm has shown a five-year period of growth of assets, sales and profits, the ratio of profits to sales revenue had declined over the period. Therefore the firm was faced with a planning problem of cost reduction, sales revenue increase, or volume reduction and margin increase, in order to achieve growth of profitability. Exporting was also seen to be important in the pursuit of profitability, although economic variables were causing problems in planning such improvements.

However, in planning growth the firm was faced with a major problem of having little flexibility with which to be able to reduce overheads. This was due to the major differences

* Derived from R. C. Parker and R. G. Fall, English Glass Co. Ltd. Copyright © 1980 by Dr R. C. Parker and R. G. Fall.

between its three product-market scopes, which required different strategies and production facilities.

Another problem of future planning was Englass's reliance on licensing and producing to contracts, which can be extremely vulnerable. Failure can obviously mean loss of business, but success can too, as customer companies may decide to produce their own components to emulate such success.

Finally, although four options for future growth were being considered as future planning alternatives, all featured major planning problems, from increased vulnerability to increasing overheads.

3 Externally caused problems

Several externally caused planning problems were also evident. An early problem had been experienced by Englass in the mid fifties. At the time the company had also participated in the fashion jewellery business, but changes in fashion and increased competition reduced profitability until they eventually withdrew from this product-market scope.

In the early sixties the firm had experienced several problems. Escalating costs were one, as were financial constraints and increased levels of competition.

At the start of the eighties financial constraints were again posing a major problem, but economic factors such as high inflation and a strengthening of the pound were causing additional problems. At the time the case was written, half Englass's European exports were to West Germany, and as the UK inflation rate was four times the West German level at that time, price competition was consequently difficult.

REVIEW QUESTIONS

1. Why is it that the personal dispositions of managers cannot be divorced from systematic planning?
2. Discuss the different types of managerial values that are likely to influence the planning of marketing.
3. 'Empirical evidence is far from conclusive in explaining managerial attitudes and is therefore of little value in understanding a company's corporate planning.' Discuss.
4. How would you suggest that a company goes about assessing the capabilities of managers involved in the planning of marketing? What problems would you envisage?
5. 'Achieving major company changes through planning can only be achieved if managers participate in that planning.' Discuss.

REFERENCES

1. Mintzberg, H., *The Nature of Managerial Work*, Harper and Row, New York, 1973.
2. Harvey, D. F., *Strategic Management*, Merrill, Columbus, 1982.
3. G. A. Steiner, 'Rise of the Corporate Planner', *Harvard Business Review*, **48**, 5, 1970.
4. Williams, T. G., *Consumer Behaviour*, West Publishing, St Paul, 1982.
5. 'Tandem's Twofold Task', *Management Today*, November 1984.
6. Johnson, G., and K. Scholes, *Exploring Corporate Strategy*, Prentice-Hall, London, 1984.
7. Christensen, C. R., K. R. Andrews and J. L. Bower, *Business Policy*, Irwin, Homewood, 1982.
8. W. D. Guth and R. Tagiuri, 'Personal Values and Corporate Strategy', *Harvard Business Review*, **43**, 5, 1965.
9. England, G. W., 'Managers and Their Value Systems', *Columbia Journal of World Business*, **13**, 2, 35–44, 1978.
10. 'Amstrad's Personal Ambitions', *Management Today*, June 1984.
11. 'Corporate Culture', *Business Week*, 27 October, 1980.
12. March, J., and H. Simon, *Organizations*, Wiley, New York, 1958.
13. C. B. Saunders, 'Setting Organisational Objectives', *Journal of Business Policy*, **3**, 4, 13–20, 1973.
14. Hicks, H. G., and C. R. Gullett, *Modern Business Management*, McGraw-Hill, 1973.
15. H. Levinson, 'Management by Whose Objectives?', *Harvard Business Review*, **48**, 4, 125–34, 1970.
16. Baron, R. A., and D. Byrne, *Social Psychology: Understanding Human Interaction*, Allyn and Bacon, Boston, 1977.
17. J. C. Higgins and R. Finn, 'The Organisation and Practice of Corporate Planning in the UK', *Long Range Planning*, **10**, 4, 88–92, 1977.
18. B. C. Ames, 'Marketing Planning for Industrial Products', *Harvard Business Review*, **46**, 5, 100–11, 1968.
19. P. H. Grinyer, and D. Norburn, 'Planning for Existing Markets', *Journal of the Royal Statistical Society*, **38**, 1, 70–97, 1975.
20. Leontiades, M., and A. Tezel, 'Planning Perceptions and Planning Results', *Strategic Management Journal*, **1**, 1, 65–75, 1980.
21. 'The hardest worker in South Korea', *Fortune*, 20 August, 1984.
22. R. J. Kudla, 'Elements of Effective Corporate Planning', *Long Range Planning*, **9**, 4, 82–93, 1976.
23. Hopkins, D. S., *The Marketing Plan*, The Conference Board, Research Report No. 801, 1981.
24. J. K. Brown *et al.*, 'Long Range Planning in the USA', *Long Range Planning*, **1**, 3, 44–51, 1969.
25. M. H. B. McDonald, 'International Marketing Planning', *European Journal of Marketing*, **16**, 2, 3–32, 1982.
26. 'Quaker Oats Retreats to Its Food Lines', *Business Week*, 25 February 1980.
27. 'How Wadkin Worked Clear', *Management Today*, May 1984.
28. B. Taylor and P. Irving, 'Organised Planning in Major UK Companies', *Long Range Planning*, **4**, 2, 10–26, 1971.
29. S. Al Bazzaz and P. H. Grinyer, 'How planning works in practice', *Long Range Planning*, **13**, 4, 30–41, 1980.
30. 'Why IBM Reversed itself on Computer Pricing', *Business Week*, 28 January 1980.
31. 'Power Complex at the CEGB', *Management Today*, May 1984.
32. 'ICI's New Yarn', *Management Today*, February 1984.
33. Higgins, J. M., *Organizational Policy and Strategic Management*, Dryden Press, New York, 1983.
34. Kast, F. E., and J. E. Rosenzweig, *Organization and Management*, McGraw-Hill, USA, 1979.
35. 'Gould's golden gamble', *Management Today*, February 1974.
36. Ansoff, H. I., *Implanting Strategic Management*, Prentice-Hall, Englewood Cliffs, 1984.
37. Gray, J. C., and F. A. Starke, *Organizational Behaviour*, 3rd edn, Merrill, Columbus, 1984.

ORGANIZATION AND PLANNING

Learning objectives are to:

1. Understand the major influences that affect an organizational structure.
2. Appreciate the matching of strategy and structure.
3. Appreciate the role of marketing orientation throughout the organizational structure.
4. Understand the alternative approaches to organizing both the total company and the marketing department.
5. Recognize major concepts that have been introduced.

The influences of managers on planning having been examined in the last chapter, attention is now directed to the organization of managers within companies and the resultant organizational structures. However, the orientation of this chapter concerns the effect that organizational structure can have throughout the stages of corporate planning, as well as changes that may need to be made to that structure as a consequence of planning.

The principle on which the organizational structure should be based is simple, namely that it should be an effective vehicle for both the strategic and operational planning of a firm's future, as well as allowing for the effective implementation and control of these plans. However, as emphasized by many writers, there is no ideal method to arrive at the 'correct' organizational structure, given the complexity of corporate planning, the complexities of both internal and external environments, and the many variables to be found in the market-place. Another simple principle is that the structure should be the most appropriate to achieving the range of objectives and strategies established throughout the organization. This is again a principle that is obvious; but again, given the complexities faced by companies, there is no ideal method that can be used to obtain such a structure.

Consequently, companies must consider several issues in formulating an organizational structure in pursuance of the above-mentioned basic principles. First, there are a number of influencing factors that are likely to affect the structure, and are prescribed as a number of guidelines within the literature by several writers. Such influences on the organizational structure are examined in the first section of this chapter. The second issue that needs to be considered is the relationship between strategy and structure. Here there is evidence to indicate that the organizational structure follows the establishment of organizational strategy, although the latter can also be affected by resistance to the changing of traditional structures. This issue is considered in the second section.

The chapter then moves on to examine the organization of overall company structures. Particular emphasis is given to accommodating both strategic and operational management, as well as the role of company-wide marketing orientation within such structures. An important issue here has recently been highlighted by Jain,[1] which is a claim that the adoption of strategic planning by many firms has had a detrimental effect on the degree of their company-wide marketing orientation. In the penultimate section of the chapter, approaches to the organization of the marketing department are examined. Of particular importance here is the facilitation of the planning of marketing at both the strategic and operational levels. Finally, attention is given to examining the adequacy or effectiveness of organizational structures.

INFLUENCES ON ORGANIZATIONAL STRUCTURE

Byars[2] has given three basic reasons for developing an organizational structure, representing three basic influences. The first is that the structure provides lines of authority for each level of managers to be able to perform their job functions effectively. Second, it allows for division of labour and the integration of each separate division, unit or department, to provide synergy within the working environment. Finally, the structure established clearly defined channels of communication throughout the number of managers employed, and should facilitate communications both vertically within the hierarchy and horizontally across departments.

The emphasis taken by Doyle[3] is that a firm's organizational structure needs to be primarily related to market performance, so that the latter should be a prime influence on structure. In this approach the structure is seen as being one of four sets of variables, all of which interact to affect a company's market performance. The other sets are given as being effective strategies, efficient operating technologies, and internal capabilities to stimulate innovation and productivity in employees (which have been covered earlier in the book). Consequently, within this approach, the required level of market performance is a major influence on the organizational structure. However, companies operating in dynamic innovative markets are likely to require organizational structures different from those needed by companies operating in steady-state markets. Such an approach to organization based on market performance was taken by the American Telephone and Telegraph Co. in the early eighties. Expanding market potential in the data processing business prompted AT and T to organize their company into two major divisions, so that one division could plan the exploitation of this expanding potential.[4]

Several writers have suggested major influences on the organizational structure, with Byars[2] listing organizational size, the environment and technology, as follows:

Organizational size The size of a company and its particular stage of growth are given as being a key influence in determining organizational structure. The basic principle is that as a firm grows in size and employs more people, the structure needs to be modified. Similarly, as additional products or product lines are developed, an augmented structure will be likely in order to plan, implement and control their marketing. An example of this has already been given above, namely, a major split in the organization of AT and T as a result of planning a major change to its organizational strategy.[4]

Although attempts have been made to model stages of growth in the historical development of firms, not all firms follow a common set of stages; they grow at different rates, and different structures are adopted at different stages anyway. However, the principle is that growth from one size to another necessitates more people, as do additional products, while resultant complexity gives a third influence on the nature of the organizational structure that needs to be adopted as a result of growth and increased size.

to changes in the organizational structure, in order to facilitate the implementation of these strategies. Indeed, the logic of the planning framework adopted in this book is suggestive of a structure to implement strategic and operational plans, as well as to continue the full range of corporate planning stages into the future.

In fact, major empirical evidence of this relationship is that structure tends to follow or be influenced by strategy, with two major sets of results coming from the extensively documented work of Chandler[9] in the United States and Channon[10] in the United Kingdom. The work of Chandler was indicative of a direction in the establishment of structure. Opportunities would be identified in particular product-market scopes or market segments, followed by decisions to pursue these opportunities. These decisions would require a range of strategies for their pursual, which would need to be integrated with strategies already existing. Such a situation would lead to a reallocation of duties to personnel in order to be able to both plan and implement these strategies, while additional personnel might need to be appointed to augment the structure. Hence, over a period of time, changes to strategy would have caused changes to organizational structure. Such an approach has been reported as being followed by the US company, the Minnesota Mining and Manufacturing Company. 3M have pursued a strategy of growth, partly by diversification. As new products are introduced a new organizational unit is developed, with a major aim of retaining an 'entrepreneurial feel for the market'.[11]

Additionally, the personal dispositions of managers (as discussed in Chapter 9) also have an effect, and again their personal influences on strategy will be transmitted, but attitudes and values concerning personal views of the most appropriate structure are also likely to be an influence. Chandler also observed that, as strategy becomes more complex, particularly with divisionaliz-ation and international operations, structures, in order to accommodate such changes, became more complex too. Indeed, he also found a tendency for inefficiency and internal operating problems within such complexities to be a stimulus for structural change. Therefore the overall indication is that changing strategies within company evolution affect the organizational structure; this process is illustrated in Fig. 10.2.

Channon's research was based on UK companies, involving a historical examination of

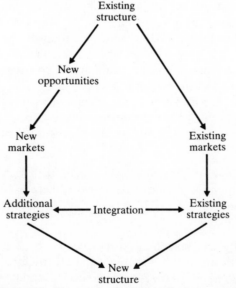

Figure 10.2 The process of strategy affecting structure

structural changes in a sample of manufacturing companies during the sixties. The investigation showed a trend away from structures based upon the individual functions towards a divisionalization based upon product-market scopes. Like the research of Chandler, this was in a period when the firms had pursued an organizational strategy of diversification. Channon also identified the same type of trend towards divisionalization in UK service companies, where again diversification was found to be associated with the changes in structure. Again the implication is that adoption of certain strategies requires certain changes to organizational structure as a consequence. Different approaches to divisionalization through strategy are illustrated in a report of the acquisition of the US company Airco by the BOC Group. The latter was described as having a decentralized structure with subsidiary companies within the countries of the southern hemisphere, with each subsidiary having its own autonomy. However, Airco was structured as a number of divisions of a single company, whose top managers were centralized at the company's headquarters in Montvale, New Jersey, so that decision making was within a centralized structure.[12]

However, writers such as Doyle[3] and Gluck, Kaufman and Walleck[13] have discussed the logic of structure affecting strategy. Doyle raises the issue that organizations must adopt to people. Indeed a company can be considered to be the range of people that work in it. In Chapter 9 the question of resistance to change was raised, which can be equally applicable to changes in structure, if they are perceived as representing a threat to personal security or status. In this type of situation it is likely that, although new strategies may be developed, they will be accommodated into current structures. Here Gluck and co-authors observe that, for many companies, the planning structure is 'force-fitted into the current organizational structure'.

Additionally, the organizational structure can be used as a component part of organizational strategy, in the form of a competitive advantage. As highlighted in Chapter 5, strength in expertise of managers can obviously represent a major company strength to be used to gain competitive advantage. A strong marketing orientation within top management could be indicative of a need to organize the company around major market groups, which in itself could give the ability to develop new or modified strategies to exploit these markets. A similar approach has been followed by the Japanese car manufacturer Nissan, of whom a major objective of has been to establish itself as leader of the Japanese industry by exceeding the market share of Toyota. Part of its competitive advantage strategy at the time of the report was a reorganization of its 50-man board of directors, including making a total of seven directors responsible for sales/marketing.[14] Therefore it is probably reasonable to claim that, although strategies are likely to have a major effect on organizational structure, in certain circumstances a certain company structure can also have an effect in formulating strategy.

The final issue in this section is that of a classification of types of companies based upon their stage of structural development as a consequence of the effects of strategy. Thompson and Strickland[15] have given four stages of structural development, which are highlighted as follows:

Stage 1 This is the initial stage of company development, with many firms being managed by a single person, or a small number of managers. There is likely to be a single business company where most personnel report directly to the owner or chief executive.

Stage 2 At this stage of development the firm recognizes a need to employ management specialists and to arrange the managers into some kind of structure. Again, at this stage there is likely to be a single business, although the functional specialisms and their staff can be reasonably well developed.

Stage 3 This classification is representative of a single product line, although markets will be sufficiently spread geographically to warrant decentralization of the business. Consequently, the structure needs to encompass a headquarters structure as well as structures to deal wtih overseas operations.

Stage 4 This classification is reserved for firms that have developed into large multi-product and multi-market organizations, whose business is in several product-market scopes. Consequently, strategies are well developed and are likely to be complex, while the very nature of the development of such companies means that they will feature complex organizational structures.

ORGANIZATIONAL STRUCTURE: THE TOTAL COMPANY

The range of influences given in the last section will provide an impetus for considering the overall organizational structure of the company in total. In addition, the overall organizational structure needs to accommodate both strategic and operational management, in order to allow for job functions, with the responsibility for managing both long-range direction and day-to-day activities. Writers such as Cleland and King[16] have suggested that traditional organizational structures of many companies have not been orientated towards long-range strategic management, but have tended to be based upon the management of the individual business functions, such as manufacturing, marketing and personnel. Similarly, Sherwin[17] has suggested that the traditional fragmentation of structures based upon the business functions has caused problems in the achievement of organizational objectives, by preventing sufficient attention being given to the integration of these functions. Britain's largest packaging company, the Metal Box Company, have recently featured a major reorganization. The firm was organized into four divisions based upon their four major markets: beverage packaging, food packaging, caps and closures, and general packaging. This concentration on markets has shifted the orientation from functions to the future direction of each division.[18]

Location of the responsibility for strategic planning within the structure is probably more problematic than locating that for operational planning. Although strategic planning is the province of the board of directors, many firms will have directors whose positions are linked directly to the business functions of manufacturing and marketing etc. Consequently, 'running' their respective departments may preclude a major contribution to strategic planning. For some companies the responsibility will be allocated to the managing director, and indeed this job function, by its very nature, merits a major involvement. However, in large companies it is unlikely that the full range of these duties could be completed by one executive. One alternative is to employ a specialist to perform the function, as an assistant to the managing director. In larger firms, operating in several product-market scopes, it may be that a corporate planning department is structured into the organization, either as an extension of the function of managing director or as a hierarchial layer between the board and the rest of the company. However, a major problem here is in deciding whether or not such specialists should perform an advisory/consultancy role, or whether they should be part of the 'in-line' responsibility for company management. A major part of the reorganization at Nissan, in its challenge to Toyota, included the establishment of a director responsible to the board for strategic planning. However, the job function also included responsibility for product planning, giving a direct link into marketing operations, and quality control, giving a direct link into manufacturing operations.[14]

Also to be considered is the degree of participation to be established for each level of management. Two considerations are appropriate here. The first is the concept that managers within the marketing department should participate in strategic planning, as well as completing their operational plans. For larger organizations it may be that there is justification for employing marketing personnel to concentrate on strategic planning, leaving the marketing department free to concentrate on operational planning. In such a situation, integration between the two sets of managers would obviously be of prime importance, particularly in relation to the personal dispositions of each executive (as discussed in Chapter 9). The way in which the marketing executives are structured into the organization will also affect the degree of marketing orientation that the firm as a whole will be able to achieve, to which fuller attention will now be given.

Company-wide marketing orientation

As will be appreciated by the readers of this book, marketing orientation is concerned with a full understanding and utilization of the marketing concept, the principles of which were given in Chapter 1. The utilization of a corporate planning framework, as developed within this book, will provide a basis for marketing orientation. The ramifications of the marketing concept within each of the stages of both strategic and operational planning, as described in the chapters of Parts Two and Three, will provide a disciplining of marketing thinking at different levels of management, while addressing the relevant stages of planning decision-making. Consequently, the establishment of job functions, throughout the organizational structure, with responsibility for the full range of corporate planning stages, with the associated marketing ramifications, will contribute to the spread of company-wide marketing orientation.

However, as marketing orientation also includes an overall philosophy towards the business, managerial attitudes and values also feature in the achievement of company-wide marketing orientation. Consequently, the establishment by the board of directors of marketing orientation as a major value within the company is likely to promote company-wide marketing orientation. Again, the example of the US company Gould Inc. is pertinent here, where the company established a declared marketing-orientated top management structure, based upon four distinct product groups to serve four market areas.[5] For some companies, particularly those in traditionally based industries, it may be that a formal marketing job function does not appear within the organizational structure. Although marketing tasks may have been performed by other executives, it may be decided that the appointment of a marketing executive would enhance, or indeed establish, their marketing orientation. Such an approach was taken by the Swiss watch industry, whose worldwide market share had fallen from 30 per cent to 9 per cent, due to the introduction of cheap quartz watches. To help restore their share a consortium, Asuag-SSIH, was established. Additionally, a subsidiary of the consortium was formed to manufacture and market cheap fashion watches. Marketing orientation was developed in the subsidiary by employing a well-experienced marketing director from a recognized marketing-oriented company in the cosmetics industry, as well as by orientating the development of their new product line to the requirements of the fashion market.[19]

However, a positive attitude to the value of marketing in achieving business success needs to be adopted by all managers. On-going education and training may need to be given to marketing executives, with the aim of updating their knowledge of methods and techniques. Non-marketing executives may also need education and training, but towards obtaining an appreciation of the value of marketing to the business. In situations where firms experience hardened negative attitudes towards the value of marketing, then additional recourse is likely to be needed to achieve company-wide marketing orientation.

Finally, Kotler[20] has suggested a number of ways to build company-wide marketing orientation. These are given as follows:

Chief-executive leadership Marketing orientation must start at the top of the organizational structure. Such leadership shows company belief in the value of marketing, emphasized by the example of the senior level of authority.

Marketing task force The suggestion is that a task force or committee should be established for a few years, charged with the task of spreading marketing orientation through the organizational structure. It is also suggested that the chief executive should be included, and so should personnel from the non-marketing functions.

External consultants Another alternative is to take advantage of the expertise and experience of outside experts, either as part of the task force, or else to specialize in certain tasks within certain parts of the structure.

Corporate marketing department The aim of this is to co-ordinate the marketing activities in companies that are organized into several divisions or SBUs. Here the aim would be to integrate all marketing into the full range of stages of corporate planning, as well as to provide advice to individual marketing departments.

In-house seminars A range of courses on marketing could be established, based upon the needs of individual groups at different levels within the structure and working in different departments.

Hiring marketing expertise Here the advice is to augment existing marketing staff by bringing in expertise from outside the company, either executives well experienced and currently employed by other companies, or perhaps newly qualified executives with either masters' degrees or professional qualifications.

Promoting marketing-orientated executives Here the suggestion is a policy to promote those executives who exhibit developments in marketing orientation in the performance of their job functions.

Installing a marketing planning system This is a ratification of the structure of this book, in that establishing the planning of marketing at both the strategic and operational levels of management provides a vehicle for promoting marketing orientation within the organizational structure.

Alternative structures

Despite the lead taken by both Chandler and Channon, little research has been forthcoming to identify the alternative organizational structures adopted by companies. However, given the range of influences as explained earlier in this chapter, it is probably valid to surmise that, for most firms, the structure is changed frequently. Indeed, it can probably also be surmised that many individual company differences within structures exist, even though broad common types are evident. Below are examined five major common types, based upon business functions, product divisions/SBUs, geographical divisions, hybrid forms, and matrix approaches.

Functional organizational structure Perhaps the simplest form of structure is where the company is organized into departments based upon the individual business functions, such as are illustrated in Fig. 10.3. This form allows for specialization within the departments, is likely to be suitable for single product companies, and is easy to administer. However, the disadvantages are that problems of inter-departmental co-ordination, integration, communication and rivalry can arise. Also, at its simplest this form tends to result in an orientation towards operational planning, with a neglect of strategic planning. Here an extra layer can be introduced as a general manager or as a staff function to modify the approach, although the tendency may still be towards insular departments.

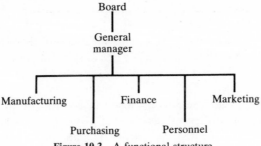

Figure 10.3 A functional structure

Product division/SBU organizational structure Here the company has several product lines that serve different markets, allowing for divisionalization of the structure to effectively serve each of these markets separately. The advantage is that each division can concentrate its business activities on both a specific product line and the specific needs of the markets that they serve. Additionally, the full range of planning stages can be specified for a particular business area. In larger firms, strategic planning may be necessary both for the company as a whole and for each of the divisions/SBUs, while operational planning will obviously be necessary for each division. The previous example of the divisionalization of the Metal Box Co. is also pertinent here. This was based upon four product groups serving four different sets of different market needs, being beverages, food, caps and closures, and general packaging.[18] The general principle of this type of divisionalization is given in Fig. 10.4.

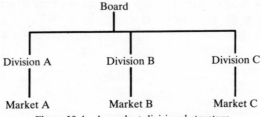

Figure 10.4 A product divisional structure

Geographic divisional structure In companies that can be classified as being international in nature, in that they market their products in many diverse countries, some form of geographic organizational structure is generally appropriate. The major advantage is that each division is able to serve more effectively the specific market requirements of a particular geographical area. Consequently, planning can be also specific to that area, while it may again be the case that for a large company each division will require strategic plans separate from those of the company as a whole, as well as developing their own operational plans. Again a previous example is pertinent, being that of the British Oxygen Company. As outlined in the last section, at the time of the report, the company was organized into autonomous subsidiary companies within countries spread across the northern hemisphere.[12] The general principle of a geographic organizational structure is given in Fig. 10.5.

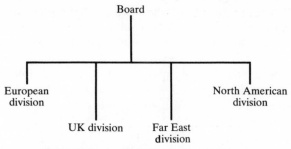

Figure 10.5 A geographic divisional structure

Hybrid organizational structures While many companies will use the three alternatives given above, many variations are featured by companies as a result of the major influences on structure, as discussed earlier in the chapter. Therefore, although there may be a divisionalization based upon SBUs, many companies would find it inefficient to duplicate all business functions for each SBU. Figure 10.6 shows a hybrid structure in which manufacturing and marketing are performed by each division, while other functions are centralized. A similar structure was utilized by the US food manufacturer Beatrice Foods in 1978. This structure featured centralized accounting, legal and administration departments at the corporate headquarters, with other functions being located in both product and geographical divisions.[21]

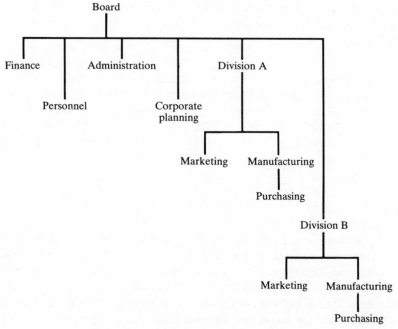

Figure 10.6 A hybrid organizational structure

Similarly, a hybrid structure could be based upon local geographical operations and home-country centralized control. Here the hybrid splits vary from geographical divisions which are merely overseas sales offices to autonomous overseas subsidiary companies, with the corporate headquarters merely representing an integrative role. The advantages of hybrid structures are their efficiency, as mentioned earlier, plus their ability to serve specific market requirements, but of major importance is their flexibility in being adaptable both to the nature of the company and to variations found in the nature of different products, markets and countries.

Matrix organizational structures This form of structure aims to integrate the advantage of specialism through functional organization, with the advantage of concentration on specific markets through divisionalization. A general example is given in Fig. 10.7.

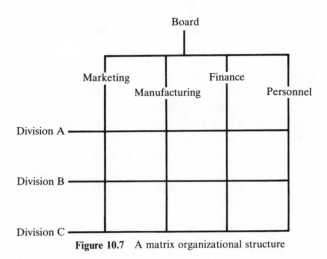

Figure 10.7   A matrix organizational structure

There are several features of such a structure. First, there are two channels of command, so that marketing personnel will be responsible to both the chief executive of marketing and the chief executive of the division in which the products they work with are located. Another feature is that each person has a dual role, namely the efficient discharge of the function in which they specialize and their contribution to the performance of the division to which they relate. However, a major problem that features in matrix structures is defining authority and responsibility. The priorities of the marketing department can obviously spread across the three divisions, with responsibility for marketing decisions in all divisions, but the authority of the chief executive of division A may be undermined in the functional departments, especially if functional resources need to be carefully allocated to divisions. A matrix structure has been adopted by Wadkin, manufacturers of woodworking machinery. At the beginning of 1980 the company was organized into three divisions, each with its own chairman. It was recognized that each division could not work as a self-contained unit and therefore a matrix structure was introduced. Of particular importance was not only the establishment of a centralized marketing department to lead the marketing planning, but also the expectation that the divisional boards would take an active part in marketing through the matrix structure.[22]

The matrix structure will also accommodate a corporate planning system. Here it is likely that strategic planning would be completed by each division, while marketing personnel would provide the marketing inputs at the interface. Additionally, each functional department would obviously be responsible for its appropriate operational planning, while the interrelationships in the matrix would allow for the integration of planning.

ORGANIZATIONAL STRUCTURE: THE MARKETING DEPARTMENT

In the last section the location of responsibility for both strategic and operational planning was emphasized within each of the different types of organizational structure. In companies where the marketing department is concerned only with operations, the strategic planning of marketing will be performed elsewhere in the structure, at either board or divisional level, or within a specialist planning department. In 1979, Doyle[3] claimed that, because of the introduction of long-range strategic planning in many organizations, many marketing decisions had been diffused and the autonomy of marketing management had been curtailed. Consequently, he was observing a tendency for decisions concerning the strategic planning of marketing to be removed from the marketing department to elsewhere in the organizational structure, leaving the marketing department with only the operational planning of marketing.

However, Doyle goes on to explain that the concept of marketing is intended to be a philosophy of business, as outlined in Chapter 1. Indeed, the focus of this book is on both the strategic and operational planning of marketing, so that marketing needs to be used as a tool of management in, as already presented in Parts Two and Three, not only the marketing department, but also higher levels of the organizational structure. This in fact was illustrated within the different approaches to the total company organizational structure given in the last section, especially in the development of company-wide marketing orientation, while the company illustrations used there are also useful in this context. A major criticism of Doyle was that many organizations have merely developed larger specialist marketing departments, neglecting to develop company-wide orientation, including the use of marketing in long-range planning.

Alternative structures

As with total company organizational structures, little research has been forthcoming to identify alternative organizational structures of marketing departments. Again, it can be surmised that many individual company differences within structures exist, even though broad common types are evident. Alternatives for the structure of the marketing department tend to reflect those for the total company, so that the major common types examined below are based upon functions, products and markets, matrix approaches, and divisionalization.

Functional structure As with the total company organization, this is the simplest form of marketing department, its structure being based upon the functions of marketing. With this type of structure, the strategic planning of marketing could be the full responsibility of the marketing manager, or it could be the responsibility of a planning department, with contributions from marketing personnel, or it could be performed by the board. The general case of the latter is illustrated in Fig. 10.8. Again, the advantage of such a structure is that it allows for specialization within the functions, allowing for strength in marketing operations. However, when a company has more than a single product then a problem arises in that there is only the marketing manager to integrate the marketing of all products.

Another problem is that the structure is orientated to a divorce of strategic and operational planning. Although the marketing manager would participate, the functional focus of other marketing executives would probably limit the value of their participation.

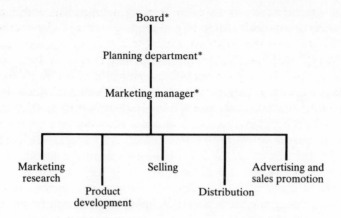

*Alternatives for the strategic planning of marketing

Figure 10.8   A marketing department functional structure

Product/market management structures To overcome the problem of integration within the department, many companies include in their structure managers to concentrate on specific products or markets. These brand, product or market managers would certainly be responsible for operational marketing planning, but strategic marketing planning could be achieved through a number of alternatives. There could be a marketing planning manager in the department who could lead strategic planning, including other marketing executives, or there could again be a planning department, or again it could be performed by the board; a general illustration is given in Fig. 10.9.

*Alternatives for the strategic planning of marketing

Figure 10.9   A marketing department product/market management structure

In this type of structure there is an extra layer of management within the hierarchy, as depicted by the managers responsible for selling, marketing services and marketing planning. The aims are that there are three specialists to allow for concentration and development of the functions of marketing. Additionally, the product managers also lead the planning for their respective product groups, allowing for operational planning as well as its integration into the strategic planning of marketing, regardless of where in the structure this is located. However, research into US firms by Cossé and Swan[23] has suggested that product managers in their respondent firms tend not to be involved with strategic planning. The implication is, therefore, that this planning is carried out at higher levels, with only a minimum participation by the product managers.

Matrix structures As with the total company, the concept of a matrix can be utilized in the marketing department. Here the aims would be to develop concentration in the marketing functions, plus integration and planning in the product groups, but to avoid additional layers of management as developed in Fig. 10.9; a general approach to a marketing department matrix structure is given in Fig. 10.10. Again there are several alternatives for the location of the strategic planning of marketing, as previously discussed.

Once more, there are two channels of command, with the product managers having full responsibility for their products (with more authority than in Fig. 10.9), while the functional managers retain overall responsibility across the product groups. However, again as in total

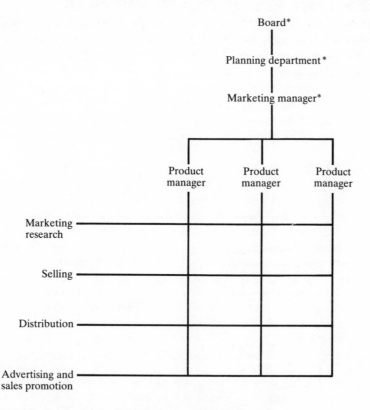

*Alternatives for the strategic planning of marketing

Figure 10.10 A marketing department matrix structure

company structures, a major problem can be that of the undermining of the authority of the product managers by the functional managers, or indeed vice versa.

Divisional structures In the last section, product/SBU and geographical structures were given as an alternative for total company organization. As indicated in that section, several marketing departments could result from the utilization of such a structure. While the operational planning would be carried out by each respective department, there could be several alternatives for the strategic planning of marketing. If each division is given autonomy, then the alternatives could be as illustrated previously in Fig. 10.9. However, another alternative is that the planning department would be located within the group headquarters, and that they would be charged with strategic planning. Similarly, some firms will structure a group or corporate marketing department into the total company structure. The aim here would be to integrate all marketing throughout the organization, including strategic planning. Finally, another alternative is to establish planning committees throughout the organization, drawn from personnel within the divisions; again, the task would be integration of operational planning and completion of strategic planning.

Case Study 14 (page 180) illustrates, within a complex company situation, many of the principles of organizational structure that have been developed in this chapter.

ADEQUACY OF THE ORGANIZATIONAL STRUCTURE

After a major reorganization of either the total company or the marketing department, due to a combination of the influences discussed earlier in the chapter, attention will need to be given to the adequacy of the new structure, including its ability to accommodate the stages of corporate planning. Byars[2] has suggested that adequacy would be reflected in the company's degree of success in achieving its objectives. However, there are obviously many interrelated variables that can affect the achievement of objectives, so that attempting to isolate the effect of just one, in this case the organizational structure, would be of limited value. Indeed, this whole concept of trying to assess the adequacy or effectiveness of the full range of planning stages is examined in the next chapter.

Also, within the literature, little attention has been given to attempting to develop methodology that can be used to assess the adequacy of structures, except, of course, for a continuous consideration of the original variables that influenced the nature of the current structure. Bates and Eldredge[24] have emphasized that regular assessments are necessary as a preventative measure, rather than waiting for a strategy failure and adjusting the structure accordingly. In principle, this is the process to be followed in controlling the implementation of plans, which is given full treatment in Part Five. The simplistic approach to assessing adequacy that is proposed by Bates and Eldredge is based upon a consideration of the following:

- The ability of the structure to be able to continue to support the company's strategies.
- The ability of the structure to be able to accommodate expected changes in the total environment.
- The ability of the structure to be able to provide the critical factors for success.

However, using such criteria appears to remain as a process of value judgement, in that the authors do not propose methodology to allow for measurement against these criteria. Further attention will be given to the adequacy of organizational structure in Part Five, within the context of control.

SUMMARY

In Chapter 10 attention has been given to the organization of managers into a structure, and the effects of organizational structure on both the strategic and operational planning of marketing.

The first section considered major influences on organizational structure that would be likely to cause modifications to the current structure. This resulted in four groups of influences, the first being the environment, market performance and competition and the second being accountability and ownership. The third was company evolution, size and technology, while the last group was based on managerial values. Attention was then given to the matching of organizational structure to adopted strategies. Available evidence is that structure tends to follow and be affected by the strategies that firms adopt. However, there is also an a-priori case that the organizational structure can affect a firm's ability to be able to adopt modified strategies, and attention was also given to this relationship.

The second section examined approaches to the organizational structure of the total company. This involved a consideration of company-wide marketing orientation before an examination of alternative organizational structures. The latter were based upon the business functions, product divisions/SBUs, geographical divisions, hybrid forms, and matrix approaches. Approaches to the organizational structure of the marketing department were then considered. These were based upon the marketing functions, product and market management, matrix approaches and divisionalization.

Finally, the chapter considered the adequacy of organizational structures. Little has been developed in the literature to assist in the assessment of adequacy, although the major problem of assessment was highlighted.

CASE STUDY 14: ALFA-LAVAL*

Case outline

Alfa-Laval is a Swedish corporate group, with worldwide operations in the form of over 70 subsidiaries in 32 countries. The company produces equipment for the following industries: farming, food, marine, chemical, engineering, metal-producing, and pollution control. The case deals with the many complexities of the organizational structure needed to accommodate these diverse product-market scopes.

Illustration

Given the complexities of organizing for such a wide range of countries, subsidiary companies, industries, products and markets, it is not surprising that a single case study document is not adequate to fully explain Alfa-Laval's organizational structure. However, it allows for some explanation of the overall group organizational structure, some of the influences on the structure, and the location of both the strategic and operational planning of marketing.

1 Group organizational structure

At the time of the case the group was organized into four major sectors: the executive group management, product divisions, market companies, and other companies. The nature of each of these was as follows:

1.1 Executive group management This was given as being the group headquarters management structure. This sector was broadly organized on a functional basis, including departments concerned with finance, personnel, research and development, purchasing, and public relations.

1.2 Product divisions This sector was organized into a structure of four product divisions, each of which was more or less autonomous with its own marketing and manufacturing. The four divisions were farm equipment, pulp and paper equipment, separators, and thermal and dairy equipment.

1.3 Market companies This sector consisted of the 70 subsidiaries companies located in 32 countries, but organized into a structure based upon the geographical areas of Africa, Asia, Australia, Europe, North and Central America, and Latin America. These subsidiaries were all selling companies, but some also had local manufacturing, while others had manufacturing facilities for the group.

1.4 Other companies This sector of the Alfa Laval group consisted of a number of subsidiaries representing a range of SBUs that were different businesses from the product divisions. The product-market scopes of these subsidiaries included refrigeration, pumps, centrifuges and environmental control.

The relationships between the divisions were described as being highly complex and not effectively established, which was recognized by the deputy managing director as being a major weakness. However, it is apparent that there is a matrix structure between the sectors, especially the product divisions and the market companies.

---

* Derived from O. Oftedal, Alfa-Laval. Copyright © 1978 The Swedish Institute of Management.

2 Influences on the organizational structure

The size of the Alfa Laval group clearly had an influence on the structure at the time of the case study. The complexities within the structure must have also been influenced by the firm's size, particularly as a result of the number of people needed in order to participate in the range of countries and products.

Developments within the marketing environment were also apparent. Flexibility was needed owing to the cyclical fluctuations experienced in the demand for dairy equipment, while increased demands were being identified for new industrial equipment. This had included company acquisitions to augment the structure, while they were moving towards supplying complete installation systems as opposed to particular pieces of equipment supplied as specific products. This also reflects the influence of technology, in that acquisitions also provided new technology, although research and development was becoming a central feature of the structure.

Evolution had also had an influence. The company was intiated with an invention to separate cream from milk. The equipment was unique to the company on a global basis, so that overseas sales were easily achieved, leading to the establishment of sales companies in many countries. Further evolution led to overseas manufacturing, which started in the United States. Additionally, Alfa Laval faced only a few competitors, so that the firm was able to grow and expand its organizational structure.

3 The planning of marketing

Each of the product divisions was responsible for its own operational marketing planning. Responsibility for strategic planning is not totally clear, although there was probably some responsibility as each division was required to develop their own product range. However, the group organizational structure included a corporate planning department to establish overall strategic planning.

Additionally, the market companies were responsible for planning their own marketing tactics. Here product ranges were provided for each of the countries by the product divisions. The result appears to be that the marketing tactics became almost totally orientated towards selling. However, at the time of the case, many executives were aware of the many weaknesses of such an approach to their marketing, including weak matching of products or markets, orientation to short-term gains, and weak new-product development.

Consequently, the group managing director was attempting to establish a new initiative for the planning of marketing, as an integrated process between the divisions and the subsidiaries.

REVIEW QUESTIONS

1. Explain why many writers emphasize that there is no ideal method to arrive at the 'correct' organizational structure.
2. Could it be that the probable relationship between strategy and structure is cyclical in nature? Discuss.
3. 'Given that we already have a marketing department there seems to be little point in pursuing marketing orientation within the organizational structure.' Discuss.
4. What is the point of trying to identify commonality in organizational structures when there are such vast differences in company situations?
5. Present the case both for and against the location of strategic planning within the marketing department.

REFERENCES

1. Jain, S. C., *Marketing Planning and Strategy*, South-Western Publishing, Cincinnati, 1981.
2. Byars, L. L., *Strategic Management*, Harper and Row, New York, 1984.
3. P. Doyle, 'Management structures and marketing strategies in UK industry', *European Journal of Marketing*, **13**, 5, 319–31, 1979.
4. 'AT and T's fast move on baby Bell', *Business Week*, 18 September, 1980.
5. 'Gould's golden gamble', *Management Today*, February 1984.
6. Hunt, J. W., *The Restless Organisation*, Wiley, Chichester, 1972.
7. Johnson, G., and K. Scholes, *Exploring Corporate Strategy*, Prentice-Hall, London, 1984.
8. 'Italy's most talked-about executive', *Fortune*, 15 March 1984.
9. Chandler, A. D., *Strategy and Structure*, MIT Press, Cambridge, 1962.
10. Channon, D. F., *The Strategy and Structure of British Enterprise*, Macmillan, London, 1973.
11. 'Eight big masters of innovation', *Fortune*, 15 October, 1984.
12. 'BOC goes West', *Management Today*, January, 1984.
13. F. Gluck, S. Kaufman and A. S. Walleck, 'The four stages of strategic management', *Journal of Business Strategy*, **2**, 3, 9–21, 1982.
14. 'Toyota pulls away from Nissan', *Fortune*, 19 September, 1983.
15. Thompson, A. A., and A. J. Strickland, *Strategy Formulation and Implementation*, Business Publications, Plano, 1983.
16. D. Cleland and W. R. King, 'Developing a planning culture for more effective strategic planning', *Long Range Planning*, **7**, 3, 70–4, 1974.
17. D. W. Sherwin, 'Management of objectives', *Harvard Business Review*, **54**, 3, 149–60, 1976.
18. 'The remaking of Metal Box', *Management Today*, January 1985.
19. 'The Swiss put glitz in cheap quartz watches', *Fortune*, 20 August, 1984.
20. Kotler, P., *Marketing management: analysis, planning and control*, 5th edn, Prentice-Hall, Englewood Cliffs, 1984.
21. 'Beatrice Foods', *Business Week*, 15 May, 1978.
22. 'How Wadkin worked clear', *Management Today*, May 1984.
23. T. J. Cossé, and J. E. Swan, 'Strategic marketing planning by product managers—room for improvement?', *Journal of Marketing*, **47**, 2, 92–102, 1983.
24. Bates, D. L., and D. L. Eldredge, *Strategy and Policy*, 2nd edn, Brown, Dubuque, 1984.

ELEVEN
PLANNING EFFECTIVENESS

Learning objectives are to:

1. Appreciate the nature of effectiveness and the problems associated with its definition.
2. Understand the performance/end results approach to assessing effectiveness.
3. Understand the multidimensional approach to assessing effectiveness.
4. Be aware of the assumed benefits approach to assessing effectiveness.
5. Be able to discuss the range of arguments both for and against the different approaches to assessing effectiveness.
6. Recognize major concepts that have been introduced.

At this point within the book, the stages of both the strategic and the operational planning of marketing have been established, the influences of managers on that planning have been examined, and structural implications of the organization on planning have been addressed. Before we consider the implementation of plans in the next part of the book, attention is directed to the consideration of whether the resultant planning is likely to be effective.

In simple terms, any planning can be considered to be effective if it has the ability to produce the required results. However, here there are two basic problems. First, a method would need to be developed to assess the 'potential ability' of the planning. Second, a method would need to be developed to determine whether or not planning had actually caused certain results, or whether other variables were also causes. Indeed, there are other problems in explaining the nature of effectiveness so that the whole concept of understanding effectiveness will be examined in the first section of this chapter, as well as the potential advantages to be gained from using planning.

The next section is concerned with one of the three major methods that have been currently proposed within the literature to assess the effectiveness of planning. This approach is based upon a measurement of the performance or end results achieved by the implementation of planning. The second major method is then examined in the next section. This is to assess the effectiveness of the planning as a process, by the examination of certain attributes within the planning, and is labelled the multidimensional approach. The final major method is based upon the intrinsic values of planning; it is concerned not with end results or the planning process, but is concerned with additional benefits to be gained as a consequence of planning. These are intrinsic in that the benefits occur as a result of planning, being both internal and external.

The concept of the effectiveness of planning is relatively new. Early attempts to measure effectiveness were limited and were based upon an examination of end results. Approaches based upon the process itself are being developed in the literature, although attention has not intensified. Consequently, there is almost an absence of company illustrations to draw upon, while there are few case studies that can be used for illustrative purposes. In the former there are only weak indications of examples of planning effectiveness. For example, Quaker Oats had planned and implemented a diversification strategy in the United States in the early seventies. However, the strategy had failed by 1980 so that they were changing their direction back to a mission based on food. Such an example is reflective of the ineffective planning of organizational strategy.[1] The UK advertising agency Saatchi and Saatchi achieved extensive growth in size and improvements to profitability over a similar time period. A major contributor to this success was reported to be 'stringent planning', which is indicative of effectiveness in planning.[2]

UNDERSTANDING EFFECTIVENESS

In this section attention is given to developing an understanding of effectiveness, despite the problems of definition mentioned in the introduction. Therefore the first consideration in this section is the range of problems associated with defining effectiveness. The second consideration is the range of potential advantages to be gained from the utilization of planning, while the understanding is completed with an overview of the three major approaches to assessing effectiveness.

Problems of definition

A range of problems in defining the nature of effectiveness has been discussed in a recent article by Greenley,[3] where four approaches were given, but all featured problems. These are labelled basic definitions, cost-and-return-based definitions, degrees of effectiveness, and definitions based on the nature of the planning process.

Basic definitions As mentioned in the introduction, this is the ability of planning to achieve a desired level of performance or end results. These are initially established within both the strategic and operational planning of marketing, in the form of objectives, strategies and tactics. After the plans are implemented the actual results are compared with the desired levels in the plans. If the actual results equal or exceed the desired levels then it is simply concluded that the planning was effective. However, the problem here is determining whether or not the planning caused the end results, or whether the many other variables within the internal and external environments were the major causes of the company performance and end results.

Another approach has been suggested by Kudla.[4] Here planning is defined as being effective if it results in capturing potential opportunities and avoiding potential problems. The problem of definition here is that current decision makers cannot know of the future consequences of the current range of decisions open to them to pursue opportunities and avoid threats. Although an assessment could be made in the future (after the implementation of current plans), this assessment obviously cannot benefit current planning.

Cost-and-return-based definitions An approach given by Ansoff and Brandenburg[5] is to define planning as being effective if the annual increments to the earnings of the firm, which result from using a particular planning process, exceed the earnings that would have been achieved without the benefit of the planning. Again the problem is determining a cause-and-effect relationship. Although increased sales revenue may have been achieved when more attention was given to the sophistication of planning other variables within the environment could again have been the major cause.

- Stimulates a co-operative, integrated and enthusiastic approach to tackling problems and opportunities.
- Encourages a favourable attitude to change.
- Gives a degree of discipline and formality to management that may not exist without planning.

The consequence of these advantages is that planning could be claimed to be useful and beneficial, even if it cannot be measured as being effective in the sense described earlier in this section. Indeed, it could be argued that these advantages are sufficient in themselves to claim that planning is effective, in that it allows for certain advantages within the management of an organization, that would not be achieved without the utilization of planning. However, if the value of planning is to develop, and if methodology within both strategic and operational planning is also to develop, then such developments must surely need to be justified by more than assumptions as to its effectiveness.

Approaches to assessing effectiveness

From the above discussions it is apparent that there are currently three available approaches for assessing the effectiveness of planning. These are as follows:

The performance/end-results approach This consists of attempting to determine the effect of planning on the performance of the firm through the achievement of objectives or end results.
The multidimensional approach This involves assessing the nature of the planning itself by looking to identify a range of attributes, the presence of which is taken to represent effectiveness.
The assumed-benefits approach This merely consists of assuming that planning is effective in that its utilization is likely to result in a range of advantages.

The next three sections of this chapter are concerned with an examination of each of these approaches in turn.

THE PERFORMANCE/END-RESULTS APPROACH

This follows the stages of planning as presented in Parts Two and Three of the book. As the approach is applicable to planning *per se*, it means that it can be utilized for both strategic and operational planning. The approach follows the logic of the stages of planning, at either the strategic or operational levels, so that planning is assessed to be effective if the performance of the plan produces end results at the levels which were initially established in the objectives. The approach can also be extended to address the effectiveness of different areas of the business. Where there are separate strategic plans for different divisions or SBUs then different assessments can be made, while the operational plans for these different areas would warrant different assessments. Similarly, it may be deemed beneficial to also attempt to assess effectiveness relative to performance in individual markets or by individual products. However, the overall approach to assessment is common. Here the basic criteria are based upon the objectives, but these can be extended to include the budget and certain measurements taken during the stage of control. For each criterion, effectiveness is assessed by comparing the actual end results with the planned levels. Full achievement in the range of objectives would give the conclusion that the planning was effective. However, partial achievement in some or all of the criteria gives rise to the problem of determining a degree of effectiveness, as explained in the previous section.

Further assessments can be made by using details given in budgets as assessment criteria, and comparing these with their related actual end results. Again, comparisons can be made for different divisions, SBUs, products, or markets, in order to identify areas of effectiveness. In addition where budgets are presented on a monthly basis, then particular periods of the year may exhibit effects on overall effectiveness. Of particular importance, in such an assessment, is the achievement in levels of contribution. Here effectiveness can be determined relative to the contribution made by a particular product or market, both before and after the deduction of operational marketing costs. These assessments would measure not only the effectiveness of the product, or that achieved within a particular market, but also the effectiveness of the associated marketing operations. In addition, assessments within the budget can also be related to sales, costs and profits by comparing these with the end results, and are likely to be more detailed than when using the objectives as criteria. Again, the advantage is in being able to be more specific in identifying sources of both effectiveness and ineffectiveness. Similar specificity can also be achieved by using control measurements as criteria. These predominantly relate to ratio analysis and marketing mix efficiency indicators, which will be discussed as part of control in Part Five. In the former, effectiveness can be determined by comparing actual ratios against those achieved in previous years, or those established by the company as being desireable. Where efficiency indicators are to be used, then again the assessment of effectiveness is by comparing actual measurements with selected standards. Again the problem of assessment of effectiveness arises where there are situations of only partial achievement of some of the criteria. The link of assessing effectiveness with control procedures will be pursued further in Part Five.

Epitomizing the major criticism of this approach is the problem of determining whether or not the end results were caused by the planning, as described in the last section. Although the levels established in the objectives and budget may have been attained, there are many variables within the overall business environment, any combination of which could have caused the levels of performance. The problem of determining a cause-and-effect relationship is that, given the range of variables and lack of control which the firm has over many of these, it is difficult for it to measure the effect of independent variables while keeping others constant. Consequently, this situation means that the effects of planning on the end results are equally difficult to determine, as any combination of both internal and external variables could have been involved. Internally, the many variables of the marketing tactics could have themselves been a major cause, regardless of the level of sophistication in their planning. Likewise, the other business functions could also have affected end results and again the net effect of, say, production improvements is difficult to determine within the combined effects of other factors. Externally, the actions of competitors, for example, can also affect end results, either favourable or adversely, and again isolating their effects from the effects of planning exhibits the same basic problem. Buyer behaviour within the

---

Studies claiming a relationship
- Ansoff et al.:[9] 1970, 93 US companies
- Gershefski:[10] 1970, 323 US companies
- Thune and House:[11] 1970, 36 US companies
- Herold:[12] 1972, 10 US companies
- Karger and Malik:[13] 1975, 90 US companies

Studies not claiming a relationship
- Fulmer and Rue:[14] 1973 and 1974, 386 US companies
- Grinyer and Norburn:[15] 1975, 21 UK companies
- Kudla:[16] 1980, 328 US companies
- Leontiades and Tezel:[17] 1980, 61 US companies

Figure 11.2 Studies of strategic planning and company performance in manufacturing companies

market-place can obviously also affect end results, owing to changes in levels of demand and purchasing patterns. Again, isolating such effects is difficult. Finally, the general social, economic, political, legal and technical environments can exert effects on end results and again the same problem is prevelent.

Given the full range of problems associated with the end-results approach to measuring effectiveness, then it is likely that the assessments described in this section are far from being solely a reflection of the effectiveness of the planning of marketing. Indeed it could be that such assessments reflect the overall effectiveness of the total company performance, of which strategic and operational planning are but a part. In addition, effects of external variables in some situations may mean that such assessments only partly reflect effectiveness within the company, as opposed to merely reflecting occurrences within the external environment.

Empirical studies

The reported studies that have attempted to investigate a relationship between formal planning and end results have been within the context of overall company performance. Therefore they have investigated the possible relationship between strategic planning and total company performance.

Greenley[8] has reported a comparison of the studies carried out in relation to manufacturing companies. The literature search for this report identified nine relevant investigations, of which five were found to claim that companies which utilize formal strategic planning achieve higher levels of performance or end results than companies which do not utilize strategic planning. However, the other four studies did not claim to have identified such a relationship. These studies are given in Fig. 11.2. From this initial view of the overall results, the conflicting conclusions obviously indicate that a firm conclusion as to the relationship of strategic planning to performance cannot be drawn. Indeed the above-mentioned article, at this stage, goes on to examine each of these studies relative to both their methodological rigor and results in order to attempt to draw a firm conclusion as to the planning/performance relationship.

However, the outcome of this examination was that a firm conclusion could still not be reached, as seven major areas of criticism were found to be common across the studies. These can be summarized as follows:

- An examination of methodology was indicative of all the studies being not particularly rigorous in their approach.
- Sample characteristics varied across all studies so that differences in results could not be deduced to be due to such differences.
- None of the studies gave evidence of an attempt to identify other variables that could also have affected end results, when they were measuring planning effects.
- All studies featured subjectivity in defining formality of planning and in differentiating between planners and non-planners.
- Indications of researcher bias were also evident across the studies.
- There was a lack of commonality of sample and methodology characteristics, giving difficulty in the cross-validation of results.
- Apart from two studies, the statistical significance of results was not reported by the researchers.

In addition to the above studies of manufacturing companies, other similar studies of other types of organizations have also been carried out. These major studies are given in Fig. 11.3. Again, there is a difference in conclusions, with two studies claiming to have found that firms with strategic planning achieve higher levels of performance than firms that do not, while the other four studies did not claim to have identified such a relationship. An examination of the nature of these studies, similar to that for manufacturing companies, also led to the same finding, that these studies do not allow for a firm judgement as to the relationship of strategic planning to company performance.

Studies claiming a relationship
– Hegarty:[18] 1976, 46 US companies
– Wood and La Forge:[19] 1979, 61 US commercial banks

Studies not claiming a relationship
– Kallman and Shapiro:[20] 1978, 298 US freight carriers
– Robinson and Pearce:[21] 1983, 50 small US banks
– Sapp and Seiler:[22] 1981, 302 US commercial banks
– Sheehan:[23] 1975, 300 large Canadian companies

Figure 11.3 Additional studies of strategic planning and company performance

Consequently, it is concluded that the research published to date is far from final in establishing a relationship between strategic planning and performance or end results. The difficulty of being able to isolate the effects of planning on performance from the effects of other variables is likely to remain a major obstacle in the pursual of this avenue of research. However, it could be argued that there is an a-priori case that, by its very nature, planning can be assumed to have some effect on end results and that the magnitude of that effect is not really important, but what is important is that it does provide a contribution to the overall efficiency of the total company performance. Indeed, owing to the very complexity of company situations, the same argument could be applied to all aspects of the business that affect its overall performance, from the interpersonal relationships of personnel to the availability of finance, but again the need for such variables to allow for the achievement of end results is almost self-evident.

However, this does not detract from the importance of planning, which remains a central concept within management, as initially established in Part One. The value of planning at both the strategic and operational levels should be apparent to the reader at this point in the book, while the failure of this avenue of research to identify a direct relationship with end results should not detract from the role to be played by planning at all levels of management. This now leads to an examination of the nature of planning itself, rather than its effects, which is the subject of the next section.

THE MULTIDIMENSIONAL APPROACH

As already established, this approach is concerned with assessing effectiveness by examining the nature of planning, rather than by assessing the end results. In examining planning, the approach is to investigate the incidence of certain attributes or features, the presence of which is taken to indicate that the planning is likely to be effective. The reliance of this approach on a range of attributes thus gives a multidimensional approach, where the assessment of end results is avoided. However, this approach also exhibits problems in its utilization, which were emphasized earlier in the chapter. As these problems need to be considered in explaining the multidimensional approach, they are restated at this point. They relate to: defining the nature of the attributes to use; attaining an adequate set of attributes; achieving a common acceptance of these and their weightings; and knowing whether or not the chosen attributes will achieve the intended results. Therefore, although this approach attempts to overcome the difficulties of the performance/end results approach, it also exhibits a set of inherent problems itself.

An early discussion of the examination of the nature of planning was given by Ackoff[24] relative to corporate planning, although methodology for assessment was not developed. Here Ackoff classifies planning systems as being either satisfying, optimizing or adaptivizing, with the last providing the most effective type of planning. This type of planning has three distinct features, as seen by Ackoff. The first is that the advantage is seen to lie in the actual process of planning itself, as completed by managers, as opposed to the end results that it produces. Hence effectiveness is developed within the process itself. The second is that the need for planning arises out of ineffective management. Therefore, by definition and as a result of this situation, the aim of planning is to improve the effectiveness of management, so that the process of effective planning becomes an end in itself, namely that of improving managerial performance. The final feature given by Ackoff is that, as knowledge of the future is based upon uncertainty, planning must allow for contingency activities. This, he claims, will add further effectiveness to planning to achieve the required levels of performance.

Four major mutlidimensional approaches to assessing the effectiveness of planning have been reported in the literature. Although all take a different emphasis, each method attempts to assess the effectiveness of the nature of planning itself rather than the end results generated. These four approaches have been developed by the following writers:

Dyson and Foster[25]	1980; developed to assess the effectiveness of strategic planning.
King[26]	1983 and 1984; developed to assess the effectiveness of strategic planning.
Heroux[27]	1981; developed to be applied to planning *per se*.
Kotler[28]	1977; developed to assess the effectiveness of marketing operational planning.

The rest of this section addresses each of these multidimensional approaches to the effectiveness of planning in turn. With the exception of the Heroux approach, the others have been designated to be used to assess either strategic or operational planning. However, as will be seen later in this section, these approaches have had little testing by applying them into company situations, so that the broad nature of the approaches by Dyson and Foster and King can be applied to different types and levels of planning. Additionally, the principles of planning *per se* can be considered to be common, so that again these two approaches can be applied to different types of planning.

The Dyson and Foster approach

This utilizes 12 attributes, the presence of which, these authors consider, will reflect effectiveness in planning. The range of attributes have been developed from earlier work by Dyson[29] and are as follows:

Integration A planning process can only be effective if the plans and analyses become the focus of the decision making of the organization.

Catalytic action Planning will be more effective if planners stimulate other participants to think about developing plans.

Richness of formulation An effective system will explore a wide range of possible futures rather than concentrating solely on a single, historically extrapolated one.

Breadth of evaluation In evaluating a plan, multiple criteria, including several financial measures and measures associated with other resources, will be used by an effective system.

Treatment of uncertainty The evaluation of plans should take account of the uncertainty in estimates of demand forecasts, costs, economic environment and other exogenous variables.

Resources planned Organizations are dependent on a number of resources, including finance, manpower, raw materials and equipment, and planning should consider them all.

Data It is important that adequate data is available for planning. Insufficient data can lead to unnecessary approximation or complete gaps in planning.

Iteration in process As the plans develop through the planning cycle, information will emerge that is relevant to previously completed parts. An effective system will recognize its relevance and cause appropriate modifications to be made.

Assumptions Planning is necessarily based on assumptions. These must be explicit, so that unrealistic and inconsistent assumptions are avoided.

Quantification of goals An effective system will quantify goals where this is appropriate, but will also recognize qualitative goals.

Control measures A static plan rapidly becomes valueless in times of change. An effective system will include a feedback mechanism leading to modifications of the plans.

Feasibility of implementation An effective system will anticipate barriers to the implementation of any given plan and avoid them, remove them, or accept that they cannot be surmounted.

In assessing the effectiveness of a particular planning system, each attribute is considered by the firm. For this purpose, a semantic differential, bipolar adjective scale has been developed, with each scale being ranked from 1 to 7 between the poles. These scales are illustrated in Fig. 11.4. When the nature of each attribute within the planning has been assessed, the outcome is a profile of 12 scores, one for each attribute. In interpreting such a profile, the approach purports that the

Integration		
1	4	7
Plans produced in isolation	Shows signs of isolation	Completely integrated into organization

Catalytic action		
1	4	7
No stimulus provided	Some prompting of other departments	Strong stimulus provided throughout

Richness of formulation		
1	4	7
Simple projection from present state	Some search for alternatives	Exhaustive search of scenarios

Breadth of evaluation		
1	4	7
Simple accept/reject rule	Assessment on small number of criteria	Multidimensional assessment of alternatives

Treatment of uncertainty		
1	4	7
Ignored	Some attention granted to uncertainties	Stochastic decision criteria used

Resources planned 1	4	7
Single	Some	All

Data 1	4	7
Minimal	Moderate empirical and subjective	Adequate empirical and subjective

Iteration in process 1	4	7
Single iteration in a given cycle	Some revision	Iteration to convergence

Assumptions 1	4	7
Remain implicit	Some made explicit others not	Clear statement of all assumptions made

Quantification of goals 1	4	7
None	Some degree of quantification	Full quantification (where appropriate)

Control measures 1	4	7
None formal	Some formal reporting	Full reporting system

Feasibility of implementation 1	4	7
Little	Reasonable	Complete

Figure 11.4 Dyson and Foster's attribute scales. Reproduced by permission of North Holland Publishing Co.

planning would be highly effective if the profile was close to (7, ..., 7), or it would be classified as being ineffective if the profile was close to (1, ..., 1).

A major problem of interpretation arises where the resultant profile exhibits wide variations in scores. Here the company can only decide subjectively how close the scores of the profile are to either the maximum or the minimum profiles. Similar problems would also arise where the profile has counteracting scores, such as scores of 1 neutralizing scores of 7. To overcome such problems, standards for comparison could be adopted, such as performance in previous years, or comparisons with other companies. In the former the advantage would be the establishment of a trend against which to compare the assessment, while the advantage of the latter would be in allowing for a relative assessment. However, the problem with trends is that environmental conditions could have changed significantly over the years, which could have caused changes to scores, as opposed to changes in effectiveness causing changes to scores. The alternative, of inter-firm comparisons of scores, could be with firms of a similar size or with those that operate in the same industry or market. A major problem here would be finding companies who not only carry out this type of assessment, but who would be willing to co-operate and compare scores. However, even if this were achieved, companies operating in the same industry and/or market are likely to approach their planning in different ways, adopting different strategies and tactics, so that again a useful comparison may not be feasible. Another major problem relates to the actual assessment procedure. As a company will be assessing its own effectiveness, it is likely that personnel involved in the planning will also be involved in the assessment procedure. Even if they are different they are still part of the company. Therefore this is a problem of neutrality of assessment, so that scores are likely to be subjective in nature, with the consequence that they may not reflect the actual degree of effectiveness.

In addition, Dyson and Foster state a number of problems which they themselves consider to be relevant. First, they recognize that the nature of the internal political climate of a company could mean that, even though their approach indicates planning to be effective, it may not produce the required results. Hence, even though the plan may be effective, the power of the individuals who need to get the plan both accepted and implemented may be such that it does not achieve the required results. This can be considered to be a problem of the effectiveness of implementation, as opposed to the effectiveness of the plan. However, Dyson and Foster deny that this is a weakness of their approach, as indeed the latter is concerned with planning and not with how the firm uses it. Second, they emphasize the previously discussed problem of achieving a comprehensive set of attributes. Finally, they stress the problem of actually measuring the attributes in some meaningful way. This relates to the interpretation of profiles, as discussed above. Although these problems do relate to some of those of the multidimensional approach given previously, there are others, namely achieving a common acceptance of both the attributes and their weightings, and knowing whether or not the chosen attributes will achieve the intended results. However, the latter relates to the inherent nature of the planning in being successful, even though the assessment may indicate effectiveness, and not the implementation effectiveness caused by the internal political climate, as discussed above.

The King approach

The basis of the approach given by King is that the effectiveness of planning must be assessed within the total context in which it operates; this concept he labels the strategic planning system (SPS). The overall assessment of the strategic planning system is given as a planning evaluation framework, of which the effectiveness of the nature of the actual planning is but one part. This framework consists of 10 attributes, the presence of which, in planning, is considered to reflect effectiveness:

Effectiveness of planning This is a measure of the degree to which the SPS has achieved its goals, as an assessment of performance/end results.
Relative worth of the SPS This is an external comparison between the firm's current SPS and standards of planning that are currently reported in the literature.
Role and impact of the SPS This is assessed in terms of whether the planning is really being used to guide decision making and whether it is fully implemented.
Performance of plans This criterion is similar to the first, but requires specific assessments for each part of the corporate planning, including all elements of all strategies and all specific objectives throughout the company.
Relative worth of strategy Here it is suggested that the assessment is based upon internal consistencies of strategies within the SPS, and the value of these strategies to pursue opportunities.

Adaptive value of the SPS This is the ability of the planning to be able to adapt to changes, either externally or internally, that are experienced by the firm.

Relative efficiency This is a measure of the resources consumed in the preparation of plans, such as man hours or cost of running a planning department.

Adequacy of resources This means ensuring that objectives and strategies are realistic relative to the resources to be made available. Alternatively, where resources are not adequate then expectations may need to be revised.

Allocation of planning resources Once the level of resource adequacy has been established, then the resources need to be allocated to different priorities within the planning. This criterion requires an assessment of this allocation.

Appropriateness of planning goals At the end of the period for which the planning was applicable the appropriateness of the utilized objectives needs to be determined in relation to the environment that prevailed during this period.

The approach to be followed is to make an assessment of planning relative to these attributes, which produces a planning system effectiveness profile. The attributes given by King are obviously similar to those proposed by Dyson and Foster, and indeed the King approach features similar problems. Although an assessment of effectiveness using the King approach at a particular point in time may show up planning weaknesses, there is still the problem of making comparisons against, say, previous years' planning and their associated assessments of effectiveness to determine a trend of effectiveness improvement. The other applicable problems, as discussed in relation to the Dyson and Foster approach, may be outlined as follows:

- Nature of the internal company climate.
- Achieving a comprehensive set of attributes.
- Measuring the attributes in a meaningful way.
- Achieving a common acceptance of attributes.
- Knowing whether or not the attributes will lead to intended results.

The Heroux approach

Rather than measuring the nature of the existing planning process, Heroux gives a series of guidelines which he recommends should be used by a company as measures to improve the effectiveness of planning. The starting point of this approach is that planning instils a degree of discipline and formality in managers, to an extent unlikely to exist without the utilization of planning. Although planning is a function of management, Heroux observes that there can be a tendency on the part of managers to see it not as an integral part of their job, but as an additional burden passed down the managerial hierarchy. This can lead to managerial perceptions of unnecessary requirements, time-consuming efforts completed for other managers, and a once-a-year exercise to be forgotten until next year. Consequently, the approach Heroux takes is to develop an understanding of planning as an integral part of management within the company.

The outcome is that he has developed a number of factors or considerations aimed at developing this understanding, as well as acting as the measures to improve the effectiveness of planning. Although he recognizes that different companies obviously exhibit different levels of effectiveness, he gives a checklist of measures to be considered, which will allow each firm to develop their own effectiveness, relative to their unique situation. These measures to improve effectiveness are classified by level of management, being given in separate check lists of measurements for senior management, middle management, and subordinates. As this approach is not taken to be directly applicable to the nature of planning, this checklist is not given here, but interested readers are referred to the original article.[27]

As already established, the Heroux approach is more of a guide to the improvement of effectiveness than a method of assessment. As such, the guidelines need to be accepted and acted upon by personnel if they are to be effective as a means to improve the effectiveness of planning. Leading on from this point, even if they are accepted and acted upon, there is still the problem of knowing whether or not effectiveness will be improved, as the approach does not include a measurement of effectiveness before and after such action. However, it can be considered that action on these attributes is likely to improve discipline and formality (an initial requirement of Heroux), although again it does not follow that effectiveness will improve as a consequence. In addition, the approach also suffers from the general problems pertinent to the multidimensional approach, as discussed in the previous two approaches.

The Kotler approach

Although this is proposed as a method for assessing effectiveness, it is presented within the context of the stage of control, which is to be considered in detail in Part Five. This approach is labelled as being concerned with the effectiveness of the overall marketing operation. Despite this, examination of the areas of the approach reveal that they are concerned not with specific details of implementation or performance of the marketing function, but rather with issues that relate directly to those involved in the planning of marketing. Indeed, Kotler emphasizes that effective planning is central to the success of marketing and this is certainly reflected in this proposed approach to assessing effectiveness.

Kotler's approach utilizes five areas of assessment, each of which includes three separate issues. The latter are the range of attributes that are considered to represent effectiveness, if they are found to be a feature of planning. Each issue is given in the form of a question, a range of answers is given for each and each answer is given a score of either 0, 1 or 2, where the score of 2 is the most favourable in representing effectiveness. This method therefore gives a maximum score of 30, representing the highest level of effectiveness. To assess the effectiveness of a marketing planning system, each question is answered and the resultant score summed. The five areas of assessment are as follows:

Customer philosophy This means defining long-run market needs, planning future products to satisfy these and planning other marketing activities to follow.
Integrated marketing organization This consists of organizing marketing personnel to be able to carry out marketing analysis, planning, implementation of the plans and the resultant control.
Adequate marketing information This involves an examination of the information system being used, relative to planning and control.
Strategic orientation This means an assessment of the extent of the planning done throughout the company.
Operational efficiency This is concerned with the control of the implementation of the plans and the allocation of resources to the stages of the plan.

A score having been determined, the final stage of the assessment is to interpret it relative to effectiveness; for this, Kotler suggests the following scale of effectiveness:

Score	Effectiveness
0–5	None
6–10	Poor

11–15	Fair
16–20	Good
21–25	Very good
26–30	Superior

However, even with such a scale, there are several problems associated with the interpretation of a particular score. The degrees of effectiveness given are arbitrary and subject to interpretation. Personal interpretations of, say, 'fair' are likely to vary from manager to manager and if this is referred back to the score then again the interpreter is faced with a figure which has no meaning within its value. As with the other multidimensional methods, there is again a problem in interpreting the effectiveness score with a standard, either from scores of effectiveness in previous years or by comparison with other firms, as previously discussed. Again, this method suffers from the general problems pertinent to the multidimensional approach, as discussed in the context of previous methods.

Empirical studies

As mentioned in the introduction to this chapter, the effectiveness of planning is a relatively new concept, especially in the utilization of the multidimensional approach. Indeed, only two studies have been identified as having been reported in the literature, being those completed by Dyson and Foster[30] and by Greenley.[31] Each of these studies may be summarized as follows:

The Dyson and Foster study This utilized the case-study method by examining the strategic planning of ten companies. However, the range of attributes included in their approach, as given in the last section, was extended to incorporate the participation of personnel within planning, by the addition of the following three attributes:

– Interest-group participation.
– Degrees of communication.
– Involvement in strategic decision making.

As with the other attributes, these were also scored on semantic differential, bipolar adjective scales, with each scale being ranked from 1 to 7 between the poles.

Each of the ten organizations was assessed for each attribute within their planning to give a profile of scores for each firm. The results showed that none of the companies exhibited a particular high degree of effectiveness in their planning, as a result of using this approach. For the majority of firms the profiles of scores were split, with a tendency for one part of their scores to be distributed in the effective section of the scale and the other in the ineffective section. In looking at the results across the firms, the authors attempted to identify the attributes considered to be the most important, in an attempt to establish the necessary conditions for effective planning. Consequently, they claimed to identify a subset that 'seems to represent a core of technical expertise', being:

– Richness of formulation.
– Depth of evaluation.
– Treatment of uncertainty.
– Data used.
– Assumptions.
– Quantification of goals.
– Control measures.

However, this application of the Dyson and Foster multidimensional approach exhibits the general problems associated with the method, as discussed earlier in the chapter. Additionally, although they claim to have identified a core of necessary conditions for effective planning, this testing has not identified a causal relationship between these attributes and the effects produced by such planning. This in turn leads back to the dilemma of using the multidimensional approach, namely how to determine whether the presence of certain attributes will lead to the desired end results.

The Greenley study This utilized the Dyson and Foster multidimensional approach. Again, the case-study method was used, but here the attributes were applied to the marketing operational planning of four UK manufacturing companies. Although the approach was designed to be used to assess strategic planning, the attributes used were considered to be applicable to planning *per se* and indeed, for each attribute, it was considered that a meaningful assessment could be made.

Each of the case studies was assessed for each attribute within its planning to give a profile of scores for each company. Of the four companies, only one could be considered to exhibit effectiveness as a consequence of this application, in that the scores were distributed in the effective end of the measurement scale. For the other firms the profiles were similar to the Dyson and Foster study in that, although some of the scores were distributed in the part of the scale representing effectiveness, other scores were located in the part representing ineffectiveness. Again it was found to be difficult to label categorically the degree of planning effectiveness of these firms as a result of using this approach. Similarly, these results also exhibit the problems associated with the multidimensional approach, as discussed throughout the chapter.

Therefore, although the multidimensional approach is an attempt to move away from performance or end results as a means of assessing the effectiveness of planning, it is obviously far from adequate, at the present time, for adoption as a reliable approach. However, the concept of assessing the nature of the planning, and the nature of the individual attributes used in the assessment, seem to be almost logically self-evident as being means to improve planning effectiveness. What is needed is extensive research into the application of these methods to companies and their subsequent development and refinement. Such empirical testing and subsequent modifications to these approaches can only contribute to the understanding of planning effectiveness.

THE ASSUMED-BENEFITS APPROACH

Earlier in the chapter a range of advantages or benefits of planning was given, representing those that have been reported in the literature. These are all claimed to arise from the utilization of planning. It was also mentioned that, as a consequence of these advantages, planning can be claimed to be both useful and beneficial, even if it cannot be measured as being effective. Indeed, this argument is the basis of this approach to effectiveness, which is that the firm merely assumes that planning is an effective component within the management of the company, at all levels within the managerial hierarchy. The argument is extended by asserting that the advantages or benefits are sufficient in themselves to substantiate a claim that planning is effective, as it is likely that they would not be realized without the utilization of planning.

These advantages can all be considered to be direct benefits that accrue to the company as a result of planning. However, a much broader benefit can be considered to arise from planning, which encompasses not only the company but also the external environment. This consists of those values, or qualities, which are intrinsic in that they are results of the nature of planning and are values in that they extend the initial advantages intended by the firm. This concept of intrinsic values has been discussed by Greenley,[8] developing from the earlier work of Vancil[32] and Camillus.[33] The intrinsic values are classified into three groups, namely those that affect the general external environment, those that operate on the company's markets, and those felt within the internal environment.

The general external environment

The logical planning of a firm's business over a future time period is seen to be of value first to the owners/shareholders, giving improved security of both investment and future returns. Long-range planning will also give an indication of the timing of future additional investments, so that owners/shareholders can plan their own future investments and returns.

The second area of intrinsic values in this group relates to the general public in contact with the firm. Effective planning can create values such as follows:

- Anticipated levels of future employment opportunities.
- A contribution to the quality of life and living standards.
- Continuous product improvement and augmented consumer benefits.
- Continuous understanding of market segments and associated needs and wants.
- Product liability, quality control and environmental pollution control.
- Effective allocation of resources, extending to the planning of efficient allocation of finite resources.

The final area of intrinsic values in this group relates to the economy of the country in which the company is located. Long-term company stability through long-range planning provides a contribution to the stability of GNP, while planned company growth contributes to planned economic growth.

The company's markets

As was seen in Parts Two and Three of the book, corporate planning focuses on markets and their particular requirements. Therefore the results of such planning can be considered to confer intrinsic values such as follows:

- Improvements to the benefits of product and service offerings.
- Effective assessment of changes in customer requirements.
- Provision of improvements to the future product range and the providing of future consumer benefits.
- Avoidance of undue pressure from the communications output through the balancing of the elements of the marketing mix.
- Development and continuation of free competition within the market-place, with the consequential customer benefits.

The internal environment The first area where planning provides internal intrinsic values is in the co-ordination of the various business functions within the company. Strategic planning obviously has value in that, if it is effective, then the total company is unified and integrated towards common aims, giving an overall framework for the co-ordination of the individual business functions.

Marketing operational planning provides intrinsic values to other business functions, in that the content of this plan provides inputs to other operational plans, providing a further contribution to co-ordination. Outputs from the marketing plan provide inputs to the production plan for production scheduling, inputs to the financial plan for budgeting and other financial forecasts, plus inputs to the manpower plan for levels of employment needed for future levels of sales. Following on from this, effective planning also provides a basis for the internal allocation of resources. Throughout the planning described in Parts Two and Three, all the decisions at the various stages of planning can be considered to result in the allocation of resources.

The final intrinsic value of planning in this group relates to the marketing personnel. Advantages of effective planning to personnel were discussed earlier in the chapter and any split between advantages and intrinsic values would be merely pedantic. However, the overall logical and rational framework given to the company by strategic and operational planning is likely to contribute to a working environment in which not only is motivation, leadership and morale fostered, but also security of operation gives a framework for overall personal development.

An illustration of the application of the three approaches for assessing the effectiveness of planning is given in Case Study 15 opposite.

SUMMARY

This chapter has addressed the concept of effectiveness as applied to planning. It started with a consideration of the nature of effectiveness. Several definitions were examined, but all featured major problems. Despite these problems of definition, a range of potential advantages of planning have been reported in the literature, and these were discussed as being part of the nature of planning. As a result of the overall examination of the effectiveness of planning, three major approaches to its assessment were identified. These were based upon performance/end results, a multidimensional assessment of attributes within the planning, and by assuming that planning will be effective.

The performance/end results approach involves attempting to identify a relationship between the level of sophistication of planning and the level of performance and end results. However, empirical evidence to date is far from conclusive in establishing such a relationship.

The multidimensional approach is concerned with assessing effectiveness through an examination of the nature of the planning. Four different approaches were reported, all of which give a range of planning attributes, the presence of which is taken to indicate that a firm's planning is effective. Empirical evidence to support these approaches is almost non-existent, although the concept of assessing the nature of planning was claimed to be almost logically self-evident.

The assumption approach is to recognize that a range of advantages and intrinsic values is likely to accrue through the utilization of planning, so that a measurement of its effectiveness is not really necessary. Again there is an a-priori case that such an assumption is valid, but again also there is a lack of empirical evidence to identify the conditions in which these advantages and intrinsic values are likely to accrue.

Overall, the concept of effectiveness is obviously extremely problematic, both in its explanation and in its assessment within company situations. Indeed, none of the described methods can be considered to be satisfactory for assessing the effectiveness of planning. However, for planning to develop its role within the management of companies then assessments in measurable terms of the effectiveness of current planning stages, explained in Parts Two and Three, must be carried out so that planning can be seen as contributing to the overall efficiency of organizations.

CASE STUDY 15: TEXAS INSTRUMENTS INC.*

Case outline

This American-based electronics organization produces semiconductors, computer systems and consumer products, with the latter ranging from calculators to digital watches and personal computers. The company had achieved phenomenal growth during the 10-year period preceeding the case study and a well-developed corporate planning system was considered to be a major contribution to this success.

Illustration

The case study illustrates that TI have utilized a well-developed planning system, incorporating many of the features described in Parts Two and Three of this book. The system features an extensive utilization of objectives, strategies and tactics, with separate planning for four different time periods, for different SBUs, and for different levels in the organizational structure. Although the issue of planning effectiveness is not addressed in the case study in a formal manner, as described in this chapter, the company is reported to perceive that planning has played a major role in its success.

The three approaches to effectiveness have been applied into the TI case as follows:

1 Performance/end-results approach

As already mentioned, corporate planning at TI was well developed, while, throughout the case study, managerial commitment and belief are emphasized, including those of the chairman and president. Associated with this approach is successful performance and the achievement of required end results. The president reported average annual increases over the five-year period up to the case as follows:

- 17 per cent for net sales.
- 19 per cent for earnings per share.
- 26 per cent for dividends paid per share.

The major organizational objective was for continued growth to become a 'large' company, with annual sales of $10 billion during the eighties. In 1960 the major objectives were to achieve the following by 1973:

- $1 billion sales per year.
- $55 million net earnings per year.

By 1973 they had achieved $1.3 billion sales and $83 million net earnings.

Although these results have been achieved within the context of sophisticated planning, there is no established cause-and-effect relationship, following the discussions given in the chapter. However, the TI directorate were convinced that planning had had a major effect on the firm's performance, reflecting an assumption approach to determining the value of planning.

---

* Derived from D. F. Channon, Texas Instruments Inc. Copyright © 1979 Derek F. Channon.

2 Multidimensional approach

From the explanation of the TI corporate planning given in the case, a search for the presence of the attributes of the Dyson and Foster approach gave the following results:

Integration The planning system was communicated as a model throughout the company, while objectives and strategies were linked through managers and SBUs.

Catalytic action TI appear to encourage participation in planning, an example being an annual strategic planning conference.

Richness The system is orientated to the future with long- and intermediate-range plans, as well as short-range plans.

Breadth This is reflected in a well-developed system of management by objectives, from the many measures of overall company performance to detailed market and product objectives.

Uncertainty Descriptions are given of assessments of both external variables and internal constraints, particularly production and finance.

Resources The tactical plans of all managers are orientated to resources, necessitating careful consideration of their allocation.

Data Information systems are not directly reported, but alternative growth opportunities are actively identified and evaluated.

Iteration Monitoring was given as being central to the planning system, while the organizational structure includes responsibility for identifying business opportunities.

Quantification It is a stated policy that the majority of objectives must be quantified, at all levels within the company.

Control Monitoring is central to TI planning, continuous checking of performance is incorporated into the plans, and control methods such as bar charts and PERT networks are used.

Feasibility This is reflected in the resource allocation process, in that allocations need to be specific, commitment needs to be justified and responsibilities are allocated to individuals.

Consequently, this brief explanation of the attributes of TI's planning indicates effectiveness, on the basis of the multidimensional approach. However, a fuller examination within the context of the company would be more beneficial, while the weaknesses of the multidimensional approach are still pertinent.

3 Assumed-benefits approach

As already highlighted, considerable emphasis is given in the case to the importance attached to planning by the directors and managers of TI. Indeed, they consider that planning has played a major role in the successful achievement of growth in sales, profits and earnings. However, a relationship between planning and end results has obviously not been established, and, although the previous section was indicative of effectiveness, a multidimensional type of appraisal is not evident.

Therefore it must be concluded that their assessment is based upon an assumption approach. However, a number of advantages and values of planning are described as being perceived by the company, as follows;

– Develops commitment to the development of opportunities.
– Provides a system of management with a hierarchy of objectives.
– Separates strategic issues from operational issues.
– Allows for a measurement of performance.
– Allows for the effective use of resources in both individual divisions and the organization as a whole.
– Provides a framework for the delegation of responsibility and authority, but also retains centralized control.
– Although a delegation framework is established, the planning also stimulates the creative thinking of managers.
– Gives a formal framework for allowing as many people as possible to participate in the planning.

REVIEW QUESTIONS

1. Discuss the alternatives to defining the nature of effectiveness within the context of planning.
2. 'It's obvious that we gain many advantages from our planning, so that we don't attempt to identify them.' Discuss.
3. What do you consider to be the major weaknesses of the performance/end results approach? Do you consider that these weaknesses conflict with the results that they are attempting to measure?
4. Do you think that perhaps there is little difference in the range of multidimensional approaches?
5. Present the case both for and against the multidimensional approach, in comparison with the end results approach.
6. 'To merely assume that planning is effective is to adopt a delinquent attitude towards planning.' Discuss.
7. How do you consider that the body of knowledge relative to effectiveness should now be developed?

REFERENCES

1. 'Quaker Oats retreats to its food lines', *Business Week*, 25 February 1980.
2. 'What makes Saatchi and Saatchi grow?', *Fortune*, 19 March 1984.
3. G. E. Greenley, 'Effectiveness in planning: problems of definition', *Managerial Planning*, 33, 2, 27–34, 1984.
4. R. J. Kudla, 'Elements of effective corporate planning', *Long Range Planning*, 9, 4, 82–93, 1976.
5. H. I. Ansoff and R. G. Brandenburg, 'Design of optimal business planning', *Kommunikation*, III, 4, 163–188, 1967.
6. French, D., and H. Saward, *Dictionary of Management*, Pan Reference Books, London, 1975.
7. Y. M. Godiwalla, W. A. Meinhart, and W. A. Warde, 'General management and corporate strategy', *Managerial Planning*, 30, 2, 17–29, 1981.
8. G. E. Greenley, 'Does strategic planning improve company performance?', *Long Range Planning*, in press.
9. H. I. Ansoff *et al.*, 'Does planning pay?', *Long Range Planning*, 3, 2, 2–7, 1970.
10. G. W. Gershefski, 'Corporate models—the state of the art', *Management Science*, 16, 6, 303–12, 1970.
11. S. S. Thune and R. J. House, 'Where long range planning pays off', *Business Horizons*, 29, 81–7, 1970.
12. D. M. Herold, 'Long Range Planning and Organizational Performance', *Academy of Management Journal*, 15, 91–102, 1972.
13. D. W. Karger and Z. A. Malik, 'Long Range Planning and Organisational Performance', *Long Range Planning*, 8, 6, 60–4, 1975.
14. R. M. Fulmer and L. W. Rue, 'Is long-range planning profitable?', *Proceedings of the Academy of Management*, Boston, 66–73, 1973; 'The practice and profitability of long range planning', *Managerial Planning*, 22, 6, 1–7, 1974.
15. P. H. Grinyer and D. Norburn, 'Planning for existing markets', *Journal of the Royal Statistical Society*, 138, 1, 70–97, 1975.
16. R. J. Kudla, 'The effects of strategic planning on common stock returns', *Academy of Management Journal*, 23, 1, 5–20, 1980.
17. M. Leontiades and A. Tezel, 'Planning perceptions and planning results', *Strategic Management Journal*, 1, 1, 65–75, 1980.
18. W. H. Hegarty, 'The role of strategic formulation of corporate performance', *Proceedings of the Midwest American Institute of Decision Sciences*, 1976.
19. D. R. Wood, and R. L. La Forge, 'The impact of comprehensive planning on financial performance', *Academy of Management Journal*, 22, 3, 516–26, 1979.
20. E. A. Kallman and H. J. Shapiro, 'The motor freight industry: a case against planning', *Long Range Planning*, 11, 81–6, 1978.
21. R. B. Robinson, and J. A. Pearce, 'The impact of formalised strategic planning on financial performance in small organizations', *Strategic Management Journal*, 4, 197–207, 1983.
22. R. W. Sapp, and R. E. Seiler, 'The relationship between long range planning and financial performance of US commercial banks', *Long Range Planning*, 30, 2, 32–6, 1981.

23. G. A. Sheehan, *Long Range Planning and its Relationship to Firm Size, Firm Growth and Firm Growth Variability*, unpublished PhD thesis, University of Western Ontario, 1975.
24. Ackoff, R. L., *A Concept of Corporate Planning*, Wiley, New York, 1970.
25. R. G. Dyson, and M. J. Foster, 'Effectiveness in strategic planning', *European Journal of Operational Research*, **5**, 3, 163–70, 1980.
26. W. R. King, 'Evaluating strategic planning systems', *Strategic Management Journal*, **4**, 1983, 263–77: 'Evaluating the effectiveness of your planning', *Managerial Planning*, **33**, 2, 4–9, 1984.
27. R. L. Heroux, 'How effective is your planning?', *Managerial Planning*, **30**, 2, 3–16, 1981.
28. P. Kotler, 'From sales obsession to marketing effectiveness', *Harvard Business Review*, **55**, 6, 67–74, 1977.
29. Dyson, R. G., *A Research Programme for Strategic Planning Under Uncertainty, Multiple Objectives and Multiple Interest Groups*, Technische Hogeschool Twente, Enschede, 1977.
30. R. G. Dyson, and M. J. Foster, 'The relationship of participation and effectiveness in strategic planning', *Strategic Management Journal*, **3**, 1, 77–88, 1982; 'Making planning more effective', *Long Range Planning*, **16**, 6, 68–73, 1983.
31. G. E. Greenley, 'Effectiveness in marketing planning', *Strategic Management Journal*, **4**, 1, 1–10, 1983.
32. R. F. Vancil, 'The accuracy of long range planning', *Harvard Business Review*, **48**, 5, 98–101, 1970.
33. J. C. Camillus, 'Evaluating the benefits of formal planning systems', *Long Range Planning*, **8**, 3, 33–40, 1975.

PART

FIVE

IMPLEMENTING AND CONTROLLING PLANS

12. Implementing plans
13. Control

OUTLINE

As the final part of the book, Part Five is concerned with carrying out both strategic and operational planning, as well as the associated control procedures. In Part One the role of planning within the context of management was examined, in that management was taken to be basically concerned with planning, implementation and control. Consequently, this part of the book addresses both implementation and control. Chapter 12 presents a framework for the implementation of plans, although the major components of this framework are also considered to be applicable during the actual planning. Chapter 13 is the final chapter of the book. It examines approaches that can be used to control the implementation of plans, but which also provide inputs to the next round of strategic and operational planning.

TWELVE
IMPLEMENTING PLANS

Learning objectives are to:

1. Understand the major components of implementation and how they relate to planning.
2. Appreciate the role of delegation and participation as components of implementation.
3. Appreciate the role of motivation and leadership as components of implementation.
4. Appreciate the need for integration during plan implementation.
5. Recognize major concepts that have been introduced.

Once the stages of both strategic and operational planning to cover a particular period of time are complete, the planning then obviously needs to be implemented or carried out over that period. The basis of this implementation will obviously be the contents of the planning documents, but the issues of the planning process that were examined in Part Four are also a basis for implementation. Of particular importance are the managerial influence on planning examined in Chapter 9, as implementation is concerned with the carrying out of specific actions and tasks from the planning by designated personnel. Indeed, this chapter is also concerned with extending the particular theme of the book, that planning is affected by human influences.

The personnel designated implementation tasks are obviously within the organizational structure, so that the presentation of this chapter needs to be within the context of the many issues concerning organizational structure presented in Chapter 10. Similarly, the effectiveness of the planning is likely to be influenced by the people who implement it, while the nature of the planning is likely to affect the approach taken to implementation. Therefore this chapter also needs to be within the context of the many issues concerning planning effectiveness presented in Chapter 11.

The first section of the chapter presents a framework to be used subsequently in presenting the body of the chapter. This framework consists of five major components and the subsequent sections of this chapter are one each for these five parts.

THE IMPLEMENTATION FRAMEWORK

Implementation requires a transition from planning to actual 'doing', requiring a change from following a sequence of planning stages to executing a range of activities. While the literature has developed in the former, writers such as Lyles and Lenz[1] provide the general observation that human behaviour within the context of planning is at an early stage of development. Their research also indicates that behavioural problems can reduce the effectiveness of otherwise well-designed planning systems. Similarly, research by King and Cleland[2] has indicated that the success of planning is less sensitive to the affects of planning techniques than it is to the managerial environment in which the planning is utilized.

Indeed, it would appear that there is a general observation of restricted attention to implementation in the literature, along with a difficulty on the part of firms in achieving the transition from planning to implementation. An example of this difficulty of transition is from the US electronics company, Gould Inc. While the CEO had found the planning of the company's change of long-range direction to be 'easy to plan', execution of these plans provided major organizational problems. These included lack of support from many executives and the defection of others, the development of adverse attitudes, difficulty in exercising effective leadership, and difficulty in achieving the necessary delegation.[3]

The major problems to be encountered in the implementation of planning have been classified by Pekar,[4] and can be summarized as follows:

– Reluctance on the part of managers to accept new planning techniques.
– A wide range of communication difficulties, especially between the different business functions.
– A lack of competent personnel to be able to both produce appropriate plans and carry them out.
– Inadequate information systems to support both plan preparation and implementation.
– Lack of outside help from consultants capable of advising on implementation.
– A general lack of commitment to planning throughout the organizational structure.
– Inadequate training of managers relative to the role of planning and how plans can be transposed into action.

As mentioned in the introduction, the adopted framework for explaining implementation is based upon five major components. The first of these is the delegation of tasks and duties from the plan documents to designated personnel. Such delegation will be throughout the organizational structure and will relate to both strategic and operational planning. The second component concerns the participation of personnel, located at different levels in the structure, in the different tasks to be performed from the planning documents. The third component is concerned with the motivation of personnel to implement the plans effectively. Again, motivation applies throughout the different levels of the organizational structure. The fourth part of the framework addresses the role of leadership in implementation. Each manager within the structure will need to provide leadership for his particular area of responsibility, but will also be affected by leadership abilities from higher levels in the structure. The final component of the framework is concerned with integration, which is also applicable throughout the organizational structure. These five component parts of implementation are outlined in Fig. 12.1. Although these components are to be examined in turn, in practice they are closely related: for example, delegation and participation are very much interrelated. This meant a difficult decision on the sequence of presentation of the components, but the approach adopted is a presentation of each, with no importance attached to the sequence.

Finally, there are three aspects of this framework to be mentioned before each component is discussed in turn. First, as already stated above, all five areas are equally applicable throughout the organizational structure. Second, they are also applicable within both strategic and operational planning. Finally, while all five are part of implementation, they are also applicable to the actual planning process itself. Indeed, as will be seen in the following sections, consideration of all five parts is seen to be necessarily paralleled in both the planning process and the implementation of plans.

Figure 12.1   The five components of implementation

DELEGATION

The simple premise on which delegation is based is that a single manager is unable to implement all activities himself and therefore needs to delegate activities or duties to various personnel. However, in order to carry out these activities, each person needs to be delegated authority in order to be able to complete the activities required of him. Indeed explanations of delegation, such as given by Stoner,[5] are based upon the assignment to other people of formal authority to carry out specific activities. This now leads on to an understanding of authority, which can be considered to be the right to take actions or decisions and the right to have others accept these. An example here comes from General Motors in the United States. A recent change was to delegate more authority down the organizational structure: each manager was given more authority to make a wider range of decisions in his planning and implementation, which previously required referral to higher levels of authority for approval.[6]

Even though an individual has been delegated certain rights, he must be able to exercise these rights and convince others that his decisions are worthy of acceptance. This ability to exercise authority is generally referred to as power, with Stoner[5] explaining power as being the ability to exert influence to change the behaviour or attitudes of other people. An individual may be delegated authority, but if others undermine this authority and he does not have the power to influence their behaviour, then the ability to exercise authority may be drastically reduced.

Once an individual has accepted an area of authority as being an integral part of his job, then he becomes responsible for that authority and accountable for his actions and decisions. Responsibility can be considered to be an obligation, in that a manager is obliged to carry out the authority delegated to him, ensuring that actions and decisions are completed. Accountability is being answerable for the results of these actions and decisions, including judgement by superiors.

The relationship of these concepts of delegation is illustrated in Fig. 12.2.

It is probably apparent to readers that the concepts of delegation are equally applicable in both the preparation and the implementation of planning, with the principle of delegation in implementation having been established. In the former, authority needs to be delegated to individual executives to give them responsibility to prepare particular stages of both strategic and operational plans. Indeed, a major consideration needs to be the way in which the various stages of planning can be delegated throughout the structure. An important concept here is the degree of participation that each manager will have in the stages of planning as a result of delegation, as

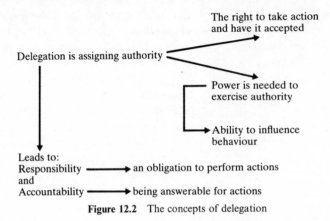

Figure 12.2   The concepts of delegation

such participation is likely to affect the commitment that will be felt towards plan implementation. The component of participation is tackled in the next section. However, the point is that specific aspects of planning need to be delegated and the scope of authority associated with the delegation needs to be determined. In addition, each individual delegated planning duties needs to develop power to complete the planning, but also needs to be responsible for its completion as well as being accountable for its presentation.

Delegation within the organizational structure

The nature of the actual organizational structure, as discussed in Chapter 10, will affect delegation to implement plans. A major principle here can be that, where the preparation of particular aspects of planning have been delegated to particular departments or individuals, then the associated implementation can also be delegated. Indeed, examples of companies 'pushing decision making down into the company' are Gould,[3] GM,[6] ICI,[7] ICI Fibres,[8] and Wadkin.[9] In the case of strategic planning, implementation is achieved through the implementation of the operational plans, so that the marketing operational plan is central to this discussion.

Regardless of the nature of the organizational structure, the issue will be concerned with the delegation of the marketing operational planning to marketing personnel, regardless of how the latter are organized. At UK machinery manufacturers Wadkin, divisionalization has meant determining the delegation of the preparation and implementation of plans, in a structure where there are group marketing personnel, but also managers in the divisions who are also responsible for marketing. The approach has been to delegate planning to the group marketing staff, but with involvement by divisional managers, although the latter are delegated authority for plan implementation.[9]

The first consideration is the communication of each person's degree of authority, how that relates to the authority that has been delegated to other marketing personnel, and how the authority of the chief marketing executive relates to the rest of the organizational structure. An immediate problem here can be a breakdown in communication, of the type experienced in everyday communications. However, a major problem is likely to be the interrelationship of authority between the individual marketing functions. For example, the market research manager may be delegated the duty of both planning and implementing the market research programme. However, other managers are likely to need to participate in this planning, and indeed may challenge the authority of the market research manager. Therefore the issue is one of establishing boundaries of authority and identifying where these may, or indeed should, overlap.

This demarcation of authority can be even more complex in firms that employ brand/product managers, marketing planners and a marketing services manager. As brand/product managers have the responsibility of managing a number of products, their jobs require them to be involved in all the marketing functions. Consequently, there can be a problem of defining their boundaries of authority relative to the authority of the individual marketing functional managers. As marketing planners tend to be designated as staff functions, there can be a problem of defining planners' authority, in that they are not included in line management and therefore tend not to be responsible for end results. This can also arise where a marketing service manager is employed; although he will have the authority to plan and implement certain marketing functions, this is done to serve other executives, who are therefore able to affect his authority. Therefore such considerations of the delegation of authority require definitions of boundaries and their effective communication.

Similar problems can also arise in that authority of marketing personnel often needs to extend into other business functions outside the marketing department. The brand manager who has authority to develop new products finds that other executives in other departments also have the ability to affect decisions on new products. Similarly, the marketing manager who is delegated the authority to determine sales objectives may be faced with a similar situation. Production planners can affect his authority relative to production capacity allocation, while financial planners may stipulate cash-flow parameters. Here the potential problems of defining and communicating boundaries of authority relate to the total organizational structure.

Power considerations

Within these potential problems of defining and communicating the delegation of authority is the meshing of the implications of power. Although the authority of marketing personnel can be affected by non-marketing personnel, the marketing department can be a major source of power, owing both to knowledge and to the importance of marketing at both strategic and operational levels of management. Knowledge of the total company environment, and particularly market trends which ultimately affect total company performance, can be used as a basis for the justification of decisions in both the preparation and implementation of plans.

The importance of the marketing function in producing power for marketing personnel is reflected in its role at both the strategic and operational levels. In the former, as expounded in Part Two, the base of power can develop out of the unique role of developing alternatives for the direction of the company. At the operational level the base of power originates in the role of the marketing function to generate revenue for the organization. Consequently, the major issue here is that, although the marketing department may be affected by other departments in the preparation and implementation of their planning, the very nature of the role of marketing at strategic and operational levels can provide a power base within the organizational structure.

PARTICIPATION

This component is concerned with the involvement of the different managers, within the organizational structure, in the preparation and implementation of both strategic and operational planning. As already stated, participation in implementation parallels participation in planning. Indeed, it is likely that participation in the preparation of plans by managers will result in greater motivation during their involvement in plan implementation (motivational aspects will be pursued later in the chapter). Although much attention is devoted to participation throughout the structure through the process of delegation, attention has also been given to the importance of participation by the chief executive officer (CEO). Steiner[10] has shown that a successful planning system that can be usefully implemented must be fully integrated into the company's management process and this can only be achieved by starting with not just commitment at the top, but also with participation by the CEO at essential points in both the planning and implementation. However, determining the essential points is probably the art of the job function of the CEO. On the one hand, the role needs to exhibit leadership for the overall direction of the firm, and needs to be seen to be involved and enthusiastic at various stages to promote motivation at other managerial levels, but it also needs to restrict participation to encourage initiative, achievement and self-motivation at all managerial levels (leadership and motivation are examined further in subsequent sections). The chairman of the Korean Daewoo Group, Kim Woo-Choong, is reported to place great emphasis on this balance. Delegation is very much part of his 'CEO style', but he also acts as a model for managerial involvement, which he supports with outstanding personal commitment to and personal sacrifice for the group's success.[11]

The nature of participation

Whether participation is in either planning or implementation, several writers have approached the nature of managerial participation. At a simple level, Pateman[12] has described classifications of participation based upon full, partial and pseudo-participation. Although such an approach may be of little value in determining the amount of participation for particular managers, it is perhaps of value to recognize that participation needs to be described for individual managers. Kloeze, Molenkamp and Roelofs[13] have suggested that the nature of participation needs to be explained in terms of the degree and direction of participation. The former means a tendency for managers to have a 'greater say in matters of decision making', or can be considered to be the component of involvement. The direction of participation means the issues of planning or implementation for which the involvement applies. In planning, the issues could involve participation in formulating, say, marketing strategy for a particular brand, whereas for implementation the issues could be participation in, say, only the advertising tactics for the particular brand. Similarly, Dyson and Foster[14] have explained the nature of participation by using three components, being:

- the groups of managers actually participating;
- the degree of communication through the organizational structure;
- the type of involvement achieved in the area of participation.

Reports of the nature of participation in companies illustrate many differences. At General Motors it seems to be similar to the Dyson and Foster components. The chairman is reported to encourage individual participation, while ensuring that the need for both participation and delegation are communicated throughout the organization. Involvement varies from project planning to a recent case that led to a total company reorganization.[6] At the other extreme are reports of the approach at the US Exxon Corporation, where it is said that individual initiatives of participation in planning are not encouraged.[15] A further example is the approach taken by American Airlines to making major decisions. These are taken by a major planning group whose members include the heads of the functional departments. Hence each department, including marketing, has a representative in the form of its senior manager to participate in major company decisions.[16]

The work of Dickson,[17] based on US companies, suggests four major components as constituting the nature of participation, being:

- interaction of personnel by getting people together in each others' physical presence;
- communication of information and different points of view as a two-way process, both up and down the organizational structure;
- influencing individual preferences and desired decision outcomes to have an effect on company decisions;
- the actual effect that the participants are able to exert on the particular decisions.

This approach is perhaps more comprehensive than the others in that the components range from the initial instigation of participation, through the actual involvement of personnel, to include also the effect that their participation has had. In recent years considerable attention has been given to the technique of quality circles used to instigate participation. Basically, this involves regular formal discussions by personnel to provide a vehicle for participation, although further attention to the technique is beyond the scope of this book.

Participation within the organizational structure

Here the issues are concerned with participation within the implementation of the marketing operational plan, the execution of which, as already highlighted, provides a basis for the execution of the strategic plan. Paralleling this is the spread of participation through the organizational structure in order to involve different managers in both strategic and operational planning, as indeed the latter is likely to affect the former.

Participation of marketing department personnel in the implementation of the marketing plan is likely to be reasonably easy to achieve. As was seen in Chapter 10, some kind of functional split in the marketing department is likely, so that personnel designated to, say, market research or advertising will simply participate in the implementation of the relevent functional tactics. However, where brand/product managers are employed, there may be a problem in determining their degree of participation in the marketing functions, producing a situation similar to that identified for delegation. Here there may be a need to specify the range of participation components, by establishing the necessary interaction and communication, determining the relative degree of influence of the marketing executives and examining their relative personal effects on plan implementation.

Additional problems of participation have the potential of occurring where the company is organized, so that the implementation of the selling and distribution functions is not included within the marketing department. In both cases it would be necessary for the marketing manager to consider the degree of participation that marketing personnel should have in the implementation of these functions, through the participation components. Again, interaction between certain managers would be needed, especially the brand/product managers, while communication of the progress of sales performance would be essential. The marketing manager would also need to consider the influence that the department would desire to exert within the sales force, as well as the effects that they consider would be necessary within the implementation of the selling tactics.

Participation in the preparation of the marketing plan would again be reflected within the functional structure of the marketing department. However, consideration would need to be given to the build-up of the total marketing plan, probably by preparing separate plans for individual brand or product groups. Intermeshing with this, though, would be the planning for each of the marketing functions. Additionally, there is the overall requirement to prepare the overall marketing objectives and strategy for the overall marketing operation, and to relate these to the strategic plan. Here consideration will need to be given to those personnel who should participate (indeed, all may have an opportunity to), and how the mechanism will be developed to consider their interaction, communication requirements, degree of influence, and the extent to which they are likely to affect the operational planning.

The final consideration is that of participation within the preparation of the strategic plan. The determination for this participation will arise out of the location of the responsibility for the strategic planning of marketing, as discussed in Chapter 10. Here it was noted that, regardless of the adopted structure of the marketing department, alternatives could include the board, a planning department, the marketing manager, or a marketing planning manager.

Although any of these alternatives can be designated as the centre for responsibility, consideration still needs to be given to the participation of marketing department personnel, given the principle of paralleling participation in both plan preparation and plan implementation. In the first and second alternatives, the principle is that responsibility is external to the marketing department, whereas in the other two alternatives the responsibility is obviously internal. Consequently, it is likely that participation by marketing personnel will vary, depending on either external or internal location. In the latter, there is likely to be more scope for individual participation, by arranging for all the participation components, especially the interaction of individuals and their ability to influence. However, where the responsibility for the strategic planning of marketing is external, then it is likely that there will be less scope for individual participation. However, it is in this very type of company situation that consideration could be given to extending the degree of participation by individual members of the marketing department. Again, the components of participation would need to be considered. Here it is necessary to give careful consideration to the degree of influence and effect that the marketing personnel can exert. Indeed, it is likely that pseudo-participation, as developed in the work of Pateman,[12] may be more detrimental than little or no opportunity to participate.

MOTIVATION

Motivation has been explained by Stoner[5] as being a process which causes, channels and sustains people's behaviour. Within the context of this book, motivation can be considered to be related to the behaviour of managers in both the preparation and implementation of plans. In both cases, managers need to be motivated so that their behaviour will result in comprehensive plans as well as efficient implementation. An example here is from the Campbell Soup Company. The chief executive has encouraged the development of several new products on the basis of a target market of health-conscious and sophisticated consumers. These products were developed by encouraging the personal initiative of brand managers, through a well-defined directional framework, which provided the motivation for the planning and launch of several new products.[18]

However, Stoner[5] points out that there are many theories that attempt to explain the factors that motivate people, and attention is now directed to an outline of those applicable to planning.

The nature of motivation

Theories of motivation, excluding those generally labelled as traditional approaches, tend to be based upon characteristics of the individual, characteristics of the individual's job, the working environment, and those that attempt an integrative approach.

Individual characteristics represent the unique set that each individual manager possess and brings with him to a particular job function. At the basic level is his personal set of human needs, although the need for achievement is probably of major importance within the context of planning. The well-documented work of McClelland[19] is indicative of a tendency for managers with a high need for achievement to easily accept responsibility, to strive to achieve difficult objectives, and to require feedback on their degree of success, all of which are obviously conducive to planning. Also to be included in these characteristics are the major managerial influences on planning that were examined in Chapter 9. These were managers' values and attitudes, their personal capabilities, their acceptance of change, and the problems they experience in planning. Like a manager's individual set of needs, these are characteristics that can provide motivation to affect behaviour. An example of individual characteristics affecting motivation was exhibited by Sir Terence Conran during the period following the Habitat–Mothercare merger. His approach to managing the new company was based upon personal involvement and extensive consultation with managers, resulting in high morale and motivation.[20]

Characteristics of individual's jobs represent aspects of the job function that are likely to affect behaviour towards both planning and its implementation. Here the well-documented work of Herzberg[21] is applicable: job satisfaction was considered to be caused by one set of motivating factors, while job dissatisfaction was seen to be affected by a different set of hygiene factors. Hampton[22] has suggested that planning can be taken to be a motivating factor within the job of management, as can participation throughout the planning system. However, he goes on to suggest that this is not sufficient, as indeed a whole range of additional factors, including rewards, recognition and advancement, are applicable.

Characteristics from the working environment have been classified by Stoner[5] as the immediate environment and the organizational policies of the firm, with the latter relating to business policy as discussed in Chapter 3. The immediate environment is given as the attitudes and values of a manager's colleagues, which again relate to both planning and implementation, plus the culture of the immediate environment. Such a culture is illustrated at Toshiba (UK) Ltd. The managing director, Geoffrey Deith, is reported as having a charismatic personality, the ability to develop team spirit and emphasize the personal importance of individual managers, while pursuing an overall philosophy of 'working together with a common purpose'.[23] Within the literature there has been debate as to whether individual characteristics, or intrinsic motives, are more important than environmental or extrinsic motives. Writers such as Mawhinney[24] have discussed this conflict but conclude that relative effects are difficult to measure and that both play important roles.

Of the theories that attempt an integrative approach to motivation, expectancy theory appears to have been given the greatest attention. As mentioned several times already in this book, this theory is based upon individuals' expectations from their work, plus their anticipation of their success in realizing these expectations. The expectancy model developed by Porter and Lawler[25] is based upon three major principles, although the full model is more complex. The first principle is that a manager comes to expect that certain patterns of behaviour, including those in planning and implementation, will result in certain consequences. The second is that these consequences will have a particular motivating effect, or valence, on that manager. Finally, a manager's expectations as to the difficulty and probable success of carrying out certain behaviour will affect his motivation to this and subsequent behaviour.

Motivation within the organizational structure

From the discussions given earlier, in Parts Two and Three, it will perhaps be obvious to the reader that planning can provide a framework for the fulfillment of managerial needs such as personal achievement. Through the utilization of management by objectives, plus participation in the formulation and implementation of strategy and tactics, managers should be able to identify their own personal achievements with that of the marketing department through the operational plans, but with overall company performance through the strategic plan. However, attention needs to be also given to other managerial needs at different levels in the structure. At the CMG computer management group there has been an attempt to remove status differences within the structure, so that each manager's status is equated to that of all other managers.[26]

Writers such as McCarthy et al.[27] have emphasized the importance of commitment on the part of managers, which can be considered to be the outcome of attitudes, values, capabilities, and resistance to change. Commitment relates to individual characteristics, but is also part of both job characteristics and the working environment. This is because not only is a manager's own personal commitment to both planning and implementation likely to affect his motivation, but also a lack of commitment by both peers and senior executives is also likely to affect his motivation to the role of planning in the company. The importance of commitment was emphasized in 1984 by the chairman of ICI, John Harvey-Jones. His claim is that managerial commitment is greater if he can get managers to be committed to ideas of their own. Hence, commitment provides motivation in that they strive to achieve plans in which they have originally participated.[7]

McCarthy et al.[27] go on to claim that this motivation can be partly achieved through a reward–punishment system, a large part of which can be achieved through planning. Rewards would include achievements within planning, such as attainment of objectives or success in new tactics, but would also include factors such as salary, bonuses and promotion, all of which can be linked into planning. Punishments can include factors such as too much tension or anxiety, reduced job satisfaction, or perhaps a reduction in responsibility or location within the organizational structure. The chairman of the UK firm Amstrad, Alan Sugar, is said to have an autocratic manner in his leadership of the company. To some managers this is a dissatisfying factor in that their potential to manage is reduced, as is their personal commitment. However, to other managers it is a satisfying factor in that they know that he will make all major decisions, which provides a framework in which they can manage their job functions.[27]

Finally, the planning framework can be considered to be a range of levels of expectations. The strategic plan represents the expectations of the company as a whole, while the operational plans represent the expectations for the functional departments of the company. For individual managers, motivation will be affected by the nature of these expectations and how their own behaviour from their job function will be seen to relate to them. A general principle is that, where they have participated in planning, where their own job functions can be seen to relate to the total corporate planning, and where the expectations of the plans are seen to be realistic, then such a situation is likely to contribute to individual motivation both for current plan implementation and for future planning.

LEADERSHIP

In developing the implementation framework earlier in the chapter, it was stated that each manager needs to provide leadership for his particular area of responsibility, but will also be affected by leadership abilities from higher levels in the organizational structure. Leadership has been described as a confounding area of management understanding, with Hosmer[28] identifying the acknowledged general inability to prepare a research design that will identify measurable characteristics of leadership. Consequently, leadership within the context of planning suffers the same condition.

Stoner[5] has defined leadership as a process that will allow a manager to influence and direct task-related activities of group members. He then goes on to describe different approaches to explaining leadership, which are based upon the traits or personal characteristics of managers, behavoural patterns that are common to effective leaders and the situational factors or environment in which the leadership must be performed.

While leadership is probably necessary to allow a manager to maintain supremacy and control over his subordinates, excessive leadership means reduced participation for lower-level managers, probably resulting in detrimental effects on their personal motivation. The example of Amstrad, given in the last section, illustrates this point. The autocratic manner of the chairman gives a high level of influence and direction over managers, and, as explained, this style of leadership can have effects on motivation.[27] Different styles of leadership have been identified and discussed in the literature, although again there are vast differences in approach. However, that given by Brodwin and Bourgeois,[29] for example, is developed within the context of strategic plan implementation and relates primarily to the chief executive officer. These authors have developed five different models of leadership style as follows:

Commander model Planning is done at the top of the hierarchy and passed down the structure with orders to implement it.
Organizational-change model Again, planning is at the top but reorganization of the structure or other aspects of corporate life, such as personnel policies, are carried out in order to allow for implementation.
Collaborative model Senior managers are involved in the planning to aim for overall commitment to its implementation.
Cultural model Middle and lower managers are involved in the planning, aiming to develop a company culture for developing and implementing plans.
Crescive model From the Latin *crescere*, to grow, the style is to stimulate and encourage participation in planning and implementation throughout the structure, so that planning 'grows from within' the structure as opposed to being 'passed down'.

A final consideration of leadership within the context of planning comes from the text by Glueck and Jauch.[30] They suggest four major ways in which leadership can be exercised, as follows:

– Ensuring that suitable people hold key executive positions. This involves analysing individual skills, including leadership, making necessary personnel changes in the organizational structure, and delegating areas of planning and implementation to executives.
– Developing appropriate leadership styles and climates. In the latter, the concern of the manager is the confidence he can place in his subordinates, plus the opportunities and encouragement that he gives them to contribute to planning. Leadership style is similar to that given previously.
– Developing the careers of executives in the organizational structure. Here profiles of required personnel are needed as a consequence of current and future planning, capabilities of current executives must be determined, promotion and recruitment forecast, executive training planned and reward systems reviewed.
– By using organization development techniques to achieve necessary changes required as a consequence of planning and its implementation. These techniques were developed in the body of knowledge concerned with organizational behaviour, and consist of methods to inform and achieve acceptance of change.

Leadership within the organizational structure

In considering leadership within the organizational structure, attention needs to be directed to that required for strategic planning, for operational planning and for plan implementation. From the above discussions, it is probably apparent that a balance needs to be achieved between the type of leadership style to be fostered and the participation of managers throughout the structure. Although a particular leadership style may be pursued throughout the company, each manager is likely to develop his own modification of that style, although this needs to be viewed within the context of the acknowledged problems of measuring leadership characteristics.

In the case of leadership in strategic planning, the type of organizational structure adopted and the location of the responsibility for this planning, as discussed in Chapter 10, will have an influence on the leadership required. A commander style is probably more effective within a traditional functional hierarchy, while the more flexible matrix-type structures are probably more conducive to a crescive style. However, there is the issue of the adopted structure, which may have been caused by the predominant leadership styles within the company, or the cause may be the structure which only allows certain leadership styles to be used. However, the point is that those executives responsible need to exercise leadership, within the given structure, in order to be able to develop credible long-range direction that has the commitment of key managers.

In the case of leadership in operational planning, the leadership styles within the functional departments are of major concern. Where the strategic plan is passed down as a framework it is likely that a commander style will be initially experienced by the marketing personnel. However, the marketing manager will need to adopt a collaborative or cultural style in order to achieve the participation of personnel, so that details of marketing tactics are credible and have the support of the personnel concerned. In the case of marketing objectives and strategy a different focus is probably apparent. Here the chief marketing executive may lead the marketing operations by establishing these himself in relation to the strategic plan, or indeed he may decide to encourage fuller participation of his staff by adopting a crescive style.

In the implementation of plans leadership is equally important, although, because the tasks differ in nature from planning tasks, it plays a different role. Rather than develop an overall style, leadership is more related to interpersonal skills of directing and influencing personnel to achieve programmes of events or specific levels of performance, as specified in the plan documents. This type of leadership has been classified as micro-level leadership skills by Wright and Taylor.[31] Such skills, which are pertinent to leadership in the implementation of planning, include the following:

Influencing-behaviour skills These get people to do tasks, and involve recognition, criticism, orders, threats, requests, advice and explanations.

Handling-emotion skills These reduce emotion when it interferes with the performance of tasks, by means of apologies or inducing reflection; or raise emotions such as enthusiasm and job satisfaction.

Gathering-information skills These enable their possessor to obtain information from personnel, control the information flow initiated by subordinates, and check for a common understanding.

Finally, the major methods given by Glueck and Jauch to exercise leadership are pertinent throughout corporate planning and its implementation. Such principles relate to the leading of personnel not only in their job functions, but also in their personal relationships within the organization, so that these approaches are appropriate to tasks of both planning and implementation.

INTEGRATION

Although the activities to be implemented were originally part of a unified whole, the previous aspects of implementation have the effect of breaking down this coordination, so that implementation is executed as a series of component parts. Consequently, part of the implementation process needs to involve the integration of the implementation of these component parts, throughout the organizational structure. Harvey[32] has highlighted a major problem of integration, this being the identification and control of conflict between individuals and departments during the implementation process. Some degree of conflict within a company is seen to be almost inevitable, and in Chapter 9 the issue of differences in managers' attitudes and values was discussed. Here the issue is that these differences, along with the breaking down of the plans into separate component parts, provide potential for conflict to develop.

Therefore the general principle is that, although plans need to be broken down into component parts in order to be carried out, integration needs to be a feature of the implementation process. There are several approaches that can be used in order to pursue integration. The major alternatives are as follows:

The planning framework Both the strategic and the operational plans obviously constitute the basis of integration in that they represent the systematic logic for the company's future. However, a problem of integration can occur at the planning stage, which can permeate through into plan implementation. Indeed, writers such as Naylor[33] have emphasized the general problem of integrating strategic planning with operational planning. In Part Three of this book attention was given throughout to the integration of operational planning and strategic planning; it will be recalled that emphasis was given, for example, to integrating marketing strategy with organizational strategy. However, if integration problems are evident at the planning stage then it is likely that confusion will be experienced by personnel, which in turn is likely to affect implementation.

Communications In simple terms, communication involves the two-way transfer of information. Therefore, we are here concerned with each manager communicating his progress in implementation to other managers. Similarly, communication of plans is also necessary to ensure that each manager is aware of future intentions of the company at both strategic and operational levels. However, Camillus[34] has reported research that indicates that a formal planning system, by its very nature, demands increased interaction between managers, resulting in improved communications effectiveness. Although formal lines of communication are established through the organizational structure, managers can personally do much to improve communications. The chief executive of Campbell Soup, Gordon McGovern, is reported as following this type of approach: when needing information he will contact the person within the company most competent to provide it, regardless of his position in the organizational structure.[16]

Organizational structure The structure represents the official and formal chain of command, giving formal working and reporting relationships between the managers. Consequently, it provides a vehicle for vertical integration, with each level of management being able to use its delegated authority to achieve integration, but also being able to appeal to the next highest level.

Rules and procedures These can range from simple departmental instructions to a well-developed set of business policy guidelines. As explained in Chapter 3, the latter provide guidelines for the overall performance of each department within the company, so that the framework also aids integration for both planning and implementation. Within departments managers may develop procedures, rules for reporting and other similar regulations, all of which would be established with the aim of integrating plan implementation.

Information systems In Chapters 4 and 6 the importance of information within strategic and operational planning was presented, while its importance in exercising control is discussed in the next chapter. The principle here is that, in order to achieve integration, information needs to be communicated relative to the progress of implementation plus any problems that may develop. Additionally, the system needs to be designed to ensure that all personnel involved understand the requirements of the plan documents. At Wadkin, the chairman uses visual aids to constantly communicate the content of their plans to managers, as well as communicating the latest information concerning the progress of plan implementation.[9]

Horizontal relationships Integration also needs to take place across the organizational structure, so that all operational plans are not only integrated during preparation, but also co-ordinated in their implementation. During implementation the marketing department will be monitoring the achievement of sales volume against the plan, but this information needs to be provided to the production department to facilitate production scheduling. Similarly, the same information would be needed by the finance department to control cash flow, while the purchasing department would also need such an input for the purchasing of components or materials. This is but one example of the horizontal integration that needs to be achieved across the organizational structure.

While such relationships are often described as 'cutting across hierarchial channels', they are often achieved by the development of informal and beneficial associations between managers at the same level in the structure, but in a different line of authority. However, it may be necessary to create official horizontal relationships through committees, task forces, or matrix linking, or by designating certain executives with a liaison role. An example of close horizontal integration comes from the French cosmetics company, L'Oréal. The marketing function has recognized a market need for a hairspray that would hold hair firmly in place, but that would be soft in texture, unlike other hairsprays. Close associations between the marketing and research and development functions resulted in the successful planning, launch and market acceptance of the required product.[35]

These five major components of delegation, participation, motivation, leadership and integration are illustrated in Case Study 16 (page 224).

SUMMARY

Chapter 12 commenced with the establishment of five component parts, namely delegation, participation, motivation, leadership and integration, representing a framework to be examined in subsequent sections of the chapter. While being given as a framework for the implementation of plans, these components were also given as being prevalent in the planning stage, and indeed their utilization during planning was seen, throughout the chapter, to have further effects on their roles during implementation.

Delegation is concerned with the allocation of duties and authority, in relation to responsibility, accountability and power. Different approaches to participation have been given in the literature. These vary from determining a simple rate of participation, to giving full consideration to four component parts that constitute participation. Approaches examined to explain the nature of motivation were based upon characteristics of the individual, characteristics of the individual's job, the working environment, and those that attempt an integrative approach.

Leadership is concerned with managers influencing and directing personnel, although it is generally recognized that leadership is a confusing area of understanding. However, four different models of leadership style were examined in the chapter. As the last component, integration was seen to be necessary in order to bring together and co-ordinate the areas of planning, as implementation through the above component parts causes a splitting up into areas of responsibility. Six major approaches to achieve integration were examined.

CASE STUDY 16: HEWLETT PACKARD (C): THE EVOLUTION OF LEADERSHIP*

Case outline

This case study follows on in time from Case Study 6 (page 61), giving a further insight into this US electronics company, whose educational computers and calculators are the products best known to the general public. In Case Study 6 it was said that HP are a people-orientated company, where individual creativity and initiative are encouraged.

Illustration

By 1981, HP had become the world's second largest minicomputer manufacturer. The chief executive officer, John Young, required diligent planning throughout the company, while maintaining a people orientation. The case study illustrates the major issues of Chapter 12 as follows:

1 Delegation

Planning was delegated throughout the organizational structure, with the CEO giving guidance more than direction. Formal business policy included trust, confidence and respect for people to complete work delegated to them. All employees are required to meet their responsibilities, but are also encouraged to share them and to be helped by others.

2 Participation

John Young is reported to rely heavily on 'consensus-style management'. Few decisions were made without the full agreement of all concerned, and executives are expected to be independent thinkers. Even if Young disagreed with a decision he would accept the superior judgement of another executive. Formal business policy included encouraging participation and working together, as well as informality, open communications, and access to higher levels of management.

3 Motivation

Young had motivated staff to develop new products and technologies, such as electronic office systems, while motivating line managers to plan and implement their launch. HP business policy included many motivational aspects. Recognition, self-esteem, a sense of achievement, and job security were emphasized. Sharing in the firm's success through profits, stock purchases, and a retirement pension was established. HP profess to develop managers through training and education, aimed at internal promotions. Two major policies are 'management by wandering around' and an 'open door policy'. The former is aimed at getting an understanding of the feelings of personnel about their jobs, while the latter is to encourage personnel to communicate freely with higher levels of management.

* Derived from R. M. Atherton, Hewlett Packard (C). Copyright © 1982 Roger M. Atherton.

4 Leadership

John Young outlined three major rules within his leadership, being diligent planning, cost effectiveness and no last-minute surprises. He had also changed the overall direction of HP, placing added emphasis on marketing as well as manufacturing, while stimulating the development of new products and technologies. He was reported to be an efficient worker who does not tolerate incompetence. Although he encourages participation, he was also able to logically discuss issues to influence managers to change their opinions. He saw himself as being good at a non-directive approach in the role of CEO.

5 Integration

Integration of the diverse operations of HP were pursued through an organizational structure split into divisions, but with well-defined lines of authority within the structure. Within this structure decentralization into smaller working groups was possible, so that common areas, including the marketing operations of the divisions, could be integrated. Additionally the 'management by wandering around' and 'open door' policies would also encourage integration. Overall, their reliance on planning, as already cited, would provide a major vehicle for integration.

REVIEW QUESTIONS

1. Why should firms experience difficulty in implementing well-prepared plans?
2. Discuss the relationship of the concepts that need to be considered when delegating.
3. 'Participation and motivation can be considered to be synonymous, so that they do not warrant separate consideration'. Discuss.
4. Do you consider that intrinsic components of motivation are more important than extrinsic components?
5. Explain the advantages and disadvantages of a range of models of leadership style.
6. What approaches can be pursued in a company to achieve integration?

REFERENCES

1. M. A. Lyles, and R. T. Lenz, 'Managing the planning process: a field study of the human side of planning', *Strategic management Journal*, **3**, 105–18, 1982.
2. D. I. Cleland, and W. R. King, 'Developing a planning culture for more effective strategic planning', *Long Range Planning*, **7**, 3, 70–4, 1974.
3. 'Gould's golden gamble', *Management Today*, February 1984.
4. P. P. Pekar, 'Planning: a guide to implementation', *Managerial Planning*, **20**, 3–6, 1980.
5. Stoner, J. A. F., *Management*, Prentice-Hall, Englewood Cliffs, 1982.
6. 'GM's unlikely revolutionist', *Fortune*, 19 March 1984.
7. 'ICI thrives on self-inflicted culture shock', *Fortune*, 16 April 1984.
8. 'ICI's new yarn', *Management Today*, February 1984.
9. 'How Wadkin worked clear', *Management Today*, May 1984.
10. G. A. Steiner, 'Long range planning: concept and implementation', *Financial Executive*, July 1966.
11. 'The hardest worker in South Korea', *Fortune*, 20 August 1984.
12. Pateman, C., *Participation and Democratic Theory*, Cambridge University Press, Cambridge, 1970.
13. H. J. Kloeze, A. Molenkamp and F. J. W. Roelofs, 'Strategic planning and participation', *Long Range Planning*, **13**, 5, 10–20, 1980.
14. R. G. Dyson, and M. J. Foster, 'The relationship of participation and effectiveness in strategic planning', *Strategic Management Journal*, **3**, 1, 77–8, 1982.
15. 'Exxon rededicated', *Fortune*, 23 July 1984.
16. 'Eight big masters of innovation', *Fortune*, 15 October 1984.
17. J. W. Dickson, 'Participation as an interaction, communication and influence process', *Personnel Review*, **12**, 1, 17–22, 1983.
18. 'Eight big masters of innovation', *Fortune*, 15 October 1984.
19. McClelland, D. C., *The Achieving Society*, Van Nostrand, Princeton, 1961.
20. 'Conran's new Habitat', *Management Today*, November 1983.
21. Herzberg, F., *Work and the Nature of Man*, World Publishing, New York, 1966.
22. D. R. Hampton, 'The planning–motivation dilemma', *Business Horizons*, **16**, 79–87, June 1973.
23. 'Toshiba's British switch', *Management Today*, March 1984.
24. T. C. Mawhinney, 'Intrinsic X extrinsic motivation', *Organizational Behaviour and Human Performance*, **24**, 411–40, 1979.
25. Porter, L. W., and E. E. Lawler, *Managerial Attitudes and Performance*, Irwin, Homewood, 1968.
26. 'How to create commitment', *Management Today*, November 1984.
27. 'Amstrad's personal ambitions', *Management Today*, June 1984.
28. L. A. Hosmer, 'The importance of strategic leadership', *Journal of Business Strategy*, **3**, 2, 47–57, 1982.
29. D. R. Brodwin, and L. J. Bourgeois, 'Strategic implementation: five approaches to an elusive phenomenon', *Strategic Management Journal*, **5**, 241–64, 1984.
30. Glueck, W. F., and L. R. Jauch, *Business Policy and Strategic Management*, 4th edn, McGraw-Hill, New York, 1984.
31. P. L. Wright, and D. S. Taylor, 'The inter-personal skills of leadership', *Leadership and Organisational Development Journal*, **2**, 2, 6–12, 1981.
32. Harvey, D. F., *Strategic Management*, Merrill, Columbus, 1982.
33. T. H. Naylor, 'How to integrate strategic planning into your management process', *Long Range Planning*, **14**, 5, 56–61, 1981.
34. J. C. Camillus, 'Evaluating the benefits of formal planning systems', *Long Range Planning*, **8**, 3, 33–40, 1975.
35. 'A makeup maker's fast, foxy rise', *Fortune*, 14 May 1984.

THIRTEEN
CONTROL

Learning objectives are to:

1. Appreciate the framework for exercising control.
2. Understand approaches for controlling profits and profitability.
3. Understand approaches for controlling both quantitative and qualitative objectives.
4. Understand the range of approaches available for controlling strategies and tactics.
5. Recognize major concepts that have been introduced.

Compared with the planning issues examined in the previous chapters, control is probably simpler to understand conceptually, although in practice it can be as complex as any area of planning. In plain terms, control is concerned with attempting to ensure that things don't go wrong during the implementation of plans. In the first chapter the concept of control was briefly examined in the context of being a major managerial activity; it was described as being concerned with the measurement of the actual implementation of activities from plans, comparing actual results against the desired results given in the plans, and taking appropriate corrective measures to ensure that the desired results are achieved.

It will be apparent to readers that control needs to be exercised relative to both strategic and operational planning. Desired results are given in both, so that both need to be controlled in relation to the time periods to which they apply. Indeed, as will be seen later in the chapter, specific methods of control can be used in relation to both strategic and operational planning. However, as operational planning covers the immediate period of time, operational control is given attention on a day-to-day basis, whereas strategic control is concerned with longer-term development. In addition, organizational structure is also likely to affect the exercise of control. Following the different approaches that can be used, as discussed in Chapter 10, the role of control will need to be established for different divisions, SBUs and markets.

Although explanations of control tend, by necessity, to be almost totally devoted to methodology, the importance of the outcome is twofold. First, as already stated above, control is taking corrective action during the time period of the plan to pursue desired and planned results. Second, the process of control generates knowledge about the performance of a company in relation to its overall and total environment. As was seen in Parts Two and Three of the book, information about such knowledge is important to the total information input for both strategic and operational planning.

This chapter is based upon five sections. In the first, attention is given to establishing a framework for control to be used throughout the implementation of strategic and operational planning. The second looks at the control of profits, the third at the control of objectives, while the fourth considers the control of both strategies and tactics. The final section addresses empirical evidence of the utilization of control methods by firms.

CONTROL FRAMEWORK

The role of control within planning was outlined in the introduction. Writers such as Mockler[1] see no clear distinction between planning and control, classifying them as an overall system to provide overall co-ordination of the process of management. Therefore an effective plan has controls built into it, but sound planning methods are required for effective control. Here the link is into the overall effectiveness of planning and in Chapter 11 control was seen to be an attribute to be incorporated into the multidimensional approach to assessing effectiveness. Despite this interrelationship, Kollat, Blackwell and Robeson[2] identify that merely planning to produce a plan does not automatically mean that control will follow. They point out that planning and control are at opposite ends of the management spectrum, with control requiring as much managerial attention as planning. Although Metal Box Company had dominated packing in the United Kingdom, a changing marketing environment led to a loss of control during the seventies. Metal Box had introduced the two-piece beverage can, but competitors could easily copy the product. Additionally, an expanding market gave ample potential for competitors, while the hot summer of 1976 attracted US manufacturers to enter the UK market. Consequently, Metal Box were unable to control their maintenance of their dominant market share.[3]

Basic considerations

Developing from the overall role of control, many writers have suggested basic considerations for the establishment of a system of control in relation to the planning of marketing. These considerations tend to be similar and those given below have been developed from the work of Wilson[4] and Greenwood:[5]

- Developing standards of performance against which to measure actual results.
- Developing acceptable tolerances to represent the amount of deviation from the standard that will be allowed.
- Measuring the actual results that are achieved by installing control methods.
- Comparing the actual results against the standards, using both quantitative and qualitative measures.
- Taking action during the current planning period to correct performance to achieve the plan.
- Taking action during subsequent planning periods as a consequence of knowledge gained about the company's environment.

This gives a logical and conceptually simple system to follow but, as indicated in the introduction, the practice of control can be complex given the many variables that can affect the achievement of plans, as emphasized throughout the book. Indeed, these many variables need to be taken into account in the system of control. Christopher[6] has claimed that many firms approach control almost totally from the standpoint of profitability, whereas, he argues, business success can be assessed only by measuring performance against many criteria and in relation to the complexities of a firm's environment.

These basic considerations for control are illustrated in Fig. 13.1. The left-hand side gives the stages of control as given above, whereas the right-hand side illustrates their links into the various stages of planning as discussed in the previous chapters of the book. The standards of

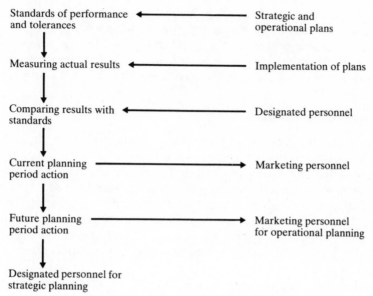

Standards of performance ←————————— Strategic and
and tolerances   operational plans

↓

Measuring actual results ←————————— Implementation of plans

↓

Comparing results with ←————————— Designated personnel
standards

↓

Current planning —————————————→ Marketing personnel
period action

↓

Future planning —————————————→ Marketing personnel
period action   for operational planning

↓

Designated personnel for
strategic planning

Figure 13.1 Basic considerations for control

performance and their associated tolerances are already established within the strategic and operational plans. Specific control in both these areas will be examined below.

The measurement of actual results and comparison with the standards occurs during the implementation of plans, but for both tasks selected personnel need to be delegated responsibility to carry out these stages. Here the responsibility needs to exist both to complete the tasks and to report the consequences. For operational control it will lie with marketing personnel, who will report to the chief marketing executive. For strategic control it could again belong to marketing personnel, or those given responsibility for strategic planning as discussed in Chapter 10, while the consequences will be reported to those executives designated within the organizational structure. Here McCarthy et al.[7] emphasize the obvious need for effective communication in reporting and discuss whether the firm should adopt a policy of exception reporting. This means each manager currently directs his efforts to areas of his responsibility that are not within the tolerances, while only reporting those measurements that are outside previously determined parameters. An example here comes from the US packaging company the Ball Corporation. It has been reported that the firm has consistently achieved highly ambitious goals, with profits deviating by no more than 5 per cent from the plan during the 4-year period up to the report. The chief executive officer claims that this is due to tight control of performance against their 10-year, 5-year and 1-year plans, the latter being a 'living document' for company management.[8]

The ultimate aspect of Fig. 13.1 is that action is instigated as a consequence of exercising control. For the current marketing plan it may be that tactics need to be modified over the coming months in order to overcome falling sales or market share objectives. This will give control of performance. In addition, in this type of situation, monthly targets for sales and market share will need to be increased in order to overcome the shortfall experienced in previous months. This will give control of achievement. For the strategic plan the consequences are likely to be apparent only on completion of the implementation of the current marketing plan. Results for the year will give an indication of any necessary revision to organizational objectives and strategy, either as modifications to the current long-range plan, or as potential changes to long-run direction. Again, personnel need to be delegated responsibility to both instigate and implement necessary action. For the marketing plan the onus will obviously be on marketing personnel, but again, consequences for the strategic plan will be the responsibility of those executives identified within the organizational structure. At ICI, for example, greater strategic control is claimed to be exercised now in the boardroom than was previously the case.[9]

Strategic and operational control

As already established, control needs to be exercised in relation to both strategic and operational planning. In addition, the system needs to incorporate the organizational structure, including any split into divisions, SBUs or markets. In Chapter 10, different alternatives for locating strategic and operational planning within different types of structures were discussed. Here the principle is that the exercise of control needs to match the arrangements for planning, so that strategic planning at the divisional level needs to be matched by divisional level control. For such organizational splits, Higgins[10] suggests the concept of management control to be used at divisional or SBU level, with strategic control being limited to control of the group's organizational strategy.

Referring back to Part Two of the book, it is perhaps obvious that strategic control will be concerned with the achievement of organizational objectives, plus the suitability of organizational strategy both to achieve these objectives as well as to provide a framework for operational planning. Additionally, in the very long run, it will also involve the continued suitability of the organizational mission in relation to changes in stakeholder expectations.

Similarly, referring back to Part Three, it will perhaps be obvious that operational control will be concerned with marketing objectives and strategy. Additionally, it will also be concerned with the control of other key sections of the marketing plan as given in Chapter 8, namely tactics, the programme of action and the marketing budget.

Within the two types of control there are obviously similarities. As a consequence, the specific methods that can be used to effect control are the same, except that they are used for different reasons in each control situation. The next three sections of this chapter are devoted to these methods, which are classified into three groups as follows:

- Control of profits.
- Control of objectives.
- Control of strategies and tactics.

Within each of these sections the differences in their application to strategic and operational control will be discussed, as part of the overall presentation of the range of control methods available.

CONTROL OF PROFITS

In this section attention is given to the control of profit as an absolute figure measured in terms of a value, as well as profitability. The latter is concerned with measuring profits relative to another indicator and requires a different approach to control. Profit is normally controlled through the use of budgets, whereas profitability is normally controlled through the use of ratio analysis.

Budgetary control

Within the operational planning of marketing, profit control would normally be tackled through the utilization of the marketing budget. In Chapter 8 this approach was introduced in that the budget was given as being a major part of the marketing plan and was identified as a method of control. In simple terms, the budget represents a monthly financial plan for the full year of sales, costs, contribution and profits, which can be presented for different products and markets. The methodology of budgetary control is to simply compare the actual figures for each month with the planned figures given in the budget and determine any variance between the two.

The major elements of the marketing budget are given in Fig. 13.2. Where there are variances between actual and planned figures the consequences are twofold, as previously indicated. First, adverse variances or shortfalls in sales, contribution, and profit will need to be compensated for in monthly targets for later months in the year, if the objectives for the year are to be achieved. Similarly, adverse cost changes will need to be examined for likely continuation. The second consequence is that the causes of the variances need to be determined and necessary remedial modifications made to the range of marketing tactics, as outlined in Chapter 8. However, an important point to emphasize here is that identifying the causes of variances may be quite complex, again due to the complexity of variables affecting the marketing environment. Additionally, determining remedial action can be similarly complex, although both issues will be examined again later in the chapter. Control of sales value and marketing costs will be given full consideration in the next major section of this chapter, which addresses the control of objectives. This leaves consideration of the absolute figures of contribution and profits at this point.

                                                January → December
Sales value
Less: Variable manufacturing costs

Manufacturing contribution
Less: Assignable marketing costs

Product/market contribution
Less: Non-assignable marketing costs

Marketing contribution
Less: Fixed costs

Net profit

Figure 13.2   Marketing budget control

Within the marketing operational plan, monthly control is obviously concerned with achieving monthly targets to give attainment of profit and contribution objectives for the year. Here the figures are simply recorded for visual inspection of the developing monthly trends, or they can be presented as simple bar charts or line graphs. The relative degree of importance of contribution over profit at the operational level appears to be developing in the literature, although different approaches are taken in firms. In Chapter 6 the different schools of thought on locating profit responsibility in the marketing department were examined, but where responsibility lies in the department then control of the absolute levels of profit for individual products and markets needs attention. Control of contribution is seen to be important by writers such as Hulbert and Toy,[11] in that the two levels given in Fig. 13.2 represent the margins produced by the marketing operations. However, in both cases, attainment of planned levels is achieved through the above-mentioned procedure, followed by remedial action to achieve required adjustments to sales value and marketing costs. Annual results of profit and contribution also need to be used to control the achievement of these aims within the set of organizational objectives. The actual levels need to be compared with those given for the corresponding year. Where there is a shortfall, then the decision may be to revise levels given in the objectives for the next five years. Alternatively, the decision may be to revise the organizational strategy, with the aim of sustaining original growth aspirations, which in turn is likely to require changes in the next round of operational planning.

Profitability control

As mentioned earlier, profitability is concerned with a measurement of profits relative to another indicator, such as sales value, or the capital employed to earn the particular level of profit. Similarly, contribution can also be measured on a basis relative to indicators such as sales or capital employed. Reference to any text on financial management will give the range of measures, given as a ratio or percentage, which normally commence their presentation with an overall profitability equation such as follows, with profit being before tax:

$$\text{Profitability} = \frac{\text{profit}}{\text{total assets}} = \frac{\text{profit}}{\text{sales}} \times \frac{\text{sales}}{\text{total assets}}$$

Here profitability is initially given as a ratio of profit relative to total assets, but which can be also split into two additional ratios. Additional profitability ratios are given in Fig. 13.3, where profit before tax is again used.

$$\text{Return on capital employed (ROCE)} = \frac{\text{profit}}{\text{capital employed}}$$

$$\text{Return on assets} = \frac{\text{profit}}{\text{total assets}}$$

$$\text{Profit margin} = \frac{\text{profit}}{\text{sales}}$$

$$\text{Return on shareholders' funds} = \frac{\text{profit}}{\text{total funds}}$$

Figure 13.3 Profitability ratios

Each of the four ratios measures profitability on a different basis. Return on capital employed measures profits in relation to the capital of shareholders' funds and long-term loans used to generate the profit. Return on total assets measures profit against the total of fixed, intangible, and intermediate assets that were utilized to generate the profit. The profit margin is an expression of the proportion of sales revenue that is achieved as profit. The final ratio from Fig. 13.3 relates profit to the sum of share capital, reserves, and the profit and loss account balance. A major problem in determining these methods is that different definitions of these four denominators are used by different writers and companies. For example, Bishop[12] has given eleven variations on the ROCE theme, all of which can be labelled as return on capital employed, but all of which would give a different result. Therefore when comparing ratios, as discussed below, it is essential to ensure that they have been determined with a common base.

At the operational level these ratios would normally be calculated at the end of the period of the annual marketing plan, or, if on a monthly basis, for a period going back the previous twelve months. The value of each ratio can be calculated for each division, SBU or market and compared with planned levels established in relevent objectives. At the strategic level the annual ratios need to be examined for consistency with the long-run requirements. Again, it may be necessary to revise levels to be aimed for in subsequent years as a consequence of this year's performance, or indeed to reconsider organizational strategy for the future.

Although objectives for each ratio are the standard for comparing current ratios, these still need to be related to a base in order to make a value judgement as to current performance. A simple approach is to establish a historical trend of ratios for each year, with the forecasts for the future extension of the trend representing profitability growth requirements. Such trends can be simply plotted on a control chart, as given in Fig. 13.4, where a separate chart for each ratio trend would be required. The chart shows the actual ratio for each particular point in time, as well as the ongoing trend. These are compared with the objective and the tolerances for acceptance, which are given as upper and lower limits on the chart. Although the objective line is given as being constant, indicating a no-growth requirement for profitability, it would obviously show an upward trend where growth of profitability is an objective. In Fig. 13.4 all ratios are given as being within the limits, so that they can be considered to be acceptable for control purposes. However, although within the limits, a downward trend of profitability is indicated, illustrating that it is the identification of trends of profitability for which control charts can be valuable.

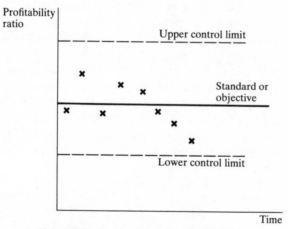

Figure 13.4 A control chart for profitability

Another approach to establishing a base for comparing current ratios to objectives is to derive them from comparisons with the performance of other similar companies. This can be achieved by referring to comparisons for a wide range of industries, published by specialist firms producing such a service, such as the ICC Information Group Ltd, where ICC refers to inter-company comparisons.[13] This service includes the presentation of industry averages for the four ratios given in Fig. 13.3, along with a whole range of other financial ratios. Hence a company operating in the packaging or confectionery markets, for example, can compare their trends for these four profitability ratios with the averages for their respective industries.

However, care needs to be taken in making such comparisons, and these warnings are given by publishers of the comparisons. The basic principle is to ensure that the ratios are being compared with ratios that come from comparable firms. Although companies may operate in the same industry they can still exhibit many differences that may affect the validity of comparisons. Such differences are:

- variations in size and economics of scale;
- capital intensity and efficiency of production plant;
- nature of organizational objectives and strategy;
- previous performance and trends of profitability;
- particular market segments of participation;
- any financial support from a parent company or other source;
- spread of the company's business in export markets;
- proportion of production carried out in export markets.

All these differences could affect the value of inter-company comparisons, so that, although such comparisons can be valuable as a base for control purposes, it must be ensured that major differences are not present.

An application of these control measures to a major British company is given in Case Study 17 (page 241).

CONTROL OF OBJECTIVES

In Chapters 4 and 6 the range of organizational and marketing objectives were examined, some of them quantitative and the remainder qualitative. Quantitative organizational objectives (Chapter 4) were given as being concerned with market spread, growth, profitability, and efficiency, while organizational objectives concerned with market leadership, customer service, personnel and social responsibility are largely qualitative. Quantitative marketing objectives (Chapter 6) are concerned with sales volume, market share, costs and profit, while marketing mix objectives can be both qualitative and quantitative in nature. However, quantitative measures of the elements of the marketing mix are more meaningfully considered in the section addressing the control of strategies and tactics. Given this split, the approach taken in this section is to tackle each in turn, as the nature of the objectives dictates the approach to be taken in their control. The utilization of objectives for the purpose of control completes the process of management by objectives, as presented in Chapter 4.

Control of objectives, both within the literature and as exercised by firms, tends to be approached by tackling each objective in turn and using the appropriate control. Integrative approaches to control within the marketing plan have been developed, although their acceptance and utilization seem to be extremely limited. For example, Barlev and Lampert[14] have proposed a model which attempts to measure and evaluate performance on the basis of the joint effects of the external environment, the product life-cycle, and inflation, in relation to sales, market share, and profit objectives.

Quantitative control

Throughout these quantitative objectives, variance analysis can be used, although ratio analysis is more appropriate for profitability (as given above) and efficiency in the case of organizational objectives, and for marketing costs in the case of marketing operational objectives.

Variance analysis The approach to variance analysis is as previously described, but again with the emphasis on the causes of variances in order to instigate remedial action. If we assume that ratio analysis will be used as mentioned, this means that variances will be used to control sales volume, growth and market share. At the operational level this involves the routine and continuous comparison of actual levels with planned levels, usually incorporating extensive breakdowns, such as by products, markets, geographical areas, customer groupings and market segments. Remedial action is generally by modifications to marketing tactics and specific responsibility and accountability is normally associated with the control of specific breakdowns of sales volume and market share. Three company examples illustrate the contrasting importance of sales volume control. At machine manufacturers Wadkin, the installation of controls, and particularly sales control, contributed to the company's recovery in the early eighties.[15] At Tandem Computers the long lead-time between sales negotiation with customers and achieving the actual sale causes control problems, as does the trend towards a smaller number of customers spending larger sums.[16] At Chrysler Cars in the United States, market share is a major concern for control. The company is reported to carefully monitor its share relative to Ford, General Motors, Toyota and Nissan, while executive bonuses are effected by, *inter alia*, changes in Chrysler's market share.[17]

At the strategic planning level, sales need to be controlled in relation to the growth required over the long term. Short-term changes may be indicative of either changes to the next set of organizational objectives, or modifications to organizational strategy to sustain the required growth. During the seventies ICI maintained control over their long-term growth objective, despite the effects on their business of economic factors, although the strategy was to alter their market spread by reducing their reliance on commodity products.[9]

Ratio analysis In Chapter 4 a range of measures was given that can be used to establish organizational objectives to attempt to control internal efficiency. The associated ratios that can be calculated in order to control these measures are given in Fig. 13.5. The utilization and

$$\text{Sales on total assets or asset utilization} = \frac{\text{sales}}{\text{total assets}}$$

$$\text{Stock turnover} = \frac{\text{sales}}{\text{stocks}}$$

$$\text{Credit period} = \frac{\text{value of debtors}}{\text{sales}} \times 365$$

$$\text{Liquidity} = \frac{\text{current assets}}{\text{current liabilities}}$$

$$\text{Departmental costs} = \frac{\text{department costs}}{\text{sales}}$$

Figure 13.5 Efficiency control ratios

interpretation of these ratios follows an approach similar to those calculated from profitability. Again trends need to be established and again the values need to be examined for consistency with long-run requirements with the view of making any necessary remedial changes. Inter-company comparisons are also available for these ratios, but again care needs to be taken in their use, as previously explained.

In Chapter 4 a classification of marketing costs was given. The associated ratios that can be calculated to control these costs are normally calculated by dividing the costs for each classification by total sales, such as;

$$\frac{\text{Advertising costs}}{\text{Sales}} \qquad \frac{\text{Product management costs}}{\text{Sales}}$$

Here the aim is obviously to control the proportion of sales that is to be absorbed by each of the marketing department cost centres. The object may be to control to a particular level or to control for a cost reduction. Although the latter may be attractive in terms of improved efficiency, it needs to be realized that reductions in expenditure can lead to reduced product development, reduced selling effort, reduced communications and reduced market knowledge. Therefore, although short-term cost savings may be achieved, the long-term effectiveness of marketing operations may be reduced, which would be detrimental to the achievement of strategic plans. For example, the Metal Box Company experienced high costs associated with holding high levels of stocks during the early eighties. However, this was part of the total service offered to their customers, so that controlling this cost would have needed careful attention.[3]

Finally, control charts can also be used for all these ratios. For the efficiency control ratios a separate chart would obviously be needed for each ratio, and again the standard or objective would be the centre line with upper and lower limits. For the marketing costs it may be useful to have a control chart for total marketing expenditure as a proportion of sales, as well as a breakdown for each of the marketing functions. However, in both cases the overall aim is again to identify trends developing in any of these ratios so that any necessary modifications can be made.

Qualitative control

As stated above, organizational objectives requiring this approach to control are concerned with market leadership, customer service, personnel and social responsibility. The first two of these were described as requiring marketing orientation within both their formulation and their achievement, as well as providing a means for developing marketing orientation. Here executive judgement needs to be used as a method of control to assess their achievement, although quasi-quantitative measures, such as percentages of units returned by customers, may be used for, say, a contribution to the control of product quality. Again, the example of the Metal Box Company is valuable here. Executive judgement would have indicated their control of market leadership in the seventies in that they dominated the market, had introduced successful innovations, such as the two-piece beverage can, and had made many advances in the technology related to packaging. However, despite this control, market changes had affected their business, indicating a need for a complete control system.[3]

Similarly, executive judgements also need to be made to control objectives involving both personnel and social responsibility. The role of marketing communications in the latter was particularly emphasized in Chapter 4. Therefore judgements need to be made as to how well the company is achieving issues such as a beneficial corporate image, success in maintaining ethical standards and useful contributions to the welfare and wellbeing of the society in which it operates.

Similarly, objectives within the marketing mix require value judgements for their control, although quantitative measures within the mix will be examined in the next section. For example, judgements need to be made on the success of product modifications, finding new uses for existing products, the necessity to follow competitors' price changes, success in selling higher margin products, success of channels in reaching target customers, and success in changing consumer attitudes through advertising and sales promotions. These judgements on the marketing mix should normally be in conjunction with the control of marketing tactics, following in the next section.

CONTROL OF STRATEGIES AND TACTICS

Even though major efforts are made towards the control of objectives, additional control can be directly achieved in relation to both strategies and tactics. Although indirect control is obviously achieved as a result of controlling objectives, it will be seen in this section that direct controls can also be valuable. Although these controls are largely based upon value judgement, attempts have been made to develop more objective approaches. The exception is the quantitative approach that can be used for marketing tactics, as mentioned in the last section. In this section, attention is given to organizational strategy, marketing strategy and marketing tactics. However, after attention has been given to control in these areas of planning, the ultimate step must be to review logically the organizational mission with the view of making any necessary modifications, which also represents a control procedure.

Control of strategies

As already mentioned, indirect control of both organizational and marketing strategy can be achieved indirectly through the control of objectives. Here modifications are 'forced' into being through the need to take corrective action as a result of developing trends in both long- and short-range objectives.

An early approach to control strategy is based upon an evaluation procedure developed by Tilles.[18] This consists of six criteria that need to be considered, the results of which will allow for value judgements to be made concerning strategy modifications, giving control in relation to these criteria. These are summarized as follows:

- Consistency of the strategy with the other stages of planning and internal policies.
- Consistency with the external environment to pursue opportunities and overcome threats.
- Suitability relative to available resources to effectively implement the strategy.
- The level of risk that the strategy represents and its acceptability to the company.
- The period of time to which the strategy relates, although this would be established within the overall planning.
- The effectiveness of the strategy in achieving its intended outcomes. Here a full consideration of effectiveness is applicable, as given in Chapter 11.

This range of value judgements is applicable to both organizational and marketing strategies, so that decisions on modifications can provide a means of control for each. Subsequent approaches to applying such qualitative criteria have done little to expand this approach, with Rumelt,[19] for example, giving criteria of consistency, consonance, competitive advantage and feasibility. However, development has taken place in assessment approaches to be used for control, although they are not concerned only with strategies. These approaches are classified under the general heading of planning audits and they will be examined later in this section.

Control of tactics

There are four overall approaches that can be used to control marketing tactics, being based upon variances, quantitative measures, marketing plan programmes and planning audits.

The approach to variance analysis is as already described. Progress of the marketing mix objectives is monitored throughout the period of the plan to identify any differences between the planned objectives and the results actually being achieved. Again, the central issue is identifying causes of variances and executing any necessary modifications to marketing tactics, through the accommodation of contingency tactics, as described in Chapter 8. Here the orientation is short-term in that control is concerned with operations being currently implemented to achieve existing levels of performance.

Quantitative measures have been developed for the individual elements of the marketing mix. Within the literature specialized texts for each of the marketing functions prescribe various indicators to be used on a regular basis to assess the efficiency of each of the functions, although considerable attention seems to have been devoted to the selling and advertising functions. Indicators for the selling function have been suggested by many writers such as Hartley,[20] with the following being detailed for members of the salesforce:

- Calls made per day/month.
- Average number of orders per day/month.
- Ratio of orders to calls.
- Average cost per call.
- Average number of new customers per month.

Indicators for the advertising function have had similar attention, with Aaker and Myers[21] advocating indicators such as:

- Cost per thousand buyers reached.
- Coverage of target audience per period of time.
- Numbers from the target audience who saw adverts.
- Numbers from the target audience who could recall the adverts.

For each of these indicators, standards need to be established, based upon previous levels of performance and those that are deemed to be desirable in relation to the full range of marketing objectives. Control is obviously achieved by again making modifications to the relevant marketing tactics, if measurements for the indicators are found to be below the established standards.

In Chapter 8 methods were discussed for establishing marketing plan programmes, with the aim of relating the specific activities of the marketing tactics to a schedule that will specify the time periods in which they will be implemented. Here control can be achieved by monitoring the implementation of the specific activities against the times given in the programme. Where activities are not completed on time, such 'slippage' is likely to necessitate changes to the schedules. This is particularly important where network analysis methods have been used, as each activity is timed related to other activities, and slippage may even result in the need for a totally revised programme. Consequently, control can be achieved in relation to time, the necessary sequence of activity implementation can be controlled and interrelationships of the specific activities maintained.

Planning audits

Auditing is concerned with examining or investigating, a process which is well established in financial management. However, the process is more precise than a simple examination, usually requiring analysis, a systematic approach, and a critical evaluation of the results of the analysis. The aim is usually to check for accuracy and efficiency.

Within the context of marketing, Tirman[22] describes audits as being overall assessments of the total role of marketing within an organization. Kotler, Gregor and Rodgers[23] suggest four features of a marketing audit, which can be explained as follows:

- It should cover all marketing aspects.
- Ideally it should be done by an independent analyst.
- A systematic approach should be followed.
- It should be on a regular basis, even if the firm has been successful.

The approach suggested by Wilson[24] differs from the above in that he sees the role of an audit as being the evaluation of the effectiveness of the other types of control, with the specific tasks of an audit being described as follows:

- Appraising existing control methods being used.
- Determining compliance of performance with that given in plan documents.
- Determining accountability that has been achieved in plan implementation.
- Appraising the adequacy of the information systems developed for planning.
- Examining the approach taken by managers to exercise control.

The use of marketing audits was developed in the seventies and the areas to be audited were suggested by several writers at that time, including those mentioned earlier in this section, with all advocating a similar approach. Indeed, this is to go systematically through the stages of planning as described in Parts Two and Three of this book and to criticize constructively the firm's performance at each stage of the planning. While the quantitative measures previously discussed can be utilized, extensive use of value judgement is made. However, the overall approach in the audit needs to be different from other control methods, as stated by Wilson,[24] in that it is a detached examination, requiring a complete overview of the total planning system. Whereas the other methods of control require measurements of specific areas of performance relative to specific planned levels, the audit produces a *gestalt* appraisal of the whole role of the strategic and operational planning of marketing. This method provides control in that it allows for an opportunity to examine the planning as a whole, as well as giving an opportunity to appraise the relationship of the individual stages of planning. The marketing operational plan can be judged for overall consistency with the strategic plan, while judgements can also be made as to how closely, for example, the marketing strategy relates to the organizational strategy.

EVIDENCE OF CONTROL UTILIZATION

The research results discussed in this section, with the exception of one, were all carried out within the context of marketing operational planning. During his investigations into British firms, McDonald[25] found that his sample firms generated a high level of information relative to markets, to allow for control of the implementation of plans. Additionally, he found that the central methods of control used were sales forecasts and budgetary control. A similar result was found by Greenley[26] in that budgetary control and sales analysis were the most favoured methods used by his repondent UK firms.

Management by objectives was used by nearly 70 per cent of the Greenley sample, while Hooley, West and Lynch[27] found that a slightly larger proportion of their sample of UK firms use this method. However, Greenley found that less than half his respondents claimed to use ratio analysis, control charts and marketing audits. In contrast, a study by Eppink, Keunning and De Jong[28] of a sample of Dutch companies, within the context of long-range planning, found extensive use of financial and accounting techniques. In particular, ratio analysis was found to be used by nearly all the companies for control purposes.

The surveys by Greenley,[26] Hooley, West and Lynch,[27] and Hopkins[29] also investigated the areas in which firms exercise control relative to their marketing operational plans, where the latter study was an investigation of US companies. All three found that control of profits and sales were of central importance across the whole of the companies surveyed, while the first-mentioned study found that a greater proportion orientate this control to products rather than to markets. Control of market share was found to be less important, with the first two investigations finding that only about half the companies consider it to be highly important to control. Control of the elements of the marketing mix were investigated by both Greenley and Hopkins, although differing results were obtained. In the former, an excess of 70 per cent of respondents claimed some control for each of the elements, whereas the Hopkins results gave lower proportions, with only slightly more than half declaring that they control the advertising and selling functions.

SUMMARY

The last chapter of the book has addressed control of the implementation of plans. In the first section a framework was presented that can be used as a basis for the exercise of control, the principles of which were given to be equally applicable to the control of both strategic and operational plans. The framework also included a classification of control in relation to profits, objectives, and strategies and tactics.

Approaches given for the control of profits were budgetary control for the absolute value of profits, while ratio analysis and control charts were given for the control of profitability as a relative measure of profits. Budgetary control was based upon budgets that are incorporated into the marketing plan, while ratios are calculated as a trend that can also be compared with ratios of similar organizations as an inter-company comparison.

Control of objectives was related to both organizational and marketing objectives. The approaches to control presented were classified as being either quantitative or qualitative in nature. For quantitative objectives, variance analysis can be used for continuous comparisons, although ratios can also be calculated to give a trend and for inter-company comparisons. Qualitative objectives are largely controlled through executive judgement, although quasi-quantitative measurements can also be made.

Control of both strategies and tactics can initially be achieved indirectly through the control of objectives. However, executive judgement also needs to be widely used. For marketing tactics, a range of quantitative measures for control are available, while programmes of scheduled completion times for the implementation of tactics also provide a means of control. Finally, planning audits were also discussed. Here the orientation is a *gestalt* approach to control, examining and investigating the total approach to planning as opposed to specific controls.

CASE STUDY 17: INTERNATIONAL COMPUTERS PLC (ICL) (A)*

Case outline

In 1969 ICL was the largest European computer manufacturing company, being ranked fifth in the world. By 1981 they were third in Europe and fourth in the world, although world sales were dominated by IBM, with a 52 per cent share in 1981, the time when the case was written. The case study follows the progress of ICL from 1969 to 1981, giving the objectives and strategies that they used and the results obtained.

Illustration

The performance of ICL over the five-year period to 1980 is given in the table, showing the growth of sales, trading profit and profit before taxation. The annual inflation rate is also given, measured by the retail price index.

	1976	1977	1978	1979	1980
Sales turnover (£m)	288.3	418.7	509.4	624.1	715.8
% change on previous year	+20	+45	+22	+23	+14.5
Trading profit (£m)	28.6	37.0	49.4	63.7	51.4
% change on previous year	+34	+29	+34	+29	−19
Profit before taxation (£m)	23.1	30.3	37.5	46.5	25.1
% change on previous year	+43	+31	+24	+24	−46
% change of RPI	+23	+17	+10	+18	+18

Apart from the declines in 1980, the company exhibited high growth over the period, returning increases in excess of inflation, indicating successful control of the implementation of their plans. Indeed, an objective to double sales from 1973 to 1978 had resulted in a trebling, while another objective to improve profits had also been more than satisfied. These levels of performance were achieved during a period when many sectors of the economy had been affected by an economic recession. They had also had to contend with high inflation and interest rates, a strong pound, rising costs and a fall in demand.

Profitability measurements

The major ratios given in the chapter to measure and control profitability are stated below for ICL for the period 1976 to 1980. Interpretations necessary to achieve control are based upon the trend for each ratio and an inter-company comparison. The latter is again based upon figures produced by the ICC Information Group Ltd.[13] This survey of industrial performance covers over 12 000 companies, classified into 25 major industries, which are split into 138 industry sectors, 94 of which are manufacturing sectors. ICL's business relates directly to one of these sectors, being that of computer equipment manufacturers.

The next table gives three ratios calculated from the ICL accounts, although return on total

* Derived from E. C. Lea and B. Kenny, International Computers PLC (ICL) (A). Copyright © 1982 by E. C. Lea and B. Kenny.

assets cannot be calculated as only current assets are given, so that total assets cannot be determined. The three ICL ratios are compared with the averages for all 94 manufacturing sectors, the computer equipment manufacturers sector and the electronic equipment manufacturers sector.

	1976	1977	1978	1979	1980
	%	%	%	%	%
Return on capital employed					
ICL	13.7	15.0	17.3	20.3	16.3
Average for all manufacturers	n.a.	n.a.	16.4	15.8	14.7
Computer equipment manufacturers	21.0	27.4	33.0	32.4	26.0
Electronic equipment manufacturers	20.5	23.3	25.5	24.9	22.1
Profit margin					
ICL	9.9	8.8	9.7	10.2	7.2
Average for all manufacturers	n.a.	n.a.	7.1	6.9	6.3
Computer equipment manufacturers	9.8	11.4	12.9	12.8	10.0
Electronic equipment manufacturers	9.4	10.4	10.2	11.1	8.2
Return on shareholders' funds					
ICL	25.8	29.2	30.1	31.7	17.8
Computer equipment manufacturers	n.a.	n.a.	40.6	39.2	32.3
Electronic equipment manufacturers	n.a.	n.a.	31.6	30.7	26.8

For the return on capital employed and profit margin ratios, trading profit before taxation was used. For the return on shareholders' funds ratio, profit excluding interest, but before taxation, was used. Information not available is indicated by n.a.

Compared with the averages given for all manufacturing company sectors, ICL appears to have performed well, while the ratio trends show increases, except for 1980. Therefore the indications are of satisfactory control, even in 1980, where their performance has exceeded other manufacturers', despite the decline. Indeed, that latter is indicative not of weak control, but of the prevailing market conditions, as mentioned in the last section.

However, when ICL's ratios are compared with those of other computer equipment manufacturers it would appear that their performance has been poor, indicating weak control. ICL, though, operates in a highly profitable sector. Indeed, of the 138 sectors, computer equipment manufacturers have achieved the rankings shown in the final table in relation to the most profitable sector for each year.

	1978	1979	1980
Return on capital employed	5th	5th	8th
Profit margin	4th	5th	6th

Consequently, in making further comparisons, the differences between ICL as a company and the companies included in the survey would need to be examined, as discussed in the chapter. However, from 1979 to 1980 the average return on capital employed for all 138 sectors fell from 18.1 to 11.7 per cent (15.8 to 14.7 per cent for manufacturers), while ICL's fell to 16.3 per cent. Similarly, the average profit margin for all sectors fell from 6.3 to 4.3 per cent (6.9 to 6.3 per cent for manufacturers), while ICL's fell to 7.2 per cent, although none of the 25 major industries achieved an increased profit margin.

Overall, the results can be interpreted to reflect successful performance relative to planned levels, being indicative of successful control over the period. Such a claim can also be made for the 1979–80 period, where ICL have been able to control reductions in both sales growth and profits earned, to levels that are favourable compared with other manufacturing companies and given the difficult trading conditions of the period. Nevertheless, such a situation has important implications for future control. Profits in 1980 had fallen to a level below that of two years before, return on capital employed had fallen nearly to a level of three years before, and the profit margin was the lowest for five years, as was the return on shareholders' funds. Indeed, the case study illustrates the approaches that ICL planned to pursue to control this decline, which were to include substantial changes to both organizational and marketing strategies.

REVIEW QUESTIONS

1. 'In this company we have comprehensive plans so that control is really not important.' Discuss.
2. Describe how control relates to the stages of planning given in Parts Two and Three of the book.
3. How would you differentiate between the control of profits and profitability?
4. What are the reasons for giving special attention to the control of strategies and tactics when it can be achieved indirectly through objectives?
5. If, part way through the implementation of this year's marketing plan, the company's trend of declining market share was found to be accelerating, what action should be considered?

REFERENCES

1. R. J. Mockler, 'Developing the science of management control', *Financial Executive*, 84–93, December 1967.
2. Kollat, D. T., R. D. Blackwell and J. F. Robeson, *Strategic Marketing*, Holt, Rinehart and Winston, USA, 1972.
3. 'The remaking of Metal Box', *Management Today*, January 1985.
4. R. M. S. Wilson, 'Accounting approaches to marketing control', *Management Accounting*, 51–8, February 1970.
5. Greenwood, W. T., *Business Policy: A Management Audit Approach*, Macmillan, New York, 1967.
6. W. F. Christopher, 'Marketing achievement reporting: a profitability approach', *Industrial Marketing Management*, **6**, 3, 149–62, 1977.
7. McCarthy, D. J., R. J. Minichiello and J. R. Curran, *Business Policy and Strategy*, Irwin, Homewood, 1983.
8. 'The five-star management of Ball', *Management Today*, March 1984.
9. 'ICI thrives on self-inflicted culture shock', *Fortune*, 16 April, 1984.
10. Higgins, J. M., *Organizational Policy and Strategic Management*, Dryden Press, New York, 1983.
11. J. M. Hulbert, and N. E. Toy, 'A strategic framework for marketing control', *Journal of Marketing*, **41**, 12–20, April 1977.
12. Bishop, E. B., 'ROCE as a tool for planning and control', *Long Range Planning*, **2**, 4, 80–7, 1969.
13. ICC Information Group, *Industrial Performance Analysis*, 9th edn, London, 1984.
14. B. Barlev, and S. Lampert, 'A performance index for evaluating marketing programmes', *European Journal of Marketing*, **11**, 1, 21–30, 1977.
15. 'How Wadkin worked clear', *Management Today*, May 1984.
16. 'Tandem's twofold task', *Management Today*, November 1984.
17. 'Can Chrysler keep rolling along?', *Fortune*, 7 January 1985.
18. S. Tilles, 'How to evaluate corporate strategy', *Harvard Business Review*, **41**, 4, 111–21, 1963.
19. Rumelt, R., 'The evaluation of business strategy' in Glueck, W. F. (ed.), *Strategic Management and Business Policy*, McGraw-Hill, New York, 1980.
20. Hartley, R. F., *Sales Management*, Houghton Mifflin, Boston, 1979.
21. Aaker, D. A., and J. G. Myers, *Advertising Management*, Prentice-Hall, Englewood Cliffs, 1975.
22. Tirman, E. A., 'Should your marketing be audited?', *European Business*, **29**, 49–56, 1971.
23. P. Kotler, W. Gregor and W. Rodgers, 'The marketing audit comes of age', *Sloan Management Review*, 25–43, Winter 1977.
24. Wilson, R. M. S., *Management Controls and Marketing Planning*, Heinemann, London, 1979.
25. M. H. B. McDonald, 'International marketing planning', *European Journal of Marketing*, **16**, 2, 3–32, 1982.
26. G. E. Greenley, 'Where marketing planning fails', *Long Range Planning*, **16**, 1, 106–15, 1983.
27. Hooley, G. J., C. J. West and J. E. Lynch, *Marketing in the UK*, Institute of Marketing, Maidenhead, 1984.
28. D. J. Eppink, D. Keunning and K. De Jong, 'Corporate planning in the Netherlands', *Long Range Planning*, **9**, 5, 30–41, 1976.
29. Hopkins, D. S., *The Marketing Plan*, The Conference Board, Research Report No. 801, 1981.

SUBJECT INDEX